MW00580854

To Denise

"All the Best"

LIGHTNING SOURCE

Mark Stein

ISBN 978-1-4507-8309-5

Proudly produced in the United States of America
January 2012
First Edition

Cover design by Ned Levine

141/250

YOU KEEP ME HANGIN' ON

2

Dedications

For Pat...my guiding light, who's been with me each and every step of the way...you have all my love and devotion.

For Rich...who gave me balance, companionship, and three wonderful gifts...Dorie, Kristopher, and Melody.

For Bob and Gayle Patterson...who gave me shelter from the storms, thank you for your friendship and your loyalty.

Chapter One

W hen the lights dimmed at the Coliseum in Phoenix, Arizona in September 1968, Vanilla Fudge was in the middle of one of its most successful tours with guitar legend Jimi Hendrix and his band, the Jimi Hendrix Experience. Often playing with an opening act, the Scandinavian progressive-rock band, the Soft Machine, and an Irish warm-up act, the Eire Apparent, the Fudge played a one-hour set before Hendrix's still revolutionary trio would provide the ear-splitting climax. This night would prove typical of many other nights in the tour: the Experience would be underwhelming, and the Fudge would prove electrifying!

Seattle-born James "Jimi" Hendrix had in a few years gone from paratrooper with the 101st Airborne to backup guitarist and side man to Wilson Pickett, to the front man for his own group, to renowned superstar, a demi-god of rockdom.[1]

Merely the introduction of a "power trio," soon copied by English supergroup, Cream, then Z Z Top, and still later Emerson, Lake, and Palmer, constituted a conceptual breakthrough in American rock. Until Hendrix, the legacy of the first "British Invasion" had left bands and fans with the assumption that the "proper" number of instruments needed was at least four—rhythm guitar or keyboards, lead guitar, bass, and drums. A singer who really played no instrument on stage, such as Mick Jagger, or who played a tangential instrument was acceptable, but the rhythm instrument was viewed as categorically essential to maintaining the background while the lead soloed. Then along came Hendrix. His full sound, interspersing powerful chords with intricate

4

leads, made listeners swear they were hearing two guitars. It was more than sheer volume—and Hendrix was loud by the standards of the day. It was a new virtuosity and aggressiveness that screamed, "Rhythm guitar? I don't need no stinkin' rhythm guitar!"

At the Monterey Pop Festival in June 1967, Hendrix, replete with flaming guitar, sexual gyrations, playing behind his back, and picking the strings with his teeth, tore up the crowd. It remains one of the classic moments in rock history, adroitly filmed in the documentary "Monterey Pop." (The filming of other acts was hardly flattering: Grace Slick of Jefferson Airplane was filmed close-up to the microphone at an odd angle, and the rest of the band was virtually never seen). Now, this American, who had gone to England to get his big break, only to return as a sensation without a top-rated record, joined the Monkees tour in one of rock and roll's most astounding mismatches. The Monkees, a made-for-television band who often didn't even play their own instruments in concert, were the darlings of adolescent (mostly white) girls. Hendrix, who oozed sexuality and whose songs were filled with references to psychedelics and drugs, appealed to a slightly different audience. Yet at the time, the marriage didn't appear quite so ridiculous. Hendrix needed wider national media exposure and to be viewed as marketable to mainstream audiences; the Monkees needed gravitas, an unquestioned musical talent. And Hendrix was something else, according to Peter Tork: "The Monkees were very theatrical in my eyes, and so was the Jimi Hendrix Experience. It would make a perfect union."[2]

For perhaps the first time in his recent musical career, Hendrix was overmatched—not because the Monkees were such musical talents, but because they were already television stars who happened to be in a band (or played musicians on TV—the kids didn't care which). When Hendrix broke into "Purple Haze," he was met with screams of "We want Davy!" referring to Monkees' singer Davy Jones or "We want Mickey" (Mickey Dolenz). It proved an embarrassment for both Hendrix and the Monkees, who had eagerly anticipated being able to watch their idol up close, night after night. Hendrix divorced the tour after only a seven dates, flipping the bird to a New York crowd and requesting that the tour release him from his contract, which management did. Hendrix finished touring with another power trio of keyboards, bass, and drums, the Scandinavian group Soft Machine.

Hendrix got his hit with "Purple Haze," had his *Are You Experienced?* album shoot up the charts, and followed up with *Axis: Bold as Love*. That did not necessarily mean critical success: Jon Landau, reviewing Hendrix's *Are You Experienced?* album for *Rolling Stone*, panned it, while Robert Christgau at *Esquire* scorned Hendrix as "a

5

psychedelic Uncle Tom."[3]

When he embarked on his 1968 tour, his business management, Stevens Weiss, also represented Mark and the Fudge. It seemed like a much better fit: both were power groups that did not hesitate to drift into psychedelics; both featured true pioneers (Hendrix on the guitar, Mark on the keyboards, and Tim Bogert and Carmine Appice on bass and drums). And as sensible as the pairing seemed, it soon proved almost as difficult as the Monkees/Hendrix union.

Beginning in Atlanta, the four bands played Red Rocks Park in Denver and Balboa Stadium in San Diego before arriving in Phoenix. By then, Vanilla Fudge opened with Mark hitting a single note, a high "E" for tuning purposes. "In the days before the strobe tuner," Mark recalled, "it sometimes wasn't easy to tune up backstage, so we came up with a really cool way to start the show. I'd hit the 'E' then Vinny and Tim would start tuning and go into major and minor scales. Then Carmine would play fills and crashes." After the "tune-up" became a roar, the Fudge would crescendo down, leaving a moment of silence before Bogert would do his quiet bass walk into the Fudge's cover of the old Zombies tune, "She's Not There." Over the next hour, the band would then pound out "Ticket to Ride," "People Get Ready," and, of course their hit, "You Keep Me Hangin' On." Then they launched into the "Break Song." This tongue-in-cheek title (for the tune that bar bands usually played prior to their break, usually lasting no more than a minute) was ironic given that the piece was a half-hour tour-de-force of solos. After a brief intro, Carmine Appice, Tim Bogert, and Mark laid down a slow, bluesy background, over which Vinny Martell scratched out his lead.

Of all the players in the two lead bands, the Experience and the Fudge, the two most self-conscious were Martell and Hendrix's bass player, the British Afro-haired Noel Redding. Neither was then on the same plane as the other five players on stage when it came to instrumental virtuosity, although in later years, Martell would see his skills grow significantly. In 1968, however, it's safe to say that as great as Hendrix was, the gap between him and Vince Martell was smaller than that which separated Redding and Bogert. Martell's role model was the ever-understated George Harrison (himself often unfairly derided as a weak musician compared to John Lennon and Paul McCartney), but Vinny had the great misfortune of coming on the scene at the same time as four of the greatest guitarists in rock history—Jeff Beck, Jimmy Page, Jimi Hendrix, and Eric Clapton. Had the Fudge appeared on the national scene two years earlier, Martell would have been renowned as innovative and bold. And Martell always cloaked his playing in heavy overlays of

6

fuzz-tones, wa-wa pedals, and other distortions, concealing his innate abilities.

Redding suffered from different expectations. Contrary to the role of someone like Jack Bruce in Cream, he was not by nature a bass player. Instead, he was a guitar player picked from English clubs and assigned to play bass in the Experience. Thus it was understandable that he have a learning curve. But of the two, Martell sang lead on some Fudge songs and was a solid harmony on almost all others, whereas Redding, as a singer, was always at best a lame backup to Jimi and a painfully weak lead singer.

The comparisons to the guitar gods coming on the scene would always affect Martell, whose solos became longer over time. In 1968, however, they were concise, appropriate, and the perfect lead-in to the full band joining back into the Break Song, ramping up to the introductory refrain again, ending on a power chord that introduced Mark's stunning keyboard work. Always beginning on a single note, quick-stroked so that it seemed he had 12 fingers, Stein jumped into a Jimmy Smith-style fast blues solo. Suddenly, he would abruptly shift into a wave of special effects coaxed out of the Hammond. Stein became a star in the age before synthesizers (Moog would introduce his famous electronic "instrument" in a 1964 paper called "Voltage-Controlled Electronic Music Modules," but he didn't have a popular demonstration until the Monterey Pop Festival in 1967, it did not see widespread use in rock bands until Leon Russell and Stevie Wonder began to use it in the early 1970s). Until the mid-1970s, though, Mark Stein on the Hammond organ came as close as anyone could to actually "bending" keyboard notes. He was so radically different than any other organists that the audience wondered if, in fact, it was a Hammond organ he played. Mark assaulted the keyboard, slapping it and sliding up and down the keys in cascades of sound; then the band launched into a double time that finally climaxed into a return to the opening riff.

Then it was Tim's turn—one of the first rock bass solos ever seen in concerts—and Bogert did not disappoint, not only playing his bass like a lead instrument, but employing Hendrix-style note bends and screams until the bass sounded like a jet escaping the runway. And after Bogert, Appice routinely delivered mind-numbing solos that vastly eclipsed the other drummers of the era. Only Ginger Baker, with Cream, and John Bonham with Led Zeppelin, were in his league, but Appice was far more innovative than either.

With the Fudge members having demonstrated mastery of their instruments, the band returned to the original riff, erupting into the grand finale. At that point, the crowds were uniformly hysterical, having not

7

only dismissed the two warm-up acts, but often forgotten they had come to see Hendrix. The Fudge left the stage with Appice forming a "peace" sign with his drumsticks and Tim, in his high-pitched voice, shouting, "Goodnight!" Yet the audience continued screaming and stomping for Vanilla Fudge.

. . . and was still screaming for the Fudge minutes later when the Jimi Hendrix Experience took the stage. (It was common in the early era of rock to move the show along, with rapid equipment changes between bands). A high Hendrix plugged in amidst cries of "Fudge!" and "Bring back the Fudge!" Irritated, Hendrix strummed the introductory notes of one of his familiar crowd-pleasers, "Hey Joe." It nevertheless took 10 minutes for the cries of "Fudge" to die out, and Hendrix did not help his cause by struggling to tune his guitar, forgetting lyrics, and looking like he had just stepped out of an opium den. Word was already out: Vanilla Fudge was stealing the show from the most sensational rock act in the world.

When the Fudge opened for Jimi in Seattle, one music critic who had claimed that the band used overdubs and other recordings to create their big sound on their debut album was exposed as Vanilla Fudge performed all their songs, with just the four musicians, live. The master of ceremonies even took the mike afterward and got the crowd to boo the reviewer.

Opening for Hendrix, as Mark recalled, "was a big 'wow.' Jimi, Mitch, and Noel were the cats." The Fudge was still on its way, but after the Red Rocks show, Mark knew that Vanilla Fudge could hold its own, and after the Balboa Stadium show on September 3, he jumped off stage and ran into the arms of his manager, Phil Basile (or "Philly," as Mark called him) and screamed for joy as Buddy Miles, who was backstage trying to get a gig with Hendrix, looked on. Later that night, Mark went down to the hotel restaurant, where Hendrix was having a pizza. He invited Mark to join him—"so casual yet surrealistic," as Mark noted. Mark Stein and Vanilla Fudge had not only made the major leagues, they were becoming an integral part of the most revolutionary and exciting episode in American music history—the time when rock 'n' roll, which was born and bred in the USA, and which had temporarily ceded its dominance to the Brits, would forever regain the artistic edge. It all formed a worldwide revolution that began with American "hippies" and radicals, but soon helped break down the Iron Curtain. As loathe as many of the die-hard rockers of the psychedelic age may have been to admit it, they and soon-to-be president Ronald Reagan were the twin prongs of a nutcracker that unleashed a wave of human freedom never before seen.

This, of course, was worlds away from everyday life in Bayonne,

New Jersey, where Mark Stein was born in 1947, on 25th Street, just a few blocks from downtown. Bayonne was a blue collar town at the base of Hudson County, separated from Staten Island by the Bayonne Bridge (at the time, a marvel as the largest steel-arch bridge in the nation), with Jersey City on the other side. It had steadily drained people, falling from a population of almost 89,000 in 1930 to just over 77,000 seventeen years later. Like most post-war American cities, Bayonne was returning to normal after the privations of World War II, its citizens having experienced full employment (either in the military or war industries) and, limited by tight rationing, unable to spend their checks freely. So people saved, and once the economy was unleashed to meet their pent-up desires, consumers flocked to buy the new subdivision-type, cookie-cutter homes made famous by Levittown, New York, or to get the latest new cars from Chevrolet, Buick, Ford, Chrysler, Rambler, or half a dozen other auto makers. With its principle industries related to the shipping trade and the docks, Bayonne made the transition from one of the leading Patrol Torpedo (PT) Boat manufacturing hubs of World War II into peacetime production. Established giants such as Standard Oil encompassed a vast swath of Bayonne, with the Pennsylvania Railroad servicing Standard with a fleet of oil tankers.

But Bayonne had also started to attract new businesses, such as Ida Rosenthal's growing Maidenform brassiere and underwear facility. It's revolutionary "I Dreamed" campaign had just started nationally, transforming how women viewed themselves and how businesses viewed women. Bayonne's prosperity made it easier to start a family. As with most of America, the "baby boom" hit New Jersey, and Mark was just one of millions of this generation, joining other Bayonne natives such as actors Brian Keith and Frank Langella and songwriter Ben Bernie, who penned "Sweet Georgia Brown," and actress Sandra Dee and songstress Edythe Wright—a fixture with Tommy Dorsey's Orchestra. Indeed, Mark was in the middle of a generational shift of Bayonne talent, followed by Todd Paradine of the "Evil Beats" and heavy metal guitarist Zakk Wylde.

Mark's dad, Irving Stein, had come from Jewish parents who settled in Elizabeth before Irving ended up in Bayonne. Louis Berkin, Mark's grandfather, had come over from Russia in the late 1800s, working the docks near Newark Bay, carrying barrels of oil until he saved enough to bring his wife Fannie to America. Both Ida, Mark's mother, and Robert, her brother, were born in the USA. Irving met Ida when he and his brothers were at a corner candy store when Ida walked by, and he couldn't resist shouting "Hey Freckles! Did anyone ever try to count all those freckles?" Ida wasn't amused, and gave Irving a dressing-down. But when she got home, she told her mother about the cute young man she met. Her mother's reaction? "Stay away from him and his brothers—they're a bunch of hooligans!" But before long, "Freckles" and Irving were a regular couple, and then after that, a happily married couple. Then came Sharon, in 1942, and then Mark.

Music was in the blood. In Mark's earliest memories, he recalled his mother singing to him, and later said "She possessed a lovely, sweet voice that brought tears to my eyes before I'd fall asleep." At age four, he was already mimicking hit songs, singing along, and outside his brick apartment next to the Mission Soda Factory on 25th Street, the Steins would sit with other families when someone would produce an AM radio. As Jo Stafford would sing "You Belong to Me," Mark would sing along, belting out the lyrics as wide-eyed neighbors looked on. But it was when Mark went to Uncle Willie's that he began to bloom. Willie had an upright piano in the living room, which he would play as Mark listened intently. Willie played the hits of the day along with popular show tunes all from sheet music and fake books. No sooner did Willie go to the kitchen for dinner than Mark jumped up on the bench and began one-fingering melodies. Mark loved visiting Uncle Willie so he could get on that upright piano again, and his skills steadily improved.

Music had already become a central part of the American fabric. Sheet music had seen a boom in the late 1800s and early 1900s, whereby music publishers sent out singers known as "pluggers" to movie theaters and public events to sing the most recent songs that the company's writers had penned, hoping to create a hit.[4]

By the 1920s, music products had a scope and penetration well beyond that of any other industry. Even as late as the 1890s, ownership of musical instruments extended to every level of society: the White House had four pianos, and when Booker T. Washington visited a poor family in rural Alabama (who couldn't even afford a complete set of eating utensils), he found an old organ.[5]

Once the phonographic revolution started in the 1920s, music ownership and consumption spread even faster. Robert and Helen Lynd, in their classic study *Middletown* of 36 cities, found that 59% of the homes already had a phonograph. In Muncie Illinois, the Lynds found that a quarter of working-class homes had a phonograph.[6]

Following World War II, music—while still not to the same omnipresent, almost inescapable degree that it would be by the 1980s—was nearly everywhere. Very soon, the transistor radio would extend the reach of music even further, to teenagers, and put it out of the reach of adult parents for the first time.

Music therefore dominated the family entertainment at the Stein household as well, which involved watching television, including such shows as "Hit Parade" and "Lawrence Welk." Mark came to admire the work of Myron Florin, whom he called the greatest accordion player of his era. Virtually every young man who ever touched the accordion must have played "Lady of Spain" at least a dozen times—it was, Mark noted, "an easy song to play triplets on"---and Ray Manzarek of the Doors recalled his Chicago childhood, when "large masses of children played "Lady of Spain" together on stages all over the city. It was not a pretty sight."[7]

It was that tune that Florin was playing in 1950 which caught Welk's ear. Welk then added the accordionist to the band. The accordion became a popular instrument for boys of the Baby Boom era because it was more portable and much cheaper than a piano, and could be played standing up, allowing for a little more showmanship. (At the time, only Liberace and, a few years later, Jerry Lee Lewis and Little Richard had any theatrics as pianists). Frankie Yankovic (unrelated to comedian/musician "Weird Al" Yankovic) had become "America's Polka King," hosting his own television and radio shows and topping the charts with his "Blue Skirt Waltz" (1949).

Stein thus became part of an American keyboardist's rite of passage, and would partly credit his speed on the Hammond to his work on the accordion. At age nine, his dad started him on lessons at the accordion school at Journal Square in Jersey City, and, as Mark noted, his father became overbearing about Mark's practice habits. He wasn't the only keyboard player to experience such pressure. Britain's Keith Emerson, slightly older than Mark, relentlessly practiced, yet could not please his father. Once, Emerson's father heard an Art Tatum record: "You should be playing like that," he said to his son.[8]

On another occasion, the two almost came to blows over Emerson's failure to get a piece of music right. For Mark, the first thing his father asked every day when he came home from work was, "Mark, did you practice your accordion?" And, for a while, Mark did.

More than that, Mark was soon singing along with the instrument, especially "Que Sera, Sera (Whatever Will Be, Will Be)," from Alfred Hitchcock's movie, *The Man Who Knew Too Much*, but already he was becoming bored with the instrument. Keyboard practice was hard on young males: Ray Manzarek recalled the tension within boys who liked music. It was either do the Czerny exercises or go out and play.[9]

Billy Joel's dad, an engineer for General Electric, had an ear for classical piano, but it was his mother who heard him "banging away" on the stand-up piano in the house and dragged him to music lessons for 12

11

years.[10] Joel didn't mind the Czerny exercises themselves, but soon resented "having to read other people's notes," and, at the same time, realized that being a musician "came in handy as a teenager to meet girls at parties."[11]

Parental support for a rocker's musical career varied wildly. Deep Purple's Ian Paice had a professional piano player for a father, and received encouragement when he decided to play drums. Legendary studio bassist Phil Chen's dad, a calligrapher, played banjo for tourists in Jamaica "for peanuts or bananas," and when Chen chose guitar, the going was tough for him as well: "I had to catch pigeons and kill them to survive," as well as stealing bread and milk from the street deliveries to houses."[12]

More than a few fathers became dictators when it came to their kids' music, with one exception: few parents liked the guitar. And where the accordion soon became a "sissy" instrument, the guitar, on the other hand, was all male. Other boys at Mark's school—#34, Jersey City—were strumming guitars, especially the new "rockabilly" songs of Carl Perkins, Buddy Holly & the Crickets, and Elvis, so when Mark saw a guitar at a friend's house, he picked it up. He quickly taught himself some chords and figures, enough to accompany himself as he started to make the transition to rock and roll and also enough to anger his Dad who had a tough time accepting his son's new-found rock and roll heart.[13]

His father was still determined that Mark would be an accordion player, even to the point of driving him to a Ted Mack "Original Amateur Hour" audition in 1957. (Ironically, singer and television star Connie Francis also debuted on Ted Mack's show . . . playing the accordion).

By the time he auditioned for the "Original Amateur Hour," Mark had become bored with the instrument, playing "Lady of Spain" without much vigor, and immediately after his slot, a five-piece group strode on stage, replete with red plaid jackets and slick-backed hair, blasting into "Night Train." Mark looked on in awe: *Now that's what I want to play*, he thought, and the accordion was relegated to the attic.

American music in the late 1950s was a universe away from where it would be even a decade later. Warner Brothers, one of the top record companies, featured such artists as Ricky Nelson, the Everly Brothers, Henry Mancini, and Fats Domino, and the folk trio Peter, Paul, and Mary. Then there were such eclectic talents as Connie Stevens (who was playing "Cricket" on TV's "Hawaiian Eye") and Jack Webb (TV's "Sergeant Joe Friday" on the show "Dragnet") reciting lyrics to love songs, backed by an orchestra. Television actors were routinely drafted to sing, even if only novelty songs. One of the biggest hits of 1959 had

Ed "Kookie" Byrnes (a teen heart throb who played a parking lot attendant named "Kookie" on the series "77 Sunset Strip") singing "Kookie, Kookie (Lend Me Your Comb)," a reference to the character's incessant hair-combing. A relatively unknown comedian Bob Newhart had a top-selling album of standup called *The Button-Down Mind of Bob Newhart*. African-Americans had begun to enter the top tier of entertainers—so long as they were not "too black." Johnny Mathis was one of the biggest-selling stars, with albums full of "color-blind" ballads; Sarah Vaughan had thirty entries in *Billboard*'s pop charts and four in the album listing before 1959"; and the "defining black LP artist was America's most popular folk singer, Harry Belafonte."[14]

Otherwise, Warner had few rock acts, and even Petula Clark, whose 1964 hit Downtown won a Grammy, was scarcely a "rocker." Bobby Darin worked for Decca Records: his "Splish Splash" was a hit, and Mark played a 78 rpm version "until the grooves wore out." "Mack the Knife," Darin's most long-lasting hit, had a flip side called "Beyond the Sea," which also impressed Mark with its big band arrangement and drum solo. These artists were nearly alone amidst a sea of musical soundtracks, including work by Rodgers and Hammerstein ("Oklahoma!," "Carousel"), Lerner and Loewe ("Brigadoon"), or Irving Berlin ("Annie Get Your Gun"). Verve Records, the predominant jazz label, had a roster that included Charlie Parker, Dizzy Gillespie, Count Basie, Louis Armstrong, and Ella Fitzgerald. Reprise, appealing to older listeners, had the "Rat Pack"—Frank Sinatra, Dean Martin, Sammy Davis, Jr., as well as Rosemary Clooney and Dinah Shore.

It was into this musical mix, full of the "doo-wop" sound that would be made hugely popular by The Four Seasons in 1961. Beginning in the mid-1950s as a lounge act known as the Four Lovers, the Four Seasons hooked up with RCA and had a number of singles that reached the mid-levels of the *Billboard* Hot 100. Eventually they ended up with the new Vee-Jay label, founded in 1953, which became a major R&B label, along with Australian Frank Ifeld, whose 1962 hit, "I Remember You," topped the charts for several weeks. But Ifeld also reflected the other stream of rock starting to form the character of the new musical medium, namely the folk movement. Such groups as the New Christie Minstrels, whose 1961 hit "This Land is Your Land" (written as a peoples' patriotic hymn by Woody Guthrie in 1940) kicked off a string of hits and allowed many of the band members to move off into other successful bands. Among the alumni were Kenny Rogers, Kim Carnes, Barry McGuire (who sang the apocalyptic "Eve of Destruction" in 1964), Larry Ramos of The Association, Gene Clark of The Byrds, as well as actress Karen Black, (and, later, former Miss America then "700 Club" hostess, Terry Meeuwsen). The New Christie Minstrels would also spin off three of their members into The First Edition a decade later. (Stein actually auditioned for the New Christie Minstrels at an open audition in Manhattan in 1963, where he sang "I Who Have Nothing." In retrospect, that wasn't exactly the kind of song for a folk group, but he wanted to show off his vocal prowess, but did not get the gig.) Ironically, later folk-activist Pete Seeger said "commercialization has actually helped folk music" and revived interest in a genre that had nearly died.[15]

Rock and roll was still largely the music of Chuck Berry, Bill Haley and the Comets, Little Richard (Richard Wayne Penniman), Buddy Holly, Jerry Lee Lewis, and of course, Elvis Presley. It was popular, but hardly mainstream yet. Dick Clark's "American Bandstand" (first aired on ABC in 1957) was popular, but the Beatles were still The Quarrymen, playing in Liverpool and the Beach Boys were still singing in their California high school. American disc jockeys were smack in the middle of the payola scandals. Even early rock, however, still had a strong strain of country through the influences of Carl Perkins and Johnny Cash, or, on the other side, of Rhythm and Blues (R&B), epitomized in the work of Otis Redding, James Brown, Ray Charles, and Fats Domino.

A musical career was thus not as much of a long-shot as it might have seemed, and Mark's dad, appreciating his son's talent, finally admitted that in the guitar, his son had found his instrument, perhaps even a vocation. Irving Stein even began acting as Mark's agent, taking him to local auditions for rock and roll shows in New York City. For Dave Wren, a music promoter, Mark played Buddy Holly and "Betty Lou Got a New Pair of Shoes" by Bobby Freeman. Now Mark felt real competition, up close. Everywhere he looked there were rock 'n' rollers, Elvis look-alikes, and bands equipped with all-Fender guitars— Jazzmasters that had become the "hot" guitar in the country. In the meantime, a curious young Mark took a walk down a hall, opening a door to find Johnny and the Hurricanes, an early rock band famous for "Red River Rock." They filled Mark with an appreciation for the energy and passion of rock at an early age.

Wren put Mark on the "Milt Grant Dance Party" show, set to launch in Washington, D.C. Another talent coordinator, Neil Scott (real name Neil Bogatz), took Mark under his wing and set him up with a rockabilly trio from the show. Eleven-year-old Mark was thrust into a television studio to lip synch a song Neil wrote for him, "Give Me A Chance." Sam Cook and Wayne Newton were on the same show, and Mark was so nervous he only remembered someone saying, "Smile, kid!" before the cameras rolled. Somehow, Mark said, "I really pulled it

14

off," and the producer told Mark's father that he might have a future in the business. Mark and his father started to jump on the tour bus that had come to Washington, and there Mark saw the proverbial "sex, drugs, and rock and roll." "There was partying like crazy," he recalled---"smoking, drinking, and women all over," and it didn't take Irving but a minute to yank Mark out. But the scene stayed with the youngster: "I couldn't get it out of my mind," he wrote and from then on, "normalcy would never satisfy me." Although he returned to school on Monday, nothing would match the thrill of playing. He briefly changed his stage name to Mark Stevens when Neil warned him that he'd face anti-Semitism. Neil kept looking for opportunities to showcase Mark, and Mark kept practicing, to the point that his grades slipped.

By the time he was in Bayonne High School, Mark was obsessed with *acapella* groups, especially black groups like the Spaniels, the Drifters, Shep & the Limelights, as well as multi-racial groups such as the Del Vikings. White groups such as the Earls and the Crests (with Johnny Maestro on lead vocals) were also all over the airwaves. Drawn to their harmonic structures and vocal blends—blow harmony, they called it—Mark found himself singing with groups near 20th Street. To Mark, it was the "breeding ground of the soul." In a scene straight out of Rocky, several black youths would gather near a hallway or around a trash can with a fire, and begin singing. Mark found that he had a really good ear, and could "give notes to the brothers to sing and it sounded so cool." They called him "Magic," short for "White Magic." One of the groups Mark enjoyed was the Creators, a black group. Mark and Ray Block, who sang baritone with some of the groups, would venture to downtown Bayonne to catch the Creators practicing, and they walked into a flat where one of the group members had painted chalk art everywhere—multicolors of street scenes, Jesus Christ, and renderings of black life. Parked on the street was the rest of the group, drinking Thunderbird wine and carrying on while this rich incredible blend of voices filled the air. In a few short years, the Creators (who would later be called the Ad Libs) would land a hit, singing "The Boy from New York City."[16]

Developing a quartet with Ray Block as baritone, Larry Morreale and Percy Fair as tenors, and Mark as the lead, the quartet began rehearsals. Then they heard another group at a Catholic Youth Organization dance called the Valitors from Jersey City. Their bass singer was MacArthur Munford, and Mark's group knew without a bass like Munford, they wouldn't be competitive. Munford must have determined that Mark's group was better than his own, and he joined them. At a benefit, the quintet sang a gospel arrangement of "Ghost

15

Riders in the Sky" then "Peace of Mind" by the Spaniels. When the lyric said "I fell down on my knees and I prayed," Mark fell to his knees and the group draped a jacket over him a la James Brown. Unfortunately, one of the Creators was there and was outraged when Mark's group did their rendition of "Ghost Riders."

Working under the name, the Valitors, the group played several gigs—rehearsing constantly at Mark's apartment. Mark told Neil Scott of the group, and he set up a recording session in New York under the name Mark Stevens and the Charmers. With a four-piece backup band, the Charmers recorded two songs "Come Back to My Heart" and "Magic Rose" and Allison records signed the group. With a demo in hand, the group heard from Bruce Morrow, a New York disc jockey who organized concerts in New York with acts such as the Shirells, the Dixie Cups, and Little Eva.

Just as it seemed Mark was getting movement in the music industry, Percy Fair was killed in a car crash. Mark remembered his mother receiving a call on a chilly fall morning as he was leaving for school, and screaming "Oh no!" "I felt the blood drain from my body, and I got hysterical," Mark recalled. Percy and MacArthur were joy riding with two girls when a truck hit them head on in Jersey City. MacArthur was the only survivor, but was fighting for his life at Medical Center Hospital. At school, Mark met Ray Block and the two couldn't go to classes—they just walked the streets in confusion and despair. At the wake, it was the first time Mark had seen anyone in a coffin, but Percy's body was so damaged that there was a veil over him. Eventually MacArthur recovered enough to receive visitors, and when Mark and the guys visited, he kept mumbling, "Where's Percy?" Morreale said, "He's dead, Mac." MacArthur began screaming and the nurse bolted in and ordered the boys to leave. It took him seven months to rehabilitate, and it took Mark almost as long to recover emotionally.

The incident shocked Mark, leaving him massively depressed. Clearly the *acapella* group was finished as well. It took time, but Mark began to move on and enjoy life like other normal kids. Spending time down at the Jersey shore, especially during the summers, or cruising by the ocean in a friend's convertible, "In My Room" and "I Get Around" by the Beach Boys grabbed his attention. The band had a beautiful, airy, almost angelic sound, and the songwriting and production skills of Brian Wilson soon became obvious to Mark. Their sound proved so different that where copy bands could emulate the Rolling Stones or even the Beatles, the Beach Boys' sound remained special, approached only (and briefly) by fellow surf music singers Jan and Dean.

Indeed, the music scene had disintegrated into a bland, non-threatening, marshmallow-grey medium when the Beach Boys came on the scene, featuring a top 40 of such forgettable songs as "18 Yellow Roses" (Bobby Darin), "Abliene" (George Hamilton IV), "500 Miles from Home" (Bobby Bare), and "The Bounce" (The Olympics). The longest-lasting hits were "Blowin' in the Wind," a folk song by Peter, Paul, and Mary, the sappy ballad "Blue Velvet" by Bobby Vinton and "Be My Baby" by the Ronettes. The number one song of the year was the lightweight "Dominique" by the Singing Nun. Against such competition, it appeared that the Beach Boys might catch the music wave. These clean cut California boys, along with the surf-music duo Jan and Dean, sang about girls, California, the sun, high school, teen loneliness, and above all, surfing and cars (despite the fact that only Dennis Wilson surfed and none of them had impressive cars). Under the name the Pendletones, Brian, Carl, and Dennis Wilson, plus their cousin Mike Love and high-school classmate Al Jardine used rented amps, drums, and guitars to record a Brian Wilson tune, "Surfin'."

Pushed by their father, Murry, who became their manager, the re-named Beach Boys (mostly Brian, with lyrics often supplied by Love) wrote its own songs. Brian would later label Murry a "tyrant" and in his 1996 autobiography, *Wouldn't It Be Nice*, claimed that Murry abused Brian psychologically and physically, permanently damaging the boy.[17]

Wilson's experience stood in sharp contrast to Mark's supportive father who, nevertheless over time became increasingly domineering. Murry Wilson promoted "Surfin'" and in 1962 signed the band to Capitol Records. (Eventually, Brian kicked his father out of the organization, physically throwing him out of a studio.) Locked into the surfer and racing motifs, however, over the next three years the Beach Boys turned out several hits, including "Surfer Girl," "409," "Shut Down," "Little Deuce Coupe," "I Get Around," "Be True to Your School," and "Fun, Fun, Fun," notching no fewer than 16 hit singles in that period. (No less than "shock rocker" Alice Cooper would later call "I Get Around" "my favorite song ever.")[18]

Their vocal harmonies were like butter, blending the high ranges heard in the Vienna Boys Choir with Love's edgy low-range lead voice. Most of all, the group (including Love, who seemed completely uninterested in the artistic aspects of music, only the money, drugs, and girls) realized, as did Murry Wilson, that Brian was a song-writing genius—and their meal ticket. Mark could hear in the Beach Boys' lyrics the same teen anxiety that most kids felt above and beyond high-school romances, including the need to get away from parents, the joy of supporting your school's athletic teams, the thrill of car racing and surfing, and the overall exuberance of youth. Whereas the Beatles did young love songs better than anyone, until their later albums their lyrics remained somewhat limited. But the Beach Boys hit on all aspects of teen life.

For Wilson, the pressures of creating and performing proved too much. Long before he entered into a personal battle with John Lennon and Paul McCartney for ascendency as pop music's songwriting and creative kings, Wilson felt the strain of artistic competition more brutally than most. Unlike Lennon and McCartney (who were occasionally enhanced by fellow Beatle George Harrison and enhanced by the production/arrangement talent of George Martin), Wilson had to do it all: no one else in the group could write. The Beach Boys' 1965 album, *Pet Sounds* seemed to establish them as legitimate competitors to the moptops (who thought it genius), but that was an illusion. The songs on *Pet Sounds* proved timeless—a direct response to the Beatles' *Rubber Soul*, which Brian found inspiring. He told his wife he would make the "greatest rock album ever."[19]

Although the album itself would be regarded as one of the greatest rock albums ever, with brilliant and sophisticated songs such as "Wouldn't It Be Nice," "God Only Knows," and "Sloop John B.," and provided inspiration for the Beatles to top it through *Sgt. Pepper's Lonely Hearts Club Band* (McCartney said it was one of his favorite albums, and said "God Only Knows" was the greatest song ever written), it accelerated the fracture occurring in the band and only reached #10 on the charts.

Wilson was not only going it alone, but his attempts to broaden and deepen the group's music were being resisted by Mike Love and the record company executives who wanted "formula" Beach Boy songs that would make money. Undeterred, Wilson plowed into his next project, or, as he described it, "a teenage symphony to God."[20]

In "Good Vibrations," Wilson produced one of the greatest songs in rock history ("Greatest Single of all Time," according to *Mojo Music Magazine*; #8 of all time according to VH1). Like everything else Wilson did, it came at great cost, literally, racking up $16,000 in debts, or more than most albums. Band members were worn out with marathon recording sessions, and Wilson hauled in the most esoteric instruments on the planet, all the while personally drifting into a psychological meltdown and gaining weight at phenomenal rates. An even more ambitious project, *Smile*, had to be halted due to battles within the group and Brian's deterioration. Ironically, critics had written them off already—Jann Wenner of *Rolling Stone* thought Wilson's "genius" label was "promotional shuck" and concluded that they were just "one prominent example of a group that has gotten hung up in trying to catch the Beatles"—when in fact the Beatles themselves were now stuck trying to catch themselves, or, at least, what they represented to their fans.

What the Beach Boys at their peak could not accomplish was to embody real rebellion—in 1968 they were still touring in their striped shirts. Their "skip-school-and-go-surfing" or "drag-race-on-a-public-street" lyrics may have concerned a few parents, and as late as the 1980s Interior Secretary James Watt would temporarily cancel a Fourth of July concert at the National Mall in Washington D.C. because the Beach Boys drew an "undesirable element," the group never came close to constituting a threat to social order.[21] Nor were they interested in rebellion: as Wilson said, "You can always write about social issues but who gives a damn. I want to write about something these kids feel is their whole world."[22]

Where the Beach Boys did have insight into rebelliousness was cars, and the inherent liberty they produced, whether it was the fuel-injected Stingray or the Little Deuce Coupe. They tapped into the angst of street-racing, which was then popular, and this was no small connection to American teens, who latched onto the same auto and motorcycle erotica slang a few years later when Bruce Springsteen half-sang, half-groaned about "suicide machines" headed for "mansions of glory." Nevertheless, despite their personal drug addictions, depressingly dark phobias and obsessions, Dennis Wilson's flirtation with cult-leader Charles Manson in the late 1960s, and Brian's inability to even leave his house at times, the Beach Boys never channeled that inner torture into public music that characterized so much of rock. Some of the absence of personal angst derived from Brian's inability to rely on other members as regular contributors, turning instead to such lyricists as Van Dyke Parks and Tony Asher. Where Jim Morrison would later sing, "This is the end, my only friend, the end," and listeners knew he didn't have long to live, and when Jimi Hendrix moaned "Manic Depression," it may have been a signal of a life out of control. But Brian Wilson hid his real manic-depressive tendencies, and the closest the Beach Boys got to the "dark side" seemed to be "In My Room." Perhaps the saddest legacy of the Beach Boys is that where Ringo Starr sang, "You've got to pay your dues if you want to sing the blues," Wilson and the Beach Boys paid their dues, but never got to sing the blues.[23]

Neither had Mark yet paid the kind of dues expected of serious rockers, although Percy's death remained etched in his psyche. That, however, did not seem directly related to a musical lifestyle and he viewed it as a tragic accident, not as a life lesson. When Mark returned to school duties, the Valitors were buried with Percy. Then, in 1963, he received a call from a band that needed a singer and rhythm guitarist.

19

Mark signed on, and soon they were each making $15 a night playing a string of bars in Union City, The Cat & the Fiddle, Phil's Kitchen, and the Rag Doll all in an area called the "Transfer Station." The band covered "Johnny B. Goode," "So Much in Love as We Stroll Along Together," and "Rumble." By the time he was a senior, Mark was in yet another band called the Dynamics playing the then-standards, "Walk Don't Run," "She Loves You," and "Do You Want to Know a Secret?"

At a college party, the band saw an early electric organ sitting in the room, and Mark hopped on it. The sound "filled the room, and the band was freaking out, saying forget the guitar: the organ is for you man!" Mark immediately bought a small organ which had the volume controlled by a lever pushed by the knee. The time Mark spent on rock guitar influenced his feel: other keyboardists, such as David Paich of Toto, grew up with classical piano training; and Manzarek's limited classical training soon gave way to Chicago-based boogie-woogie, which allowed him to develop his left-handed bass lines used in the Doors' music. Mark, on the other hand, combined a rock-and-roll touch with a blues attitude—early, and unrefined, but emerging.

Upon graduation, Mark was directionless, finally enrolling in Pace College. It wasn't long before the lure of music pulled him back, this time with a group called the Valets. Booked by a talent agent named Thomas Truelove, who soon teamed the Valets with a singer named Mike Zara, the group did the club circuit in New York and New Jersey. A singer who worked with Xavier Cougat named Rick Martin then convinced Mark to join his group, Rick Martin and the Showmen, which featured a Peggy Lee-type lead singer named Michelle Paris ("hot looking, but not much of a singer," Mark recalled). Martin also provided Mark a chance to sing lead on such tunes as "Ebb Tide," "You've Lost that Lovin' Feelin'," and "Soul and Inspiration," allowing Mark to refine his street soul into a more polished show-business voice. The group auditioned at the Headliner, one of the hottest clubs on the west side of Manhattan, and got the gig. For Mark, it was both a dream come true, and a new world of work: six nights a week, six sets a night—36 sets a week. "You talk about getting your chops together!" Mark acknowledged. For a while the band really cooked: "We'd play 'Shout' by the Isley Bros., and Rick would get on his knees—the whole dramatic trip." When he got overly theatrical, drummer Joey Brennan would hurl drumsticks at him and the band would crack up. But Martin also had a bad habit of making up stories on stage to enhance the band's image, including a fable about Brennan being born in England and hanging out with the Rolling Stones. Brennan finally confronted Martin and insisted he stop, providing yet one more source of dissatisfaction between the band and Rick. Michelle Paris soon left, replaced by Nicky Reynolds, a "platinum blonde bombshell in tight silver pants" who had been singing with Johnny & The Jays, but whom Martin lured to the Showmen. Mark eventually found himself involved romantically with Nicky. Beneath the surface, however, the band was falling apart.

By that time, country, folk, soul, blues, all edged together around a radical new sound, Leo Fender's sharp-edged twangy guitar. Clarence Leonidas "Leo" Fender (1909-1991), a Greek-American who couldn't play guitar and couldn't even tune a guitar, had begun working with new solid-body electric guitars after the decline of the "big band" era of World War II.[24]

Whether Fender based his design on the Rickenbacker guitar (founded by Adolph Rickenbacher and George Beauchamp in 1931, using the name to connect with Adolph's distant cousin, World War I air hero Eddie Rickenbacker) is uncertain. The first Fender model did feature a detachable neck and a single, large pickup. Originally named the "Esquire," Fender's guitar debuted in 1950, but Fender already had a more advanced two-pickup model in mind. Called the "Broadcaster," Fender's two-pickup model appeared in 1951. While the pickers grinned, the competitors frowned, particularly Gretsch Guitars, which had a drum line called the "Broadkaster," forcing Fender to rename the guitar the "Telecaster." Fender kept the "Telecaster," but worked on improving the guitar based on comments from musicians, designing a new guitar with more pickups, a vibrato bar, and a more comfortable body, released in 1954 under the name "Stratocaster." It became an instant hit.

Fender's guitars were much more aggressive sounding, providing a choppier, more edgy sound than the other great American guitar, the Gibson "Les Paul," developed specifically to compete with the "Stratocaster." Gibson Guitar Corporation hired jazz guitarist Les Paul as a consultant in 1950. He had a solid body design, although controversy about how much his original "Log" design found its way into the final Les Paul concept. Strings were mounted on top of the guitar body, as opposed to running through the body, and after 1957 the two-coil humbucker pickup was added, which (through reversed polarity, greatly reduced interference—i.e., "the hum"). The "Les Paul" had a warm, smoother, more forgiving sound than the "Strat," and while most guitarists eventually would use each for different songs, certain sounds were initially associated with one or the other. Surf music, in particular, was the home of the "Telecaster"; blues, the "Les Paul."

Meanwhile, it wasn't long before Fender applied himself to a similar edgy-sounding bass guitar, which would prove a key ingredient to Rick Martin's band in the hands of Tim Bogert when the draft took their bass player, Jo Granelli. Martin needed a replacement, and told Mark about a fellow he had heard of from Ridgefield Park. Without so much as a rehearsal, they picked up the scrawny Bogert, bedecked in librarian's glasses, at his house and headed for a job in a Jersey club. Although rocky at first, Bogert quickly picked up the tunes and impressed everyone with his talent on the bass. Influenced by Motown bass player James Jamison of the Funk Bros., Bogert began to change the very nature of bass playing, making it essentially an equal, lead instrument.

The country stood on the brink of a cultural explosion. Music had a radical new instrument with a new sound, several streams of music—much of it (country, folk, R&B, and rock) rebellious in nature— and the largest generation in American history coming into puberty. These trends collided with a fourth: a radical turnover in talent from the original rock 'n' rollers. Already, however, Buddy Holly, Ritchie Valens, and the "Big Bopper" were dead; Jerry Lee Lewis had become a pariah due to his scandalous marriage to a 13-year-old who was his cousin; and Little Richard had been born-again, playing only gospel music between 1957 and 1963. Carl Perkins's "Blue Suede Shoes" was already an "oldie," and at any rate was increasingly identified with a new subvariant of rock called "rockabilly." On top of that, Perkins was three years older than Presley, four years older than Orbison, and almost a decade older than up-and-comers such as Gene Pitney and Ricky Nelson. As they say of dogs, in teen years, that made Perkins ancient. And the King? Elvis was waning as a "rock star." He was increasingly absorbed with making movies, and his songs came substantially as tie-ins to his current film. "Jailhouse Rock" was a classic, but more often the material proved second-rate and forgettable.[25]

Both Bing Crosby and Frank Sinatra had made the transition from music to Hollywood, and Sinatra in particular remained able to duck into a studio from time to time and come out with an "easy listening" hit. Elvis, however, went into an artistic funk for years.

A few others filled the gaps left by some of the founding giants. Roy Orbison, already a Texas songwriting whiz, recorded "Only the Lonely" in 1960, but despite his powerful impact on the Beatles and others, Orbison was hardly a household name at the beginning of the decade. Crooner Gene Pitney—also an adept songwriter---would have his first hit in 1961 with "Town Without Pity," the same year his main competition for teen heartthrob/singer, Ricky Nelson, released "Hello Mary Lou" (a song Pitney wrote).

A few others filled the gaps left by some of the founding giants. Potential heirs to the Elvis throne Pitney and Ricky Nelson would have solid hits in 1961, yet neither they nor Orbison came close to Elvis's on-stage magnetism. Nelson was constricted by his ongoing television series, as well, where each week he ended the "Ozzie and Harriet Show" with a song. Both he and Pitney were too smooth, too preppy to be rock rebels. The departure of the Little Richard/Elvis/Jerry Lee Lewis triumvirate from live touring produced a vacuum and whatever filled that vacuum had to be electric.

Thus the scene was open to not only new sounds, but new stars. And the East Coast had its share of contenders for the lead role, but increasingly in the form of bands, not individuals. Hundreds of groups like Rick Martin and the Showmen vied to seize the moment. Mark got word of one such hot group, called the Young Rascals, who were appearing at The Barge in Long Island, but it was a while before he and drummer Joey Brennan could check them out. They finally saw them at a discotheque in Manhattan called The Phone Booth—a moment that Mark described as "changing my life." Sitting close to the stage, Mark and Joey watched in amazement as drummer Dino Danelli played with great passion and power as he twirled his sticks between beats, as guitarist Gene Cornish played cool rhythms and drew deep sounds from his Gibson L-5 hollow body. Up front, a skinny Eddie Brigati captivated them with a high soulful voice, his long hair quite a change from typical American Beach Boy groups. But it was a former pre-med student and keyboard player Felix Cavaliere, on his Hammond B-3 organ, that inspired Mark.

Cavaliere had come to music through a classical background, and, like Mark, started early. He had absorbed music in jazz clubs, where, again like Mark, he was won over by the Jimmy Smith Hammond sound. A New Rochelle trio with bass, keyboard, and drums provided regular inspiration, while Smith, Cavaliere thought, translated the Hammond to rock. Working with Joey Dee and the Starlighters, Cavaliere couldn't afford a B-3 or even a C-3. Indeed, at the time, a Hammond organ was a rare commodity: "the only place to even see a B-3," Cavaliere noted, "was at Macy's."[26] Nor was the Hammond Organ Company interested in rock and roll. At a time that Gibson and Fender guitars, and Ludwig and Rodgers drums were beginning to sponsor rock acts, Hammond not only recoiled at its instrument being part of rock, but resisted even linking the organ to the famous Leslie rotating speaker that gave the Hammond its distinct sound. "For a while," Cavaliere pointed out, "Hammond wouldn't even let the L-5 (predecessor to the B-3) be sold together with a Leslie speaker."

Neither the Hammond organ company nor irate Baptist preachers could stem the flow of rock. Before long, Cavaliere had a band playing weddings (although he only had a piano at the time). Working gigs in Germany, Cavaliere saw the Beatles up close, and it was in Germany he met Joey Dee. Locating some talented singers and musicians, Cavaliere formed the Young Rascals in 1965 and had a record deal within six months. At the time he had not found a suitable bass player, so he played the bass pedals with his feet, becoming the first mainstream rock act without a bass guitar.

Though a talented keyboardist, Cavaliere technically was hardly in a league with Jimmy Smith, as, indeed, few were. But his style and his willingness to explore the Hammond B-3 as an instrument that only yielded a single sound placed him in a category of his own. Just as guitarists such as Jimi Hendrix and Eric Clapton would later explore a variety of sounds on the guitar—trebles, basses, fuzz tones, wah-wahs—Felix experimented with all the Hammond's capabilities. It was an insight that led a generation of keyboardists, including Billy Joel and Mark Stein, to see the Hammond differently. (Joel would later remark, "Felix was my idol.")[27]

Instead of a thin, cheesy sound associated with the Vox or Farfisa, Cavaliere introduced the B-3 as not only a solo instrument but as a virtual one-man orchestral medium.

Aware of the Young Rascals as local icons, Mark had his own gigs to play, and the work kept coming. Rick Martin took the group to Cocoa Beach, Florida to play the Satellite Lounge—Mark's first time on a plane—and the locale was pleasing. The band had rental cars and the motel was close to Cape Canaveral, allowing the group to watch rocket launches. At a local coffee shop, Mark spotted newsman Walter Cronkite who had come down to cover one of the launches. A much different lift-off was occurring, though, one that would send shock waves through the music industry like nothing since Elvis first gyrated on stage.

In February 1964, the Beatles had arrived in America to appear on the Ed Sullivan Show. It was a climactic moment in American music, not only drawing record television audiences, but sparking the "British invasion" of Beatle wanna-bes (some of them performing Lennon and McCartney castoff songs) to the United States that soon redefined the industry. Formed in Liverpool as the Quarrymen in 1957 with John Lennon and Paul McCartney, followed by George Harrison who joined the following year, along with Stuart Sutcliffe on bass and Pete Best on drums, the band went through a series of names before settling on the Silver Beetles. Later this was refined with a play on the word "beat" to simply, The Beatles. The boys played local clubs before taking a career-changing gig in Hamburg, Germany where they performed six nights a week and were pushed to become showmen and entertainers, not just

24

musicians. Steadily adding new songs to their list, they were forced to incorporate a variety of material, all the while pressed by the dance crowds to keep it up-tempo and energetic. Sutcliffe, one of the weaker members musically, was ribbed about his playing by Lennon. At the same time, he had artistic aspirations, and left the group in 1961 leaving the innovative McCartney to take over duties on bass.

Hamburg turned Lennon, McCartney, and Harrison into solid musicians, which in turn later fed their songwriting talents. Over the years, star after star would testify to the value of those early, dingy clubs in forging one's "chops"—music slang for the ability to play with skill.[28]

After returning to Liverpool, the band began its famed stint at the Cavern, where Best was replaced by Ringo Starr in 1962. Starr (Richard Starkey) had actually met the band in Hamburg while he was playing with Rory Storm and the Hurricanes. Over the years, Ringo would be both ridiculed and admired. One critical characterization was that he was "not even the best drummer in the Beatles," but percussionists from Deep Purple's Ian Paice to Billy' Joel's drummer, Liberty DeVitto, were inspired and instructed by Ringo's drumming.[29]

Among his other skills, Ringo knew virtually every type of drum beat, from a slow blues to a cha cha, and always underplayed. Later, in an age of solo virtuosity typified by John Bonham's "Moby Dick" or Ginger Baker's "Toad" solos, such restraint was viewed as a sign of incompetence. But in 2010 DeVitto insisted, "Ringo is so underrated it's sick. He is the ultimate in what a drummer should be."[30]

Not only did the band bring in a new drummer, but the Beatles incorporated a heavy dose of R&B, particularly Sam Cooke and Ray Charles, into their act—something the American surf groups were slow to do, and was exactly the kind of music that Mark Stein and Felix Cavaliere were drawn to across the Atlantic. Melding American rhythm and blues with standard English rock music continued the fusion that had begun in the United States with Presley, Little Richard, Chuck Berry, and Buddy Holly, in which R&B would be given a "white" makeover for mainstream Caucasian audiences. As Ian Paice of Deep Purple later described the transatlantic crossing of musical styles, "We took it back to you after we got it."[31]

This was no small matter. Already, in the United States, the process was under way in reverse as Detroit assembly-line worker, Berry Gordy, had conceived of a new type of record company.[32]

His Motown label took raw African-American acts and gave them high-class clothes tuxedos and evening gowns, provided them with standardized (non-threatening) choreography, and instructed them in public speaking so they would be accepted easily by mainstream white audiences. As Motown producer Mickey Stevenson recalled, "We wanted to kill the imagry of liquor and drugs and how some people thought it pertained to R&B."[33]

Gordy soon had a dozen top groups, including the Supremes, the Four Tops, and Smokey Robinson and the Miracles under his management. Gordy was coming at the market 180-degrees away from Elvis and the Beatles, but with the same strategy: get the best from the musical styles and appeal to the largest audience possible. His strategy worked. During the 1960s, Motown released 535 singles, of which 357 made the charts and 174 reached the top ten.[34]

Motown also featured a remarkable high-school wizard of an engineer, Tony Bongiovi (also publicly known as "Bon Jovi"), whose lack of an electrical engineering degree made it impossible to get a job in the large New York market. He landed a gig at Gordy's studio and commuted back and forth from Detroit to New York City as he mixed Motown's acts. Since the studio had one of only three eight-track machines in the nation, the richness of the Motown sound not only became unique, but nearly unmatched. Moreover, Bongiovi noted, Motown used the same small stable of musicians in almost every number, lending a cohesion and familiarity to the sound that studios in New York—even with an eight-track machine—could not match.[35]

"When you worked at Motown," Bongiovi recalled, "you couldn't go outside" because of the equipment: no one else could duplicate the sound. Better still for Bongiovi, at Motown, producers and not just engineers could run the equipment. Motown constituted one of those remarkable accidents by which unexpected pockets of music genius and power, including Nashville and Muscle Shoals, both of which were far outside the mainstream of finance and marketing, developed in the American music scene.

Meanwhile, by the time the Beatles came to America, they not only had a new sound, but a different look. Their hair, absurdly short by subsequent "hippie" standards but considered radical and "long" in 1963, gave them a stunning (yet uniform) look, but also their grey and black suits sent the message that these rebels might excite you, but wouldn't hurt you. Whether American parents were ready to trust their teenage daughters to them or not was yet to be determined, but the suits—a Brian Epstein management decision—made the Beatles anything but the "biker" rebels so popular in the 1950s. The group also gained from the timely introduction of 33 rpm records, known as "LPs," which had comprised a smaller part of the market until 1963. The Beatles *Please Please Me* album (later released in the U.S. as *Introducing the Beatles* on Vee-Jay Records) was among the pioneering LPs that was introduced. As music historian Jonathan Gould observed, "LPs were the first records to be sold in foot-square cardboard jackets faced with glossy cover art, which served as an alluring advertisement for the music within . . . . [allowing the cover to become] a companion piece to the listening experience: a contemplative object that functioned like a fan magazine," putting a face to the voices on the album.[36]

Virtually all American rockers acknowledged the Beatles as critically influential in their music. Bob Dylan "knew they were pointing in the direction of where music had to go."[37] Steven Tyler of Aerosmith recalled "When I saw the Beatles on Ed Sullivan on a Sunday night in 1964, that was it."[38] Standing outside his school the next day, Tyler heard a friend say he was going to grow his hair long and "be like the Beatles," whereupon Tyler replied, "Not me man. I'm gonna be the Beatles."[39]

Quiet Riot bassist, the Cuban-born Rudy Sarzo, whose family had escaped Castro's regime, watched the Ed Sullivan Show and Rudy, heard "the sound of freedom," even as his father said, "The long hair reminds me of Fidel and his rebels. I bet you they're Communists, too!"[40] Rock bassist Jimmy Haslip, a latecomer to Beatlemania, only became influenced by the Fab Four in 1967 when he began playing bars and parties and noticed that Paul McCartney was left-handed. Dave Mason of Traffic, who went on to a solo career, recalled the "raw, brand new sound" of the Beatles—"everyone copied them."[41] The Beatles, as Rare Earth's Pete Rivera observed, were "England's Elvis."[42]

Most specifically identified "I Want to Hold Your Hand" as the first Beatles song that caught their ear. Vinny Martell, Vanilla Fudge's guitarist, was a student at Broward Junior College in Florida and heard the song then.[43] Sugarloaf's keyboardist and singer, Jerry Corbetta, recalled he was going to a high school junior prom when he heard "I Want to Hold Your Hand" and "was mesmerized."[44]

Even the quirky and cutting-edge twisted genius, Frank Zappa, who claimed the Beatles were "just a good commercial group," and that they "were only in it for the money," nevertheless felt compelled to play "I Want to Hold Your Hand" in 1971 when his band, the Mothers of Invention, played shows in London.[45]

A few musicians remained unimpressed by the Beatles. Doors' guitarist, Robby Krieger, "thought they were silly. I didn't like them," he said after watching their Ed Sullivan appearance along with hundreds of other kids in a big auditorium.[46] Chuck Negron, later one of the three frontmen/singers of Three Dog Night, similarly "didn't get it" when it came to the Beatles, and like many remained grounded in rhythm 'n' blues and black music.[47] Most of the artists who asserted that the Beatles had little influence on them fell into the category of bluesmen, such as

27

Negron, or had a strong background in jazz, as was the case with David Paich of Toto.[48]

A young Eric Clapton, having just taken up guitar, recalled the beginnings of Beatlemania in England with disgust. "All over the country people were dressing like them, playing like them, sounding like them, and looking like them," he wrote. "I thought it was despicable . . . because it showed how sheeplike people were, and how they ready they were to elevate these players to the status of gods, when most of the artists I admired had died unheard of, sometimes penniless and alone."[49] Clapton's comments about the "status of gods" would prove particularly ironic, for within a few years, "Clapton is God" graffiti appeared everywhere on English walls and in train tunnels.

In fact, the Beatles had deliberately striven to defrayed the hero-worship that had accompanied Elvis by claiming to be just "one of the guys," or, in this case, four. Their movies portrayed them as "ordinary blokes," bemused by stardom. They successfully skewered the very concept of an entertainment industry, of entertainers as mythic heroes. McCartney said "we don't believe in our fame the way Zsa Zsa Gabor believes in hers," and all four engaged in relentless self-mockery---until Lennon's notorious "bigger than Jesus comment" in 1966, which suddenly exposed Lennon's arrogance. Their portrayal of themselves as "mates," a true group lacking a star, was reflected in their song selection, where they (for a time) went out of their way to include George Harrison-written songs on every album, and to let Ringo have at least one lead per LP. It was supremely appealing to class-free America, with its Horatio Alger stories of rags to riches, and who better to exemplify such a story than four average lads from England, where, of course, society still suffered from such social stratification?

The impact of the Beatles on America was bigger still, though: the Beatles introduced to the United States not merely a music form (which, of course, was distinctly American to begin with) but an entire art experience, transforming Dick Clark's teenage dance music into a set of shared cultural values. As music historian Elijah Wald put it, the most fundamental change within 20th century music was the shift "from being something people played to something they consumed. . . ."[50] Yet Wald erred when he claimed that this shift also involved music transforming from "part of a larger experience to being a thing that is often heard alone and out of any set context."

Indeed, it was just the opposite. While listening to music—thanks to recordings—now made it possible to enjoy music without the physical presence of the players, the context was entirely social. Just as virtually every living American could describe what he or she was doing when John Kennedy was shot or when the terrorists flew planes into the World Trade Center, so too could almost every American alive in the 1960s recall the first time "I Want to Hold Your Hand"came on the radio. Music, thanks almost entirely to the Beatles, transformed itself from a limited cultural experience into an all-encompassing social experience. Even Wald admitted as much, noting "If you are not aware of the Beatles, you cannot hope to understand any music of the 1960s, because they were ubiquitous and affected all the other music."[51]

Even if some musicians remained free of their influence, those musicians were still heard by an audience that was acutely conscious of the Beatles. They were the dominant sound of the era.[52]

It is absurd, however, to claim that the Beatles snapped the country out of a gloom produced by the Kennedy assassination. Slate writer Fred Kaplan, looking back in 2004, correctly noted that none of the teenage girls cheering the Fab Four were unleashing their anguish over Lee Harvey Oswald's shots in Dallas. Rather, "the Beatles took hold of our country and took it to a different place because . . .our parents didn't get it."[53]

Moreover, pre-Beatles music suddenly sounded, well, old, while almost all post-Beatles music sounded young and new.   Mark Stein, like most other rockers of the era, similarly cited "I Want to Hold Your Hand" as the first Beatles song he heard—"there was excitement everywhere over this new sound, all over the radio," he noted.[54]

"It seemed like every month you couldn't wait to hear their next single on the radio," and fans would line up outside record stores for the latest release. Felix Cavaliere, touring in Europe with Joey Dee and the Starlighters, heard a different, more raw, and overwhelmingly electric side of the Beatles in their live performances. "The screams were deafening, and continued throughout the performance," he recalled. Even at that time, before "Beatlemania" reached America, "it was an astounding, almost eerie atmosphere."[55]

For Mark, though, the Young Rascals were as almost as exciting as the Beatles. He became a regular at the Phone Booth wherever the Young Rascals appeared, sitting as close as he could, stage right, to Felix, watching his every move. "By my third scotch and soda," Mark noted, "Felix would be covered with sweat from all the energy he put out." The rest of Mark's band likewise was awestruck by the skills of Dino Danelli and Eddie Brigati. The Phone Booth was one of those 1960s clubs---now made a cliche by the "Austin Powers" movies--- known as a discotheque (or, simply, a "disco"). Later, in the era of John Travolta's white suit and the Bee Gees' falsettos, "disco" would come to mean that absence of live musicians, but in the mid-1960s, they not only

29

featured live bands, but usually suspended cages containing "go-go dancers." The focus, nevertheless, was on the band. Each night, Mark would marvel at Cavaliere's technique, and almost as important, at his imposing Hammond B-3 organ. He decided he had to have one of these monsters, despite the price tag.

In 1966, locating an organ store in Elizabeth, New Jersey, Mark and his father plopped down $2,995 for a Hammond B-3 and a rotating 122 Leslie speaker, only to realize that the Stein house could not contain such a large instrument. Mark promptly parked the organ on Tim Bogert's porch in Ridgefield, oblivious to the potential detrimental effects of weather, heat, and cold. Tim, Joey, and Mark would play daily, as Mark unlocked the mysteries of the drawbars and presets. Once he had done so, he began to emulate Felix and relentlessly listened to Rascals music. He also studied Jimmy Smith and Brother Jack McDuff, a gospel blues B-3 player, practicing constantly until he could make the organ work within the band. Bogert copied Paul McCartney of the Beatles and listened to Motown; Joey, to the Rolling Stones.

As Mark came to master the B-3, he started to realize something Felix had already discovered: the stage presence of an organist was vastly different than that of a guitarist. "There were no phallic symbols" associated with the organ, Cavaliere would dryly note. An organist is locked in place—even the stand-up keyboardists, such as Mike Smith of the Dave Clark Five, couldn't move away from their instrument. What Felix Cavliere pioneered, and what Mark Stein perfected, was the use of hands and gestures to give the impression of movement and action. Later, Mark would wave one hand while singing, akin to those in Pentecostal congregations. It simultaneously attracted attention to the keyboardist, and freed him from being a static player. For the first time, with Felix and Mark, the massive Hammond organ almost became a mobile instrument, and the keyboard player became an equal showman in the band. The key word was "almost." Without the use of cameramen on stage, or mirrors, no one could watch an organist actually play. But while drummers were stationary, at least the audience could see them work their craft, and Dino Danelli had been the first to twirl his sticks while actually drumming, creating a breakthrough for percussionists similarly locked into a single spot on stage. Carmine Appice would later not only copy Danelli's stick twirl, but mimic Mark's hand gestures with his own, making a peace sign out of his drumsticks and waving his off stick-hand high.

By 1966, then, Mark Stein was rapidly fashioning his own stage persona, building upon Cavaliere's path breaking sounds and stage presence. His fellow band members were likewise growing into their instruments at a time when rock and roll was about to make an American revival. Yet Tim, Joey, and Mark knew they still needed a guitarist, so they made regular trips to NYC to scour the Headliner, the Peppermint Lounge, the Metropole, even a place called the African Room. An agent handed Mark a card, "Vince Martell—Guitarist and Singer for All Occasions." The next day, Mark called the number, finding that Vince lived in the Bronx. Joey and Mark planned to drive to Vince's house to meet him, when they took a wrong turn off the west side highway and found themselves smack in the middle of Harlem. The winds of racial hostilities were prevailing at that time, and the boys suddenly found themselves in a Bonfire of the Vanities moment, and after some abrupt turns and tires screeching, they managed to get back on the highway headed for the Bronx. Before long, they arrived at the address, a set of attached two-story houses, and rang the appropriate bell. From above, they heard "Yo!" and "this guy with this thick head of hair" was looking down at the pair. Mark, Joey, and Vinny hit it off right away. Vince Martell, whose real name was Vincent Martemucci, hit it off with the Jersey kids right away. The next day, he came to Tim's house and set up, breaking out his red Gibson 335 and began to play the Beatles' "Ticket to Ride." Tim freaked! Brennan and Stein were beaming instantly they knew that Vinny was the cat. "So here was the beginning of it all," Mark recalled. "We practiced, listened to Motown . . . Rascals, Stones, Beatles. We were doing 'Mustang Sally,' 'When a Man Loves a Woman,' 'Get Off My Cloud,' and everything else" they could copy.

When not rehearsing, the four hung out together and hit every club they could find. One band in particular caught their attention, the Magnificent Men, an all-white soul band with great vocals and a "killer brass section," which was the first white act to play the famous Apollo Theater in Harlem. There was another Jersey group called the Pilgrims, a Rascals clone band which regularly played Ondine's, a disco on the east side at 59th Street by the bridge; and a Los Angeles-based band that had "strange music," called the Doors. "I wasn't ready for them," Mark said, but "in retrospect, geniuses all. The poets, the mystical players---it was the totally alternate image of power funk sounds from the East Coast that we were into." Decades later, Mark became friends with Doors' guitarist Robby Krieger and organist Ray Manzarek, who possibly coined the single most memorable organ lick in history with his line in "Light My Fire."

While Robby Krieger had dismissed the Beatles, Manzarek took a different view, calling the British invasion an "irresistible force," "a juggernaut," adding "we were all in awe of their success, if not their musical accomplishments." Immediately American musicians "saw the

31

headlines" about the Beatles and the other groups and "drooled. . . . My mind did a cartwheel at the possibilities," Manzarek wrote.[56]

Yet the Beatles were somewhat baffled by their impact on America. "They've got their own groups," mused McCartney. "What are we going to give them that they don't already have?"[57] In reality the Beatles were giving back rock and roll to the nation that invented it, reminding Americans who they were.[58]

Vanilla Fudge had not been born yet; and many early American rock legends were still finding their way. But the milieu was set; the ingredients, not just for the Fudge, but for American rock, were being mixed. Even folk hero, Bob Dylan booed offstage when he first went electric at the 1965 Newport Folk Festival, had confirmed the shift to electric music. "People were horrified," said Peter Yarrow of "Peter, Paul, and Mary." "It was as if it was a capitulation to the enemy—as if all of a sudden you saw Martin Luther King, Jr., doing a cigarette ad."[59]

In fact, such revulsion disappeared quickly. The electric, powerful sound of rock and roll, which began in America, which lost steam in America, and which was reenergized from across the Atlantic, was forging a music movement that would change the world.

YOU KEEP ME HANGIN' ON

Chapter Two

Perhaps one of the ironies of rock and roll is that it owed as much of its success to a non-musician as to any of the greats who ever played or sang. Pennsylvania-born Alan Freed, a Cleveland, Ohio disc jockey, rightly deserves much of the credit for popularizing rock as a cultural medium. Freed spun records at Cleveland's WJW station in the early 1950s, starting a show of his own called the "Moondog House" that featured black music for a make-believe kingdom of hip listeners.[1]

In 1952, he organized a dance/concert called the "Moondog Coronation Ball" with five acts, sometimes considered the first rock concert. But in a scene that eerily anticipated Woodstock, too many kids showed up and the overcrowding nearly caused a riot. The concert was shut down, and Freed gained priceless publicity. Not long after that, Freed lost a suit involving the use of the name "Moondog."

His fame, however, had already spread to New York City, where he relocated with a new job at WINS radio station. On his show, Freed "rang a cowbell, banged a telephone book, and bellowed a Negro-inflected patter into the microphone as he spun the platters."[2]

As Clark Welton of the New York Times put it, Freed had a "teenager's mind funneled into 50,000 watts." During his early stint at WINS, he recorded a half-hour show called "Radio Luxembourg" for European audiences, where it reached the Beatles and influenced them with songs by Little Richard and Chuck Berry. In 1958, he left WINS for WBC, but was fired a year later when he refused to sign a statement saying he had never accepted "payola," or the popular and illegal

34

practice of taking bribes to spin certain records. The Federal Trade Commission had found a golden apple in the payola scandal, putting 40 staffers on the investigation and in 1960 finally charging 106 record manufacturers and distributors with deceptive act or practices to "suppress competition." "Sure we paid disc jockeys," said one distributor. "We met competition."[3]

Because of his prominence, the brunt of the investigations fell on Alan Freed. He finally admitted on air, "Payola may stink, but it's here and I didn't start it . . . . I know a lot of ASCAP [American Society of Composers, Authors, and Publishers] publishers who will be glad I'm off the air."[4]

In testimony before the House Special Committee on Legislative Oversight, Freed was asked if he would accept a Cadillac as a gift from a record company. "It would depend on the color," he replied. The government was not amused. Freed was indicted by a Grand Jury for evading taxes related to the income he got from payola.

Some rock historians claim the payola scandal forced radio stations to introduce the famous Top 40 format to avoid the appearances of corruption, with station managers agreeing to limit their play to the Top 40 songs on the *Billboard* charts. But this interpretation is circular, because position on the charts required airplay, and in any event, if true, bribery could merely be shifted to *Billboard*'s editors. A somewhat more sophisticated interpretation about the demise of "payola" and the rise of Top 40 involves the prevalence of the automobile. No manufactured item was more in demand after World War II than the car, which, given the postwar prosperity, became common place. As consumers in the millions soon owned cars (already, before the war, one in four Americans had an automobile, compared to only one in 37 in Nazi Germany), travel between states and even regions became commonplace. Food selection and eating habits dramatically changed as pizza appeared in the Midwest, Asian food in the South, and Mexican food in the Northeast.[5]

Freedom of movement brought with it a rapid destabilization of American society—long thought by historians to be "boring" and "dull" in the 1950s. Quite the contrary, between the threat of the atomic bomb and the bubbling of racial tensions, all combined with the smashing of geographical restraints offered by the car, suddenly Americans faced an overwhelming array of new choices and opportunities. Entrepreneurs stepped in to offer familiarity and reassurance that, in fact, some things would stay the same no matter where one traveled, led by Kemmons Wilson with his Holiday Inn Hotels, Ray Kroc with his McDonald's food chain, and Top 40 music, which provided a well-known base of songs for everyone throughout the nation. The car radio was key. Invented in the

1930s, by the 1950s it had become a standard item, used enthusiastically by teens when they could get the family car.[6]

The car radio allowed teens to take their music with them to spaces free of adults, including drive-in movie theaters (pioneered in the 1930s, but coming of age in the 1950s) and the famous drive-in diners.

More important, the industry had already developed popularity measures that relied more heavily on sales than on radio play. Prior to 1955, record popularity was measured by three separate indices, including radio airplay, jukebox plays, and sales In 1958, however—before payola----that changed with the advent of the Billboard Hot 100, labeled "the industry's fastest and most complete programming and buying guide" to pop music.[7]

Eventually, *Billboard* created a separate singles play chart based on a point system that gave sales more weight than radio plays. *Billboard*'s list was not simply a rock and roll list, but reflected the diversity of American music. Still, rock quickly established itself as the main component of *Billboard*'s songs.

As for Alan Freed, despite a string of television and movie appearances, the payola scandal ended his career. Whether he took bribes or not, the incentive was there: continuing lawsuits involving conflict of interest in which his co-authorship of songs such as Chuck Berry's "Maybelline" meant that he could earn more royalties by playing the song more. Freed was charged with commercial bribery and pleaded guilty in 1962, receiving a fine and a suspended sentence. Although he would later return to radio in the 1960s, Freed would be eclipsed by more bombastic disc jockeys such as Robert Weston "Wolfman Jack" Smith (1938-1995), a Freed fan who gained fame in 1962 by broadcasting from XERF in Ciudad, Mexico. The station's massive signal penetrated across the border—reportedly killing birds that flew too close to the tower—where he perfected an act based on bluesman "Howlin' Wolf" (Chester Burnett), complete with wolf howls and a gravelly voice. Jack eventually ended up broadcasting from a variety of locations in the United States, becoming such a character that he played himself in numerous movies, including George Lucas's *American Graffiti*.

Both Freed and Wolfman Jack turned an underground, mostly-black music form into a socially acceptable teen cultural touchstone, which too featured its own televised dance club ("American Bandstand"), fan magazines, and folk interpreters in the form of the disc jockeys. Rock insinuated itself into the mainstream through clothes and other item marketing, and by 1957, some 78 Elvis Presley items grossed $55 million.[8]

Ironically, though, interest in rock music was simultaneously

YOU KEEP ME HANGIN' ON

declining. In 1960, just as payola was declared illegal, the #1 song was "A Summer Place" by Percy Faith, and sales overall were down 5%; by 1963, even though the number of baby boomer teenagers had surged, record receipts rose a measly 1.6%.[9]

Few of the founders and top performers anticipated the new wave of sound and inspiration traveling across the Atlantic. As powerful as the influences of Motown and the country/folk movements were, American rock was still in a react and respond mode to the British invasion (which gained notoriety as a term when first used by CBS newsman Walter Cronkite in February 1964 during a segment about the Beatles). Over the next two years, joining the Beatles on American shores were the duos of Peter and Gordon and Chad and Jeremy, individual pop singers such as Petula Clark, Cilla Black, Lulu, Dusty Springfield, and Donovan (Leitch), plus a slew of rock bands ranging from cute (Herman's Hermits, Freddie and the Dreamers) to pleasant (Gerry and the Pacemakers, Wayne Fontana and the Mindbenders, Billy J. Kramer and the Dakotas) to edgy bands such as the Rolling Stones, the Troggs, the Kinks, and the Animals. Fashions from Carnaby Street, replete with bell-bottom trousers, scarfs and frills, wild designs, and, of course, longer hair accompanied the British musicians as they stepped onto the tarmac.

The Beatles' influence was apparent in some American acts, particularly Pacific Northwest group, Paul Revere and the Raiders, with handsome lead singer Mark Lindsay. The Raiders had re-recorded an earlier hit, "Louie Louie," penned by Richard Berry in 1955, and then covered again by an Oregon group, the Kingsmen in 1963. If any band learns a single song to begin its career, "Louie Louie" is that song. It is one of the simplest three-chord tunes ever written. The Kingsmen's version shot up to #2 (despite the fact that the lyrics were slurred to obscure the profanity), but Paul Revere and the Raiders went to the same studio to record their own version of the song, which caught the ear of Columbia Records. Columbia signed the Raiders, and briefly their version dominated the West Coast until Columbia's A&R head, Mitch Miller, who was no fan of rock 'n' roll, pulled the plug on promotion of the record. Miller, a New Yorker who got his start with an oboe-and-English horn band, had played a principal role in Charlie Parker's classic album, *Bird With Strings*, and was would later be credited with having "an alchemical gift for transmuting esoteric instrumentation and unlikely song choices into musical gold."[10] He then had his own television show, "Sing Along With Mitch," in which a bouncing ball hopped over on-screen lyrics for the audience at home.

Despite initial success, the Kingsmen struggled while the

Raiders found producer Terry Melcher and saw their ticket to stardom in becoming an American Beatles knock-off band. In 1965, their second hit, "Just Like Me," captured the British feel of bands such as the Kinks and Manfred Mann. Schooled in the performance tradition of Motown, the Raiders used almost-comical choreography, combined with Revolutionary War uniforms while at the same time pushing out edgy songs such as "Kicks," "Hungry," and "Good Thing." Along the way, they also connected with Tommy Boyce and Bobby Hart, who, outside of the Motown trio of Holland-Dozier-Holland, the Barry-Greenwich-Spector team that will be discussed shortly, and the writers of show tunes, such as Rogers and Hammerstein, became America's top song-writing team. Boyce and Hart penned a string of 1960s hits, including "Come a Little Bit Closer" (Jay and the Americans), "Last Train to Clarksville" and "(Theme from) The Monkees" (the Monkees), "(I'm Not Your) Steppin' Stone" (the Raiders and the Monkees), plus their own "I Wonder What She's Doing Tonight."

Other clean-cut groups, such Brooklyn-based Jay and the Americans, recaptured the Gene Pitney sound with "Only in America," "This Magic Moment," and "Cara Mia." Lacking the comedic elements of either the Raiders or the Monkees, the group experienced a shorter life-span than the other bands. Another more traditional-looking group, the duo known as the Righteous Brothers (Bobby Hatfield and Bill Medley) achieved immortality with their 1965 song, "You've Lost that Lovin' Feelin'" (recorded with a young Cher singing background vocals and revived in the 1986 smash movie, *Top Gun*).

By then, American entertainment businessman Richard "Dick" Clark, had tapped into the new rock phenomenon in much the same way Lawrence Welk had appealed to the young adults of the 1950s, but instead of accordions, horns, and violins, the central instrument now was the guitar. Clark (b. 1929) literally started his career in 1945 in the mail room of Utica, New York's WRUN radio station, where he worked his way up to be a weatherman and news announcer. He left for Syracuse University, then landed jobs at Utica and Syracuse television and radio stations, hosting a country music show for a time. His break came in 1952 when he took a disc jockey slot at WFIL in Philadelphia. The radio station had an affiliate television station that broadcast a show called "Bob Horn's Bandstand," and Clark was occasionally tabbed to host the show as a substitute, taking over the show full time in 1956. When "Bandstand" was picked up by the new American Broadcasting System in 1957, renamed "American Bandstand," Clark started to become a household face. Untinged by the "payola" scandal of 1959—although as a shareholder in the Jamie-Guyden Distributing Corporation, Clark was tangentially connected but never charged---Clark showcased two aspects of American life: the latest rock and roll music and teenagers having fun. In each show, Clark introduced the nation's top records as the cameras followed teen couples (eventually, blacks and whites) onto the dance floor to display the latest moves, including Mark's own sister, Sharon. "Bandstand" reached into neighboring states and a group of teens from Snyder High School in Jersey City were picked, although naturally the camera stayed with the regulars, some of whom became TV personalities in their own right.

"Bandstand" became one of the first reality shows on television, following on a daily basis the romances of the dancers as well as exposing American youth to the latest songs. Where as younger kids they may have run home from school to watch "Howdy Doody," the teenagers now turned on Dick Clark. Shows soon featured at least one "live" performance, where a singer or band lip-synched a current hit, and usually introduced a new song to the public in a segment where teens would rate the tune for its hit potential ("I give it a seven---I liked the beat, but didn't care for the lyrics"). For six years, "American Bandstand" ran daily, switching to weekly in 1963, and then, the following year, moving to Hollywood. Clark also gleaned another element that would later prove key in the Beatles' success, which was appearance. Rock historian Glenn Altschuler noted Clark was "150 percent deliberate' in cultivating a wholesome image. Donning a coat and tie on the theory that 'if we looked presentable, normal and the way they [adults] think we oughta look, they'll leave us alone,'" Clark presaged Brian Epstein and Berry Gordy, Jr. as understanding the central role of physical appearance in tempering rock's threatening image.[11]

Whether Clark completely understood the music or not was debatable---one colleague said Clark "didn't know Chuck Berry from a huckleberry," but that was irrelevant. He grasped the cultural transformation inherent in rock music.[12]

"American Bandstand" only clarified what was becoming obvious, namely that music—rock and roll music—was becoming a central part of the culture. Imitation is the sincerest form of flattery: "Bandstand" soon had a competitor in NBC's "Hullabaloo," a prime-time show which premiered in January 1965 and featured a bigger budget, slicker presentation. "Hullabloo," directed by Steve Binder, was a half-hour rock concert in which dancing teens were replaced by professional "Hullabaloo Dancers," but were essentially window-dressing for the rock acts. Clark was replaced by weekly guest hosts such as Paul Anka, Frankie Avalon, Sammy Davis, Jr., and the acts included the Rolling Stones, Sonny and Cher, the Supremes, the Animals, and

Dionne Warwick.

When it came to the structure of the music business, rock was entirely revolutionary. By introducing singer-songwriters, including Bob Dylan, Joni Mitchell, the Byrds, the Rolling Stones, and of course, the Beatles, the old "Tin Pan Alley" method of having professional song-writers whose work other people merely performed was swept away. As then Byrd, and later member of Crosby, Stills, Nash, & Young, David Crosby, recalled, "In some ways, the growth of the music business paralleled that of the movie industry. It was founded by ground-breaking independents exploiting a new technology." And while that business was "consolidated by giant vertically integrated conglomerates that owned the talent, the means of production, and the channels of distribution," Barry Gordy, Clive Davis, Ahmet Ertegun and other music moguls did the same in the recording industry.[13]

If songwriting could be about individuals or bands, rock and roll at its roots was about bands, and almost all bands began the same way— putting together a dozen or so songs, finding grooves or a particular sound that worked, then getting gigs. Mark, Tim, Vinny, and Joey had the talent, they had put together a repertoire of popular songs, and now they needed work. As their sound evolved, it naturally took on the characteristics of many other East Coast acts, replete with soulful vocals and heavy guitar (as opposed to the twangy "surf" sound popular on the West Coast). But the East Coast soulful sound was only one thread in a rich tapestry of sounds emanating from garages across the United States in response to the British invasion.

Many of these bands featured keyboards, although few employed the powerful B-3. Instead, most groups featured stand-up keyboardists using the tinny-sounding Vox Continental, the Farfisa, or even the cheap Panther organ. Sugarloaf's Jerry Corbetta, whose hit "Green Eyed Lady" was carried by a jaunty B-3 solo (one of the longest recorded on a single at the time) recalled starting on a Farfisa before graduating to the Hammond B-3.[14]

Question Mark and the Mysterians snagged a #1 hit in 1966 with their song, "96 Tears," which featured a repetitive Vox riff mastered by every aspiring keyboard player since. The hit was steered to the top by Mark's old teenage friend, manager, and producer, Neil Scott. Scott was one of the top promotion men in the business and at that time worked for Cameo Records.[15]

Keith Emerson saw a keyboard player using a "Bird" portable organ that impressed him, and he knew "I had to get my own instrument."[16] But when he arrived to pick up the "Bird," the salesman showed him a Hammond L-100 and he realized, "That was the sound."

His father agreed, and sprang for the extra money.[17]

Most keyboardists of the 1960s had to be content with the cheaper, stand-up organs, including Paul Revere and the Raiders' keyboard player and founder, Paul Revere Dick, a restaurant owner from Boise, and Mike Smith of Britain's Dave Clark Five. Alan Price of the Animals also played the Vox, which was a strange-looking instrument with the black and white keys reversed, standing on two chrome Z-shaped legs. As Doors keyboardist Ray Manzarek enthusiastically recalled his first encounter with a Vox, "It was sleek and loud. . . . A keyboard player could then compete with those maniacs of loud . . . the guitar players."[18]

One of the few exceptions to the electronic organ trend was Les Maguire of Liverpool's Gerry and the Pacemakers, who played a traditional (non-electric) piano.

West Coast surf music may have emphasized twangy guitars, but the California-based group the Doors scored a #1 song with "Light My Fire" (1967), which featured keyboardist Ray Manzarek playing the new Fender Rhodes Piano Bass as well as his Vox Continental organ. Manzarek recalled the Doors' first contract featured little money, but free equipment from Vox:

> Vox made the organ that the Animals and the Dave Clark Five used. The red-and-black Vox Continental Organ. Alan Price played one with the Animals, and he was good . . . and it was very groovy . . . . It was sleek and loud. You plugged it into a guitar amp and cranked the sucker. A keyboard player could then compete with those maniacs of loud . . . the guitar players.[19]

Mark Stein, therefore, who had tapped into the keyboard trend had nevertheless landed on a new sound in rock, the more powerful, more prominent Hammond B-3 organ, not only shared with Felix Cavaliere but also Matthew Fisher of Procol Harum, who also developed a distinct approach to the instrument heard on the band's hit, "A Whiter Shade of Pale," which had a massive, cathedral sound. A young Stevie Winwood with the Spencer Davis Group also created his infamous distorted B-3 on their hit, "Gimme Some Lovin'" which endowed the instrument with an edginess. With Mark's soulful voice and his increasingly radical keyboard sound, the group had potential like few others.

What they did not have was management. Through a local band called the Pilgrims, Mark was put in contact with songwriter Jeff Barry (b. 1938), who had, with his wife Ellie Greenwich (and, at times,

41

producer Phil Spector), wrote "Chapel of Love," "Be My Baby," "Then He Kissed Me," and "Da Doo Ron Ron," becoming one of the more successful songwriting teams in pop music. Working with Spector, Barry-Greenwich helped define the "girl groups" such as the Ronettes, the Crystals, and the Shangri-Las. The two would also later discover and produce Neil Diamond (though he wrote his own hits, "Solitary Man," "Cherry, Cherry," "Kentucky Woman," and "Girl You'll Be a Woman Soon"), as well as wrote Tina Turner's "River Deep, Mountain High." Barry hung out in Tin Pan Alley, where he interacted with other rising composers, including Carole King, Jerry Goffin, and Shadow Morton.

The Pilgrims' manager, Frank (Fat Frankie) Scinlaro, set up a meeting between the boys and Barry, who asked the obvious question, "What's the band's name?" At that point, they hadn't decided on a name, so, playing on the wildlife nicknames (Beatles, Animals, Byrds), he came up with the Pigeons. Scinlaro then escorted the group to a club called Clay Cole's Place on the east tide. Cole, a New York disc jockey, founded the Clay Cole Show (1959-68), which was a successful counterpart to American Bandstand. Briefly, it eclipsed even Dick Clark's show as the hot venue for new groups, although Cole featured comedians (such as Richard Pryor and George Carlin) as well as music acts. As the boys watched the performances, Scinlaro informed them they were going to go onstage and play a few songs. They would use the house instruments, and be introduced as the Pigeons. Scared and nervous, the band pulled it off, playing "I Who Have Nothing" and "Midnight Hour," leading Barry to agree to handle them. He instructed Fat Frankie to find them a gig.

Scinlaro quickly booked them at the Choo Choo Club in Garfield, New Jersey, located so close to the train tracks that the sound of a passing locomotive would intrude on the (loud) rock music. There, they were re-signed to several months' worth of work. Playing four nights a week, the Pigeons got tighter and individually improved on their instruments. Equally important, they learned how to deal with club owners, for whom it was not "about the music," but about selling liquor. Thus songs that made people drink were far more desired than great musical numbers that displayed virtuosos. Mark and the boys also got the opportunity to watch and back up other acts on "Star Night" at the club, every Tuesday, when celebrities would come in. Screaming Jay Hawkins, The Dovells, The Shirells, Little Eva and many others played the Choo Choo. The acts would hand out chord charts at afternoon rehearsals which was a learning experience in and of itself from an "on the job training" perspective. "Most of us knew the lion's share of the material by ear from hearing their hits on the radio," Mark recollected, "but following the songs reading 'block charts' gave us discipline."When the Pigeons were on stage, the Young Rascals' Eddie Brigati, who lived close by, was often in the audience, and proved a big fan of Mark's. One night, Sal, the club owner, pulled Mark aside, saying, "There's someone here who wants to meet you." Sitting at the bar in the corner was guitar legend Les Paul, who signed a napkin, "To the Pigeons who will be famous someday."

Just as it appeared Mark and the Pigeons had found their groove, and had discussed Barry signing a production and songwriting agreement with them, one of those rock and roll things happened: Joey came in late for a rehearsal and Barry, convinced the band wasn't serious, took off. "It was a simple as that," Mark recalled, "and the relationship was over." Frankie, however, was still there, managing the Pigeons and other groups. One night, he brought a band to the Choo Choo to play a few songs on the Pigeons' equipment. Frankie had raved about, the Vagrants, who had a large guitar player named Leslie West. As Mark reminisced, "the Vagrants went on stage and played a song called 'My Babe' by the Righteous Brothers, and even though they sounded good, Frankie stopped the show," claiming something was wrong with the sound system. "You have to see them in their own habitat," Frankie told Mark.

A few weeks later, Frankie got the Pigeons a gig opening for the Vagrants at The Eye on Long Island. While Mark thought the Pigeons had played well, the crowd didn't respond and "we went back to the dressing room a bit shaken." Mark went out among the crowd and got ready to see the Vagrants. As he recalled, "little did I know that what was about to take place was going to truly blow me away and change my life. That night showed me the greatest band I ever saw. The way they moved, the energy, the drama…it was unreal!" They rearranged songs in ways Mark had never heard, playing the theme from Exodus, turning it into a "huge rock opera," then shifted gears into a slowdown version of Bobby Darin's "If I Were a Carpenter" that was "so soulful it would almost bring tears to your eyes." The Vagrants' star was lead singer Peter Sabatino, whose energy and excitement awed Mark. "He'd be soaked with sweat and when he would shake his head with his long hair into the lights, the sweat would fly and add to the drama." But they also had a burly, powerful guitar player named Leslie West, who would later become a star in his own right. Then there was the Hammond B-3 player, Jerry Storch, who created massive sounds and thunderous wind ups. "They took my breath away," Mark remembered. "I mean, the Rascals were great, but these guys took it to a whole new level." Mark drove home thinking the Pigeons were done, yet strangely enough, he also felt inspired. As Mark would later say, "we are but the sum of our

43

influences," and the Vagrants had now done their part to shape Mark's music and his vision.

The Pigeons' maturation unfolded against a backdrop of the Cold War, something Mark knew about tangentially, but which had little impact on his daily life or political views. Mark recalled, "I was ten and in the back seat of my parents' car on the way home from the Roosevelt drive-in theater in Jersey City—we had just seen Springfield Rifle, with Jimmy Stewart—and dad was listening to the radio when news came on that the Soviet Union had launched the first satellite into outer space, Sputnik." Like many youngsters, that was Mark's first awareness of a nation far away that had to be reckoned with. But what that meant, he wasn't sure, until in the fall of 1962 the Cuban Missile Crisis nearly brought the world to nuclear war. "I was in high school, and didn't understand what was going on, but it was my first real fear of Russia and communism," he recalled. "So there it was, this great, ominous, dark country."

As transcriptions of the tape recordings made within the security meetings of the Kennedy administration would later show, from the President on down, most expected war to come at any moment. Kennedy's brilliant, in retrospect, "middle ground" of a blockade (as opposed to an invasion of Cuba on the one hand, or letting the missiles stay, on the other) proved essential allowing Soviet Premier Nikita Khrushchev time to offer a face-saving deal to remove the missiles in exchange for Kennedy's promise not to invade Cuba. Of course, the White House jumped at the chance—after the Bay of Pigs, JFK had no intention of trying to invade Cuba again anyway—and the world came back from the brink.[20]

The Pigeons' guitar player, Vince Martell, had just gotten out of the U.S. Navy and barely missed seeing action in the Cuban blockade. An engineer, 3rd class on the U.S.S. *Hunting*, an auxiliary ship, Martell had just returned from testing sonar gear in the Bermuda Triangle and were "loading stores," as Vinny recalled. "We got the order to get under way," but were abruptly recalled as Kennedy and Khruschev arrived at a peaceful conclusion to the crisis.[21]

Mustered out, Martell's first thought was to play music. He had played guitar since age eight—everyone in Vinny's family played an instrument—played drums in a Catholic school drum and bugle corps. While in the Navy, he saw Ray Charles perform in Norfolk, and had a band with several other sailors while stationed there. Vinny did not want to stay in Virginia, so he returned to New York before joining his parents in Florida. Obtaining a Gibson ES 335 cherry red guitar, Martel joined the Porkys in Ft. Lauderdale, then played local clubs with the Bondsmen,

44

where he backed up Bobby Vinton. (Vinny was not the only rock star to serve, if before Vietnam: Doors keyboardist Ray Manzarek enlisted in the Army in 1961, and despite trying to get into the film unit, ended up a "rifle-toting mud hog" stationed in Okinawa and Thailand, where he developed a fine appreciation for marijuana!)[22]

Mark, who himself faced the Selective Service, by now focused on obtaining manpower for the Vietnam War. Playing at the time with Rick Martin, Mark was called in for his physical. "Here I was," he said, "lovin' life, playin' in a band, making money, and I thought, 'If I end up in the Army, this will disappear.'" He called a local doctor, who wrote notes about how bad his feet were, and Mark brought them to the physical. Whatever the notes said, it worked: Mark was classified 1-Y at first (available for service in a genuine emergency) then re-classified 4-F ("physically unfit for service"). Mark's attitude was that of countless numbers of young American men who could not see a direct threat to the nation from a small country across the globe, and who were caught up in their lives.

As the battlefield shifted from the Caribbean to Southeast Asia, making the case for military service became even harder for the nation's recruiters. The Vietnam War was only just escalating—John F. Kennedy had put in 17,000 U.S. advisors, with more than 25,000 troops stationed in the region. Kennedy was assassinated before he paid a political price for Vietnam, but there is no denying his role in starting an almost irreversible buildup. After his assassination and the Gulf of Tonkin incident, Lyndon Johnson committed the U.S. military to widespread operations, increasing troop levels to over 150,000 initially. They would eventually reach over 550,000, still far below what the Joint Chiefs of Staff had insisted would be necessary to do the job in 1964.[23]

Despite the sometimes desperate scholarly gymnastics used to try to claim that JFK would have "pulled out," the evidence suggests that had he lived, JFK would have pursued much the same policy in Vietnam as did his successor. What directions the anti-war movement would have taken under that circumstance is purely speculative, but given the romantic myth associated with Kennedy's "youth," it is entirely likely that the anti-war forces would have been blunted, and certainly it would have been more difficult to portray JFK as detached and as bloodthirsty as Lyndon Johnson.

Nevertheless, what did unfold was a widespread, broad-based opposition against the war that linked itself to the civil rights movement already well under way in America. It was inevitable that music would become one of the movement's major forms of expression. What is surprising is not only how long it took, but that rock music's influence within the antiwar movement seemed to peak only after public attitudes had already shifted against the war.[24]

The war placed several distinct stresses on rock musicians. First, with the Selective Service system, virtually all young, healthy males were subject to the draft and, hence, possible deployment to Southeast Asia. This exposure weighed on most musicians of the day, almost all of whom sought ways to escape military service. A few served, mostly before the war. Vince Martell and Ray Manzarek were exceptions.[25]

Another was Jimi Hendrix, who had been arrested for riding in stolen cars, was given a choice of jail or the army, and he enlisted in May 1961, completed boot camp, then was assigned to the 101st Airborne at Fort Campbell, Kentucky. His friends and officers remembered him as a poor soldier, was a habitual offender in missing bed checks, and thought about little except playing a guitar.[26]

He later reminisced about his parachute training ("once you get out there everything is so quiet, all you hear is breezes") and told Dick Cavett only that he had been stationed at Fort Campbell. But on other occasions his comments were mixed. In 1962, he took pride he was in the 101st, saying "I'm in the best division: the 101st Airborne. That's the sharpest outfit in the world."[27]

He met Billy Cox, who would be his bass player in Band of Gypsies, at the post recreation center, and the two formed a band called the King Casuals.

In an interview in 1969 with *Melody Maker* where he mentioned his military experience, Hendrix said he disliked the army.[28] Yet later that year, in a second *Melody Maker* interview, Hendrix was pressed by European reporters to comment on the Vietnam War. He shocked them by comparing Vietnam to D-Day: "Did you send the Americans away when they landed in Normandy? . . . No, but then that was concerning your own skin. The Americans are fighting in Vietnam for the complete free world . . . ."[29]

Unlike many of his contemporaries, Hendrix could vacillate between drug-inspired pantheons of dragonflies and "sixes turning out to be nines," then turn around and utter common-sense, down-home wisdom worthy of the *Farmer's Almanac*. "Of course war is horrible," Hendrix said in 1969, "but at present, it's still the only guarantee to maintain peace."[30]

His album, *Axis: Bold as Love* contained astounding realism for the hippie crowd: "Castles made of sand, fall in the sea, eventually." Music critics uniformly interpreted his rendition of the 'Star Spangled Banner' at Woodstock to be an apocalyptic parody, yet there is considerable reason to believe that it was a heart-felt American tribute done as only Hendrix could perform it.

Folk music, much more than rock, had emerged as the protest music du jour, with such 1950s artists as Pete Seeger and Peter, Paul, and Mary still mixing politics with their musical appearances. Perhaps for that reason, many within the counterculture movement expected Bob Dylan to emerge as the anti-war champion. Dylan, supposedly following in the footsteps of Woody Guthrie, had issued his third studio album in 1964, "The Times They Are A-Changin'," which seemed an appropriate youth anthem. "Come senators, congressmen please heed the call," Dylan moaned in his nasal whine, and "don't stand in the doorway, don't block up the hall . . . There's a battle outside and it's ragin'." He called on "mothers and fathers throughout the land" not to "criticize what you can't understand . . . you old road is rapidly agin'." Wish as they did for Dylan to lead, the footsoldiers of the "movement" were sorely disappointed. Dylan himself never thought he was political, and expressed as much to singer John Cougar Mellenkamp.[31] As '60s culture critic, Peter Doggett observed, "the more oblique and fantastic his lyrics, the more they intrigued his followers."[32]

One radical New York student gained acclaim by performing a 1960s version of "channeling" Dylan, using acid to decipher the muse's lyrics for the world. "I decided to devote myself," Alan ("A.J.") Weberman said, "to explaining the Secret Language of Rock to the world." This led him to conclude that such oft-used phrases in Dylan's lyrics as "morning" and "nightfall" really meant drugs, "rain" was code for violence, and "Maggie's Farm" stood for the evil capitalist system.[33]

Weberman posed an eerie resemblance to those other possessors of Rosetta Stones, including interpreters who were certain "Lucy in the Sky With Diamonds" stood for "LSD," despite John Lennon's protestations that the lyrics were taken from a painting by his son, Julian. (McCartney would later tell the BBC that it was "pretty obvious" the song was inspired by LSD, but Lennon stood by his comments until his death).[34]

In San Francisco, the Jefferson Airplane was similarly ambivalent about activism. "We didn't give a shit about politics," recalled Paul Kantner. We created our own special space [and] felt that we didn't have any responsibilities . . . . We wanted the freedom to make our own choices."[35] Not surprisingly, this freedom and liberation distinguished the Airplane's music. Grace Slick would later call it "a little sloppy, actually, it wasn't precise . . . . It wasn't like, how come you didn't sing that flatted fourth?"[36]

When it came to politics, however, the assumption that the Airplane—or any rock and rollers—would automatically "fight the power" crashed into reality. In 1967, when several British intellectuals and authors sent a telegram to the prime minister calling for his government to renounce the American bombing of Hanoi, no rock and rollers signed up.[37]

This, of course, was the flip side of "livin' life, playin' music, and making money": there was little enthusiasm for joining any cause, movement, or organization, whether it was the U.S. Army or Abbie Hoffman's Yippies. Nor was the power of music as a revolutionary force proven yet.

What was not debatable was that rock music had swept through the entire culture, providing a common language to a generation. Within that common language were numerous musical "dialects" or tastes. They went a long way towards predicting someone's personality—almost a litmus test of sorts for compatibility, as former *Rolling Stone* editor Fred Goodman described:

> It was a lot like administering a psychological test. First you'd check to see if the basic language was there—the Beatles, the Stones, and the British invasion bands; Motown and Stax; the San Francisco groups; Dylan. After that, you'd probe special interests for signs of sophistication or character flaws. For instance, a passion for a perfectly acceptable but lightweight group like Steppenwolf showed a certain genial rebelliousness but suggested a lack of depth; a girl who listened to a lot of Joni Mitchell could probably be talked into bed but you might regret it later; a single-minded focus on the Grateful Dead and the New Riders of the Purple Sage was a sure sign of a heavy dope smoker; anyone with a record collection that traced the blues further back than John Mayall and the Yardbirds was an intellectual. It was, I recall, a remarkably accurate system.[38]

It also provided a vast canopy under which different musical styles could emerge and thrive. As the Vietnam War escalated, Mark had escaped the draft on medical grounds and Vinny had already served, giving the band a stability, certain in the knowledge that no one would be leaving soon. But Mark sensed it was time to grow or pack it in, especially after seeing the Vagrants. Dissatisfied with what he called "straight ahead music," Mark realized that "although we were a good top 40 cover band, there was something more serious to pursue." At the time, the Pigeons had scored a recording session with Luther Dixon, a hot Motown producer who saw the band at the Choo Choo Club and said he wanted to record some tracks for them. They located a New York studio and recorded Wilson Pickett's "Midnight Hour" and a Doc Pomus song called "About Me." Dixon thought the song would be perfect for Mark's voice. After the session, Luther told the band he'd be in touch, that he would try to set up a deal for the band, and departed for Detroit with the tapes. Months later, he called to say that he had overdubbed some horns and would send the boys a copy.

Then . . . nothing. Two years later, after Vanilla Fudge had success on the charts, an album appeared called *While the World Was Eating Vanilla Fudge,* by Mark Stein and the Pigeons. Mark's lawyer stepped in to squash the album—"a glorified demo," as Mark called it—and while the record became something of a collector's item, Luther Dixon disappeared permanently. So, as it was, Mark's vision was to have a band that had the soul and harmonies of the Rascals, combined with the symphonic like arrangement capabilities and dynamics of the Vagrants. Mark, Vince and Tim blended well vocally, but Joey wasn't really a singer and his "Charlie Watts" style of drumming didn't lend itself to the music they wanted to pursue. We broke the news to him and immediately started on our quest for a replacement. Weeks later, Mark and Tim paid a visit to the Choo Choo club to watch Thursday's Children, a band that featured Dean Parrish on vocals. They had on drums an Italian kid from Brooklyn named Carmine Appice. He had an incredible foot equal or even beyond Dino Danelli's, demonstrated some astounding counter rhythms, and above all played with great power. Mark and Tim sat as close to the drums as they could and after the set went back and asked him to talk "so we went outside" in the crisp night air and pitched him on what we wanted to do and he got really excited, Mark recalled. He was a singer too and "we hit it off right away," Mark said. "Do you want to be a Pigeon" Mark asked "Fuck yeah!" Appice replied.[39]

Mark's father knew the owner of this bar near 50th Street and Broadway in Bayonne, and he set it up so the boys could rehearse in the back room. Carmine could drive in from Brooklyn, Vinny was staying with Mark, and Tim could come in from Ridgefield. Meanwhile, Irving Stein talked to the owner of a popular club in Oceanside, Long Island called the Action House. Phil Basile, known to the boys as "Philly," agreed to audition the band within one week. One week! Practicing like banshees, picking tunes and selecting the lead singer for each, the Pigeons flew into a week of frantic rehearsal. But the vocal harmonies just came together—"everybody listened to the same groups," Mark noted, including the Impressions, the Temptations, and the Righteous Brothers. The blend was there from the beginning, and it didn't hurt that Mark, Carmine, and Vinny had similar vocal sounds. Only Tim was significantly different, but that also worked to the group's advantage, in that he ended up singing the high end with his high tenor voice.

The audition went well and the Pigeons played the Action House. Before long, Philly put the band on weekends. Here they were, in the heart of Vagrant country, and that band remained the Pigeons' local idols. Virtually every musician who had ambition drifted into the Action House at the time—Billy Joel's drummer, Liberty DeVitto, recalled opening for Vanilla Fudge (as the Pigeons were soon re-named) there, and was so intimidated by the sound he could barely go on stage. Yet before long, his band "took on the personality" of the Pigeons-turned-Fudge.[40]

"We got the same clothes . . . . [and] our guitarist copied Vinny." But neither the Vagrants nor the Pigeons were alone in taking top songs and turning them into production numbers, as virtually every band on Long Island had hit on the same approach. Each, however, had the same goal: to someday be the best of the lot. Other top names played the Action House, such as Question Mark and the Mysterians, and Wilson Pickett. On the night Pickett appeared, he asked the audience, "Now, who wants to come up and sing with me?" Mark's friends all pointed at him, whereupon Mark "jumped on stage with him and did a duet." As for Question Mark, that band re-introduced Neil Scott into Mark's life. Scott, who had drawn Mark into his early show-business jaunts, was on his way to becoming the top promotion man in the business with Cameo Records, and had steered |96 Tears high up on the charts. Scott would continue to drift in and out of Mark Stein's musical life.

Meanwhile, Phil had become the band's de facto manager, signing papers in Phil's office at the Action House. While signing the management contract, Philly instructed them, "remember, first you gotta crawl then walk and then you can run." Basile's assistant was Shelly Finkel, who actually booked the bands. Sending the band to Newport, Rhode Island at a club called Dorian's, the band found another place where it just fit in, soon becoming a regular there along with the Action House. The Cowsills, who lived in the area and whose hit, The Rain, The Park, and Other Things made them teen heart throbs, frequented Dorian's and loved the Pigeons. The father of the group wanted to manage the band, but the boys felt great loyalty to Basile, and opted to stay with their current management.

Another Rhode Island club where the Pigeons were popular was the Bastille, where they not only performed their own material but often backed up bigger acts. Once Freddy Cannon came in, only to find Bogert was bored with his songs. "Tim and Freddie locked horns," Mark remembered, but finally worked it out and we rocked on "Tallahassee Lassie" and "Palisades Park" for him. The Left Banke also appeared at the Bastille, performing their hit, "Walk Away Renee." The band was making enough money to pay the bills, but chafed at backing up other artists. Already they were putting together some of their soon-to-be famous arrangements, such as "People Get Ready" and "She's Not There."

After playing another club, though—Ungano's in New York's upper west side—the careers of the Pigeons nearly came to a hasty end. Mark, Tim, and Vinny were walking in the city and a car screeched up to the curb. Tim shouted something at the occupants, who came running out of the car and grabbed Bogert. He had managed to insult plain-clothes police, who pulled something out of Bogert's pocket. (Mark was never sure if it was a small knife or not). They arrested Tim on the spot and hauled him off. Mark yelled, "Christ, we're in a band and we're playing Ungano's tonight." The cop yelled back, "Not tonight you're not!" Bogert was the guest of the city for the night, forcing the band to play without a bass player, and requiring Mark to play bass on his pedals.

From that low point, however, the band was close to its breakthrough, which came in the winter of 1966 when Mark and Tim sat in a car idling in front of the Cheetah Club. Over the radio came the Supremes and their hit, "You Keep Me Hangin' On." So Mark said "Tim, it might be really cool to slow this down." We looked at each other and felt it in our guts. Mark thought about it for a few days and called Vinny and Carmine and we started hashing out the arrangement. Vinny had developed a "rock raga lick" that was perfect for the intro and Mark supported that with some nasty bottom end Hammond stuff leading up to this almost haunting fluty sound which echoed the melody of the verse. Then Carmine and Tim added the groove, and the vocal arrangements came quickly. "We were excited," Mark said. "We knew we had something great." They couldn't wait to start playing it in the set, but then people didn't know what to make of the song at first. They couldn't dance to it—but, Mark noted, "they couldn't dance to half our stuff"— but the band knew there was a bigger picture. Audiences began to sit on the dance floor to watch the Pigeons play. "Our dynamics were mighty. We'd be rocking at a roar and suddenly like a great wave hitting the shore there would be nothingness. The style played a big part in the drama of a Pigeons' performance. After a two week gig in Miami at a club called the Par-T Lounge, the band returned to the Action House where it was hitting its stride. No longer intimidated by any of the other local bands, the Pigeons had their own following—even Vagrants' fans started to frequent the Pigeons' shows.

Basile and Finkel—who later in his career would become a major manager of boxers in all weight classes, including several champions, including Mike Tyson and Evander Holyfield ---thought it was time to bring in the "big guns." They invited the hot New York producer George "Shadow" Morton to see the band. A New York native, shipped to New Jersey by his mom to get him out of the local gang scene, Morton, like Mark, began singing in *acapella* groups when he was young. Morton wrote and co-produced the Shangri-La's' hit "Remember (Walkin' in the Sand)," which featured a young Billy Joel playing keyboards on the demo, and their #1 song "Leader of the Pack." Morton's production techniques resembled the "Wall of Sound" already developed by Phil Spector on the Ronettes' 1963 hit, "Be My Baby." Operating out of Gold Star Studios in Los Angeles, noted for its reverb and echo effects from its hard walls and specialized microphone placement, Spector employed a "Wagnerian approach to rock and roll," or "Little symphonies for the kids," as he labeled it, Spector employed a large band backed up by an even larger symphony orchestra in the studio.[41]

His mainstay studio band, called the "Wrecking Crew," consisted of, among others, Hal Blaine on drums, Leon Russell on keyboards, and Glen Campbell on guitar. But they were only the beginning: Spector would line up five guitars, two bassists, and layer on line after line, literally burying the lead voices.

Morton had heard the Pigeons at the Action House, where the band was playing its first album arrangements. Then Mark began the lone notes on his B-3 and Morton stopped: the music soon exploded into the Fudge's classic version of "You Keep Me Hangin' On." Morton was knocked out because he had witnessed the show that would ultimately become the first Vanilla Fudge LP, but didn't fully realize how great it was until he recorded the band. He signed them immediately, telling Shelly Finkel, "Listen, this has to be the greatest group I'm ever gonna hear . . . ."[42]

As the Pigeons became Vanilla Fudge and gained popularity, Basile got 25% off the top. While struggling to keep the Fudge under his control, he tried to edge Finkel out of the action. Shelly responded by taking Vinny and Mark out to dinner and plied them with hookers: "He bought dinner and bought the women," Mark laughed. Finally, Phil took the boys to the car one night and pulled out stacks of receipts: "Look at all the money I gave you," he said. "What did Shelly do for you?" In fact, Basile had paid the boys out of his own pocket for a time. At one point, Mark's parents got involved and met with Phil, and the band remained with Philly, who continued to press their careers forward.

Armed with a full studio deal, Morton normally would have emulated Spector with the Pigeons' sessions, but without that financial backing, he took the boys to a studio in Mira Sound in New York City, which was in the basement of a hotel (or, as Mark more correctly labeled it, a whorehouse). Mark, Vinny, Tim, and Carmine set up and started playing while Morton recorded them in monotone. Morton later recalled he was less concerned with perfection and more concerned with the band's energy and emotion. The band was tight from so many club gigs that they recorded "You Keep Me Hangin' On" in one take! They hustled into the booth where Shadow and engineer Joe Vineri looked mesmerized, playing the track over and over. It was originally seven minutes long, and the two kept muttering, "It's a symphony." Morton called it the "best time I had in a studio," and the Vanilla Fudge album of course became a hit. (Later, when Liberty DeVitto brought his own band to Morton's studio, Shadow "put on [the Fudge's] 'Ticket to Ride' at volume 13 and said, 'This is what I want you to sound like!'"[43]

As Mark put it, "the buzz got loud in a hurry." Instantly Shadow told Atlantic Records president, Ahmet Ertegun, about the band, even playing him the acetate of the music without the vocals just to whet his whistle. Basile quickly put together a record deal through Phantom Productions (a combination of Shadow's company and Atlantic) while the band kept recording other numbers, such as "People Get Ready" and "Ticket to Ride," still recording some at a studio called Mira Sound but also laying down tracks at Ultra Sonic Studios on Long Island, where they recorded most of the vocals. Morton arrived one day with a song called "Take Me for a Little While," written by Trade Martin and originally recorded by Eve Sands. After working their soulful power-magic, the song took on a whole new character, and later would prove to be a favorite among Fudge fans and which was tagged as the flip side to "You Keep Me Hangin' On." It made the album, which was released in August 1967, but not without a struggle. Morton recalled a phone call from Ahmet Ertegun, the head of Atlantic, who informed Shadow, "I can't put this out. Every song is over three minutes, and there's not one original song on it." Morton simply hopped on a plane to Los Angeles where a colleague, Artie Rip, was promoting a single. Rip was visiting stations, record in hand. Morton asked if he could piggyback, just to talk to the managers.

Unaware he was being set up, Rip agreed. Morton gave out Vanilla Fudge albums to the disc jockeys and said, "see if you get any response on this." At one station, the disc jockey actually didn't handle any records at all—a "kid" behind a booth did. So Morton gave the young man the record and proceeded to ply the DJ with booze. Every time he looked into the booth, which was both playing live and being taped for replay that night, the kid gave Shadow the "keep it going" sign.

By the time the disc jockey got curious, the engineer had played the entire album, and recorded it for a second playing that night. The response was stunning. Shadow called Ertegun and said, "You need to ship 350,000 copies of the album to California." When it dawned on the outraged Ertegun that he had been outmaneuvered, he reluctantly shipped the LPs. It was the first time in history that a rock LP was released without an accompanying single. Nevertheless, to ensure the group's main song, "You Keep Me Hangin' On," got AM airplay, producer Arif Mardin edited it down to three minutes without losing any of the power or unique sound.

Prior to the release, Ertegun told the Pigeons they had to change their name to something more powerful. While rehearsing at the Action House, a female singer from a band called The Unspoken Word shouted out, "Why don't you call yourselves Vanilla Fudge?" It was a nickname her grandfather had called her because she ate so much vanilla fudge ice cream. Ahmet hated it, saying the band would never make it with that moniker, but it fit perfectly: here was a white band playing black, soulful music with a whole new psychedelic, symphonic twist. Their success proved that even Ertegun was not perfect in his assessments. Where he was prescient was in his appreciation for the sound of Vanilla Fudge. Every week, famous disc jockey Murray the K had his "pick the hit" show, in which he premiered five new songs. The seven-minute version of "You Keep Me Hangin' On" was featured with a new song by the Beatles and three other tunes. Listeners would decide the winner with their phone calls. It was amazing to the boys merely to hear their song on the radio, but then when they came in ahead of the Beatles in top place, the buzz in the industry became deafening. It also was another indicator within American rock that the Fab Four no longer reigned supreme—that they could be dethroned, however temporarily, by a bunch of kids from Jersey, Brooklyn, and the Bronx. Morton and Ertegun did their part: when the LP was released, the trade magazines Cashbox and Billboard featured full page ads saying "Vanilla Fudge: The Most Awaited Album of the Year!"

Jerry Wexler of Atlantic Records took notice of the Fudge's success. He already had Buffalo Springfield, Cream, and Aretha Franklin, "also had his eye on the future, as forecast by the sales performance of . . . Iron Butterfly and Vanilla Fudge [both on Atlantic/Atco].." Both groups were heavier than Springfield or most other bands—save Cream—and, except for "Inna-Gadda-Da-Vita," rarely had #1 hits. But their staying power was impressive, and forced Atlantic to begin signing bands with similar appeals.[44]

Meanwhile, as fame began to swim in the boys' heads, a few of the realities of life also began to dawn on them when they slowly discovered that Phil Basile was affiliated with the Luchese crime family. The mob had begun an intense infiltration of the record industry, including companies, radio stations, and tour bookings. Mark started to notice that the LP was constantly on the air at WNEW in New York City, where Scott Muni was the hottest disc jockey around. He not only played songs from the album—not just You Keep Me Hangin' On—but even introduced Vanilla Fudge at shows. Muni was "good friends" with Basile, and it didn't hurt that Paulie Vario was the local boss who owned Vanilla Fudge and also owned a club in Brooklyn called Tempo City. The Fudge soon played there regularly, with Neil Diamond as the opening act. From a purely business angle, however, Vanilla Fudge made Vario plenty of money: the club was always packed and, in return, everywhere the boys went they were treated like royalty—not only because they were a popular band, but, as Mark said, "who we were hooked up with."

Anyone who thought that the Fudge—or any other group—owed their success solely, or even mainly, to mob influence or payola was sadly mistaken. In reality, several factors coalesced to put Vanilla Fudge (and other "album bands," such as Pink Floyd, the Allman Brothers, King Crimson, or Emerson, Lake, and Palmer) in the right place at the right time. First, the long-term transition from singles (or "45s") to albums within the industry was nearly complete. The long-playing record (LP), spun at 33 revolutions per minute versus the 45 revolutions per minute of the single, made it possible to "create one's own musical environment," making pop music more segmented than ever.[45]

In 1949, the Broadway play South Pacific produced seven different performers doing "Some Enchanted Evening," but no one version of the song ever cracked the top charts. Singles on the other hand, had already imposed their own changes on the industry, giving rise to the infamous "one hit wonders," because any "street-corner doo-wop group could get a top ten hit while still in high school without making any professional appearances. . . ."[46]

It also, however, set the mainstream music profession—with its unions, publishing contracts, professional songwriters and musicians—against rock and its amateur origins.

A second phenomenon unfolded for "album" bands such as the Fudge: the length of the songs made them naturals for "underground" radio, the network of FM stations that fancied themselves as countercultural rebels. Typical AM singles seldom ran more than two minutes and forty-five seconds, but Vanilla Fudge songs averaged five to seven minutes. With the heavy sound, the Fudge soon became the darlings of the 60s drug culture—"it was a foregone conclusion," noted Mark, "that we were all acid heads." (In fact, while the boys smoked reefer, none had even tried LSD yet, let alone become regular "trippers"). Just as Cher, who was straight, emerged as an icon of the male homosexual community, so too the drug-free Fudge were seen as leaders in the drug-music subculture. "I remember doing interviews," Mark recalled, "and there was almost this disappointment when we were found out to be straight."

Then there was the simple reality that Vanilla Fudge live was one of the best acts in the business. They hadn't started that way, but by the time the album came out, the band had begun to perfect a show that few acts wanted to follow. As an indicator of the types of jealousies the Fudge would face, in July 1967, just before the album came out, the buzz from advanced airplay on WNEW FM landed Vanilla Fudge a spot opening for the Rascals at Long Island Arena. This was a big event for a group of upstarts. It was a packed house, and Scott Muni, the disc jockey from the station, had played the tracks relentlessly (with lots of "palm greasing" by Basile, no doubt). But the Fudge didn't get much of a sound check and three songs into the set, Mark's Hammond lost power. Their single roadie searched frantically for the problem, switching wires, but the band had to keep playing—without the organ! Mark was mortified and thought the group had been sabotaged. They never learned who unplugged Mark, but "judging by the sly smirks of a few stage guys that worked for a band with a hit called 'Good Lovin',' one could only surmise!" Mark stormed into the dressing room, screaming, when Tim gave him a hug and said "Stop taking it so hard, you creative son of a bitch!." Then, Sid Bernstein, known as "the man who brought the Beatles to America" and the personal manager of the Rascals, came in put his arms around Mark, and said, "Kid, one day you're going to look back at this and laugh." Looking back some 40-odd years, Mark asked, "Am I laughing? Well, yeah, but with a sadness in my heart that it went away so swiftly."

The Rascals, the Vagrants, and now Vanilla Fudge constituted the vanguard of an East Coast sound that featured precise and powerful arrangements, soulful vocals, and a blend of keyboards and guitars. A much different sound emerged on the West Coast, much of it originating in San Francisco, that emphasized an unstructured style, used more guitars, and lacked the black vocal elements. Groups such as We Five, the Beau Brummels, Jefferson Airplane, the Grateful Dead, Moby Grape, Big Brother and the Holding Company, Quicksilver Messenger Service, Blue Cheer, Country Joe and the Fish, the Sons of Champlin, Creedence Clearwater Revival, and Sly and the Family Stone all came from San

Francisco or northern California. Associated with the Haight-Ashbury counterculture, the bands' sets usually included extended improvisations (the essence of rock and roll) and long, meandering solos perfectly attuned to drug highs. The Grateful Dead, in particular, developed a reputation as an off-the-cuff "jam" band. West Coast music also—Tim Bogert and Jack Bruce aside—tended to allow the bass guitar to wander freely; and while there was not as much black influence, oddly there were a number of interracial bands, including Sly and the renowned horn band, Tower of Power. Where the East Coast groups sought to win over audiences by skill and soulful vocals, West Coast groups eagerly tried anything, including gimmicks. Blue Cheer once played up its sheer volume, reputedly recording one album on a pier because its amps were too loud for a studio. Tower of Power's horns became so famous that they were in demand by Huey Lewis, Rod Stewart, the Monkees, Cat Stevens, Santana, Toto, Poison, and Jefferson Starship. A few groups, including the Beach Boys—who had come up earlier—and the Doors, the Byrds, and the Eagles, all from southern California, developed a somewhat different, more precise, sound. But the northern California/"West Coast" music was instantly recognizable. Over time, as a rule, the twain never met—it was unusual to find band combinations of West Coast/East Coast musicians because the styles differed so greatly.

No single person advanced West Coast music, and, by extension, rock and roll, as Bill Graham. A German-born Jew, Graham as a child ended up in France with other Jewish orphans and escaped with a few other children, even though others in his family died at Auschwitz. Put in a foster home in the Bronx, he changed his name from Wolodia Grajonca to Bill Graham, graduated high school, then received a degree in business from City College before going into the Army in 1951. While serving in Korea stringing communication lines, he received the Bronze Star and the Purple Heart, then after the war worked as a waiter in the Catskill Mountains. Moving to San Francisco in the early 1960s, Graham became associated with the San Francisco Mime Troupe, which he soon managed. He got his start as a concert promoter when he staged a benefit concert for the group's legal fees.

Graham soon found himself at odds with those who favored "pure" art and wanted to avoid any business structures, while he "would preach to people, business-wise, about what their obligations were."[47]

After promoting another benefit at the Fillmore Auditorium in 1965, Graham got a lease and in 1966 began producing concerts at the Fillmore. He specialized in San Francisco counterculture groups such as Jefferson Airplane, Janis Joplin, Country Joe and the Fish, and the Grateful Dead, although one of his first big shows involved a Chicago group called the Paul Butterfield Blues Band. His chief rival, former associate in the Butterfield concert, Chet Helms of the Family Dog Production company, had founded Big Brother and the Holding Company with Janis Joplin and had set up shop for alternative concerts at the Avalon Ballroom in 1966. Family Dog specialized in wild, psychedelic posters, an eclectic mix of musicians, and more free form concerts than the Fillmore.

Graham, on the other hand, rejected the "music for music's sake" approach. He understood that survival and longevity required a certain commitment to the bottom line. He especially encountered the "everything-should-be-free" ethos in New York City when he started the Fillmore East in 1968. Counterculture papers would chide him about making money. "Why do you people have to pay for your paper?" he asked. "You want mine to be free?" referring to concerts, "Okay. I want yours to be free" referring to their papers.[48] "I was the antihero," he noted, but "the artist on stage always dictated the price of the ticket by his financial demands."[49]

When MC5, one of the most radical bands on the scene—known as "the people's revolutionary band"---played the Fillmore East, they had all their equipment stolen out of a van in the alley. Graham noted in his biography, "The people's band had all their equipment stolen. By the other people, I guess."[50]

At its apex, the Fillmores achieved legendary status. Graham recalled that once in the bathroom he overheard two guys talking. "I forgot. Who's playing here tonight?" one asked. The other responded, "I don't know man. What's the difference? It's the *Fillmore*."[51]

Graham soon took concert promotion to a larger scale, forming a booking agency that produced the Rolling Stones tour in 1972, then several Stones' tours thereafter. Left-wing in his political persuasions, he never lost sight of the reality that someone had to pay for performances—they didn't spontaneously happen. Graham admitted "I had no real personal knowledge of the rock scene of that era. I had been into Latin music all my life [and] didn't even listen to the radio. . . ."[52]

But he did care about musicians, relentlessly labored to remind them of their obligations to paying customers, and helped launch the careers of Santana and Eddie Money. Ironically, the powerful Atlantic Records guru Ahmet Ertegun heard Santana in San Francisco and was unimpressed. "They can't play. Furthermore, they won't sell."[53]

Despite the presence of the Fillmore East, the sounds on the two coasts remained distinct for some time. And unlike the Fillmore West, which gained a reputation for helping create the San Francisco Sound, the Fillmore East was where groups played, not where they were made.

Certainly East-coast groups such as the Fudge—after they had enjoyed record success---played at the Fillmore West, too. When the Fudge made their appearance there, they arrived to find the backstage doors locked. Tim Bogert began kicking the door, trying to open it, when Graham appeared, incensed. "What the hell do you think you're doing? You never do that to my club!" But he let them in, and the Fudge played a whale of a show.

Vanilla Fudge, the first album, had been out only two months when the band opened for the Mamas and the Papas at the Portland Coliseum. Stations were playing the whole side of the album straight through—a practice that was unheard of unless your names were John, Paul, George, and Ringo. Giddy with excitement, the band drove by the Coliseum to see the marquee, "The Mamas and the Papas—SOLD OUT," but . . . no mention of Vanilla Fudge. It was already 2:00 p.m., meaning that the managing agencies back east were closing, so the group sped back to the hotel. Phil Basile called Ron Terry, the band's booking agent. "Man," Basile said, "the Fudge doesn't even have their name on the marquee." Seemingly endless minutes passed before Basile received the return call: "Tom Hulett, the promoter, said the Mamas and the Papas never put another band's name on the marquee." Philly started to protest, but Ron cut him off. "This is their first big show. Don't make a big deal of it, just tell the Fudge to get onstage and KICK ASS."

It didn't prove that easy to "kick ass" in Portland. First, the band scrambled after hanging out several hours in the dressing room after an initial sound check, then, when the "on-stage in five" call went out, the boys shot down the stairs to a long hallway where they could see 20,000 screaming Mamas and Papas fans. The local disc jockey took center stage to announce, "Good evening Portland! Please welcome for their first appearance here in the northwest, from New York. . . Vanilla Fudge!" The band walked on stage, with Carmine sliding behind his drums and Tim and Vinny, guitars in hand, strode to their amps where roadies plugged them in. Mark moved behind the B-3 and grabbed the microphone only to notice . . . the audience was booing them loudly. He turned to the rest of the band and threw up his hands in disgust. "How could these people be so rude?" he thought. "Our first album just came out and they really don't know what we're all about as we haven't played a single note." His fear turned to anger, and Mark screamed into the mike, "Listen, Portland. We came three thousand miles to play for you and we're gonna do it whether you like it or not." A sudden silence followed, then turned to cheers. The Fudge put on a good show, and Mark was satisfied with the performance when it was over.

Down the hallway from the dressing room, accepting the good

59

wishes of the entourage of people swarming the stairs, Mark could see Mama Cass Elliott and Michelle Phillips warming up. Cass gave Mark a brief nod, then the two were joined by John Phillips and Denny Dougherty—the Mamas and the Papas. Mark watched as they held hands, then headed down the hallway to play. "They had such a look of joy and confidence," Mark recalled, "that it gave me a sense of warmth." The roar from the auditorium told him the headliners had arrived on stage.

But there was little time for reflection: Philly was already hustling the boys back to the hotel room to speak to the proverbial "some people." Scheduled to open in Seattle the following night for the Fifth Dimension and Sonny & Cher, Tim asked "Aren't we supposed to go to Seattle?" He then grumbled, "I wish you'd get your shit together." Philly's eyes bulged, but he controlled himself. "You worry about the music and let me worry about the business. You guys are going to make so much fucking money!"

Tension between Tim and Phil had started before the West Coast tour, almost from the instant the band signed with Atco Records. In addition to already being a terrific bass player, Tim Bogert was highly intelligent—"beyond the rest of us," Mark would say—while Philly was a tough street guy who had made it partly on the basis of his Mafia ties. Along the way, there had to be an explosion or two of egos. Such blazes seldom burned for long, but it created yet one more issue for the young musicians to deal with. On that night, however, the matter dissipated and the boys engaged in typical rock-band wild partying at the hotel. Mark fell asleep, awakened by his roommate Vinny who shook him and said, "Philly wants to talk to you." Still groggy, Mark took the phone: "You guys have to be in the lobby in 45 minutes. We're going to Seattle." Hustling to the lobby, they saw Tim and Carmine eating doughnuts and drinking coffee from the breakfast cart. In minutes, they were standing out in the chilly air of Portland when a cab pulled up. As the cabbie sped them to the airport, he began to chat. "You guys in a band?" "Yeah," Mark beamed, "Vanilla Fudge. We were on the bill with the Mamas and the Papas last night." The cabbie deflated them with his response: "Can't say I've ever heard of you." Following the initial boos of the previous night, it was a lesson in humility for Vanilla Fudge.

Seattle offered a much different experience, both good and bad. The hotel was no cut-rate affair, but upscale. Like all hotels of the day, it put rockers on a separate floor if possible so as not to disturb other guests. As the band walked in with their long hair, paisley shirts, and bell bottoms, they got their share of catcalls and jeers. Hendrix would later respond to this harassment in one of his songs: "You white collar conservative pointing your finger at me . . . . I''m gonna let my freak flag fly!" The seminal film, *Easy Rider* (1969), portrayed the potential violent ending to such rebellious "flag-flying," but that too would change as, before long, a majority of young men had long hair and parents began wearing bell-bottoms (which, by then of course were out of fashion). While the rebels of the day paid a price in verbal (and sometimes physical) abuse for their look and dress, like all rebels they won when their styles and music went mainstream. It posed an interesting dilemma for future would-be outsiders, who subjected themselves to skin piercing and (occasionally) wall-to-wall tattoos: when 50-year olds routinely wore earrings and grannies sported tattoos that sagged with age, exactly how rebellious was it?

For those who had to endure the ridicule and outright hostility, though, the promise that their impact on culture would be long-lasting was little recompense in the 1960s. However, such attitudes tended to form musicians into a fraternity of shared experiences. Virtually every important artist, from Lucille Ball—once told after an audition to "find another occupation, any other"—to Elvis Presley, booed off the Grand Ole' Oprey stage, to Dylan's appearance at Newport, encountered criticism, negativity, and rejection. The up and coming Bruce Springsteen had his dark moment when his managers played *Greetings from Asbury Park, N.J.* for record executives and were all met with grim looks. Mike Appel, Springsteen's manager at the time, actually went to every label so he could collect rejection letters that he intended to paste on the wall. Like Hendrix and Cream, Springsteen felt little love from the critics at first: Dave Marsh, in Creem magazine, described the Boss as a performer who "doesn't give a shit how big a fool he makes of himself."[54]

In addition to criticism and rejection, another commonality among rockers was the universal language of the day, marijuana. It literally opened doors. While in Seattle, Mark headed   for his hotel room only to smell cannabis, and he followed the odor to the end of the hall, where he then heard a guitar playing and the sounds of a party. Someone saw him through the open door and shouted, "Come on in and join us dude!" Mark entered to find the room littered with beer bottles, food, and all kinds of stuff scattered everywhere. He knew these guys. "Are you Moby Grape?" he asked. "That's us," came the reply.

Mark literally had stumbled on one of rock's legendary shooting-star bands, for the Grape, formed in 1966, had that magical and fatal word, potential. As Jefferson Airplane biographer, Jeff Tamarkind observed, "The Grape's saga is one of squandered potential, absurdly misguided decisions, bad-luck, blunders and excruciating heartbreak, all set to the tune of some of the greatest rock and roll ever to emerge from San Francisco. Moby Grape could have had it all, but they ended up with nothing, and less."[55]

One of the main three-guitar groups on the scene—Buffalo Springfield, with Steven Stills, Ritchie Furay, and Neil Young was the other—Moby Grape had generated a buzz before their first self-titled album was released in 1967. Where other multiple guitar bands featured either a straight rhythm player or alternating leads, the Grape introduced layered guitars playing different licks, even different styles, yet woven together masterfully. Moby Grape, their influential album, would rank on *Rolling Stone*'s "500 Greatest Albums of All Time," and the hit song from that record, Omaha, featured all three guitarists dueling. ("Omaha" would also make the magazine's "Top 100 Guitar Songs of All Time"). The Who's Roger Daltrey, who scorned American groups, once said "The Mothers of Invention and Moby Grape are marvelous, but the rest are a lot of rubbish. It's time someone told the truth about the American scene. [They have a talent for writing songs.] But groups themselves are nothing on stage."[56] (Daltrey's bandmate, guitarist Pete Townshend thought Moby Grape were "terrible.")[57]

David Rubenson, one of the early Fillmore insiders, recalled "the best band [in San Francisco in 1966] was Moby Grape. Bar none. . . . Steve Miller, Sons of Champlin and Moby Grape were *staggering* bands."[58]

The Grape's fame, however, was approaching flameout, as debilitating experiments with acid would eventually land Skip in Bellvue Hospital. It was a tripping Skip Spence Mark encountered in Seattle: A "thin, long-haired guy sitting halfway out the window, looking like Renfield in a Dracula movie, screaming 'Eeeeeaaaah! Eeeeaaaah!'" "Is everything okay?" Mark asked. "Dude," came a voice, "don't worry about him. Skippy's just trippin'." When Mark addressed Spence directly, he was greeted with a desperate look: Spence's eyes were bulging and his teeth protruding out. Mark hadn't seen a bad acid trip before, and was taken aback. He walked toward the door when someone shouted, "That's Skip Spence, our guitarist. By tonight, he'll be coming down and ready to play. You a musician?" "Yeah," Mark replied, "I'm the organ player and singer with Vanilla Fudge." "Vanilla Fudge? So you're on the bill with all the other bands tonight. We just flew in from Portland, and I'm looking forward to it."

Mark was still rattled when he got to the Fudge's hotel room, telling the other guys about the strange, window-sitting Spence, "tripping his brains out and freaking me out." Within two years, Spence would completely melt down, convinced he was the anti-Christ and holding a hostage with an axe at the 52nd Floor of the CBS building where, according to guitarist Peter Lewis, "They had to wrestle him to the ground."

But that was only the beginning of the Grape's collapse as a band: their manager, Matthew Katz, kept the band's name tied up in litigation, preventing the members from working. Guitarist Bob Moseley eventually was homeless, as was Spence (once he was released from Bellvue); Lewis ended up in psychiatric care as well.

Moby Grape presaged a disease that would also affect Vanilla Fudge later, namely a legal issue over the use of the name. Katz had been personally paying for rent and other living costs during the making of the first album, and he used that as a reason to strong-arm the members into including a clause in their contract that gave him the rights to the name. Buffalo Springfield guitarist, Neil Young, was in the room at the time, quietly looking down and playing his guitar, but Grape guitarist Peter Lewis later said "I think Neil knew, even then, that was the end. We had bought into this process that we should have known better than to buy into.[59]

Worse, in 1973, while Moseley and Spence were mentally incapacitated, the Grape's remaining members signed away rights to Katz for the group's individual songs. Katz already had the rights to the name Moby Grape, meaning that not only were members denied years' worth of royalties, but that when the band toured, they had to do so under similar-sounding names such as "Moseley Grape" or "Legendary Grape." It was a cautionary tale for the Fudge band members, not so much with management, but later, for each other.

For the present, though, Vanilla Fudge was near the top of the mountain and could smell the crisp air of success. It didn't hurt that a new outlet for more exotic music that "didn't fit the format" had appeared in July 1964, when the Federal Communications Commission changed its regulations for AM and FM radio stations, forcing station owners to develop new programming for FM stations, and exposing FM for the first time to the rock and roll audience. Now, disc jockeys could play long songs previously disallowed by the narrow 2.5-minute AM formats, and even play entire album sides. And this, in turn, permitted rockers to consider "theme" albums where one song deliberately tied to another, thus encouraging the listener to take in the entire side of an LP, as opposed to just their favorite song. Advertising, then, was worked in around the music, rather than music being subjugated to ads. While the Fudge certainly were not the first to take advantage of this trend, the longer play times substantially benefitted the group's extended classical intros and mood setting, and gave a permanent home to the long version of "You Keep Me Hangin' On."

Meanwhile, on the road at the Seattle water park where Vanilla Fudge prepared for the concert, Mark stood in awe of the musicians around him—not just the Fifth Dimension and Sonny and Cher, who were the headliners, but even "down ticket" acts such as the Grape and the American Breed. While getting something to drink, Mark noticed a familiar figure at another table sitting by himself, Sonny Bono. Mark introduced himself and asked if he could sit, and Sonny invited him to grab a seat. Bono said, "Ahmet is very excited about your band. He thinks your album will do very well." It was reassuring to know that Atco's organization was behind the Fudge. "Where did you come up with that sound?" he asked. Mark replied "We try to get the most out of our instruments and we've been hearing the symphonic sound, so when a song turns us on, we rearrange it." Suddenly flash bulbs went off and the press appeared. Mark asked, "Sonny, what did you think of 'Bang Bang'?" Sonny said, "I was wondering when you were going to ask that. The last time I was in New York, Ahmet sat me down and said, 'Listen to this cool version of 'The King and I' [the band's intro riffs to 'Bang Bang']. I made him play it a few times, and didn't know what to make of it at first."

Salvatore Phillip "Sonny" Bono, born in 1935 to Italian immigrants in Detroit, had moved to California and worked with Phil Spector as a writer, promotion man, percussionist, and personal assistant, writing songs for Sam Cooke before working with Jack Nitzsche to pen the hit "Needles and Pins" for Jackie DeShannon (then, later, the Searchers). Becoming romantically involved with one of the backup vocalists, Cherilyn Sarkisian, known as "Cher," the duo known first as "Caesar and Cleo, then as "Sonny and Cher," had a string of hits with "I Got You Babe" and "The Beat Goes On." "I Got You Babe" immediately went to number one, and sold a million copies, making it Atlantic Records' biggest hit up to that point. Covering the Byrds' "All I Really Want to Do," Sonny and Cher's version did even better than the Byrds' version, reaching number 15 on the charts. Sonny also arranged and produced Cher's solo works. Mark and the Fudge were immediately attracted to the Bono songs, and besides re-arranging "Bang Bang" would embark on a disastrous theme album based on "The Beat Goes On." Sonny and Cher saw their marriage hit the skids even as they filmed a weekly television show, "The Sonny and Cher Show," which ran on CBS for three years.

After the demise of the duo, Sonny struggled, working around the periphery of show business, doing a solo album, and appearing in a few bit parts in movies. After trying to open a restaurant in his home town of Palm Springs, wherein he encountered massive red tape and bureaucratic obstructionism, Bono ran for mayor and won. Serving from 1988 to 1992, Bono created the Palm Springs International Film Festival. He then ran for the U.S. House of Representatives in 1994 as part of the "Republican Revolution," signed on to the famous "Contract With America," and became one of the leading fundraisers in California. A bill extending copyrights was named for him, the Sonny Bono Copyright Term Extension Act.

Bono retained his show-business sense, and was among the first to recognize that Speaker Newt Gingrich—a masterful tactician—had become a celebrity, and as such, he told Gingrich, "The rules are different for celebrities. I know it. I've been there. I've been a celebrity. I used to be a bigger celebrity. But let me tell you, you're not being handled right. This is not political news coverage. This is celebrity status. You need handlers." Possibly the most touching image of Sonny Bono— usually captured with his broad smile beneath his thick moustache—was the video of him weeping while hearing testimony on the Waco assault in which the followers of David Koresh were burned to death and shot by police and FBI. Bono would die in January 1998 when he crashed into a tree while skiing: such "impartial" sources as the *Rolling Stone Encyclopedia of Rock and Roll* implied that he was using drugs when he died, but the autopsy proved otherwise.[60]

Sonny Bono, though, was one of those show-business figures who seemed to always be present during key moments in the evolution of rock and roll, even if he wasn't the prime mover or even the focus of attention, while his former wife reinvented herself countless times from hippie chick to TV entertainer to Hollywood actress to Vegas headliner.

Although years later Las Vegas might have offered a perfect career change for Mark and the Fudge—as it did for so many other 60s and 70s-era bands—that was the furthest thing from the boys' minds at the time. They were entering the top echelon of American rock musicians, and were about to embark on their biggest and best-known tours, sharing the stage with Hendrix, Alice Cooper, Led Zeppelin, Three Dog Night, Creedence Clearwater Revival, Iron Butterfly, the Who, and countless others. Vanilla Fudge would soon find out that attaining stardom is one thing—keeping it, something entirely different.

Chapter Three

As the Vanilla Fudge album sailed from #130 on the charts to #33 with a star in Billboard in one week, indicating a hot seller, the band was primed for amazing success, but the Los Angeles market was critical. Mark recalled that the last stop on the tour was the City of Angels, at the famous Whiskey a-Go Go on the Sunset Strip. Buffalo Springfield and the Doors—who were enjoying a home field advantage---offered yet more competition, and Mark, in retrospect, "never remembered us fitting in." (The romantic notion that there was no jealousy among rockers, or that all musicians "respected" each other was more Woodstockian hooey: Eric Clapton noted in his Autobiography how "contemptuous" he was of West Coast groups such as the Jefferson Airplane, Big Brother, or the Grateful Dead: "I thought most of the so-called psychedelic stuff . . . was pretty dull.")[1]

On the day of the Whiskey show, while the band was outside the venue, Mark recalled arguing with the clubowner, Elmer Valentine, about equipment during the load in while actor Steve McQueen stood there staring at the band, arms folded, as if to say, "You're on our turf now." Over 40 years later, Mark could "still feel the hostility." He admitted in retrospect the band was young and immature, and probably gave off some attitudes that were less than productive. Nevertheless the Fudge played to a packed house that night and after the show they were swarmed in their dressing room by local luminaries, such as Dewey

Martin, the drummer of Buffalo Springfield who befriended the Fudge later on, actor Sal Mineo—famous for his role as legendary drummer Gene Krupa in *The Gene Krupa Story* (1959) and co-star to James Dean in *Rebel Without a Cause*---and a host of DJs from local stations, as well as the usual promo men from the label who ranted about reports of strong album sales in Europe as well. Soon there was talk of touring overseas. Before the Fudge knew it, they were on their way to England.

"It was our first trip to the UK," Stein recalled: "I was hanging out at one of the spots called The Speakeasy." Over the sound system the Who's "I Can See for Miles" was playing and Mark loved the sound of the vocals. It struck a chord with him, "maybe because it just reflected a time for me in my life when everywhere around me in the club I would see the likes of Mama Cass at one table, Jeff Beck and Dave Mason at another." The Fudge played at Finsbury Park—40 years later to become infamous for one of the most radical Islamic mosques in the western world---with Traffic and the Herd (young Peter Frampton's band), and the Spencer Davis Group (with Stevie Winwood). Although limited to only 20 minutes and stuck playing on other groups' gear, and without a sound check, the Fudge's first live appearance in England had everyone buzzing. It seemed the whole of London was there to see Vanilla Fudge.

Of those in attendance was a young Jon Lord, who had just formed a new group with guitarist Ritchie Blackmore called Deep Purple. Lord recalled of the Fudge performance, "They knocked me out," and he began copying Mark. Lord told everyone of Deep Purple, "We are going to be an English Vanilla Fudge."[2]

In fact, Lord's "newly consummated love for the . . .maverick neoclassicists," as Deep Purple's biographer put it, did not wear well at first. The band's "musicianship had not yet caught up to their American counterparts, and they were labeled the 'poor man's Vanilla Fudge,'" particularly after they appeared on a packed ticket at the Roundhouse with Jeff Beck, Ten Years After, and Joe Cocker.[3] Still, Lord's appreciation for the Fudge was shared by Purple drummer Ian Paice, who recalled the Americans were "a breath of fresh air—their longer songs inspired us, showed us what we could do."[4]

Soon, Paice admitted "Deep Purple wasn't them. What was natural for them [wasn't natural for us]," he observed, but in 1968, the two bands would play together on a Canadian tour where Paice and Appice struck up a working relationship as drummers. Paice had taken up drums after seeing Gene Krupa in the movies. "I tried to copy him with knitting needles," Paice recalled. Then, like most musicians, the Beatles grabbed Paice, particularly Ringo with his Black Oyster Pearl set. But Appice was the epitome of rock drumming for Ian Paice, noting his "instinctive grasp of what makes rock." Where Carmine would pound, "I tended to go 'swingy'," he said. Indeed, on one of the Canadian gigs, Carmine's gear got lost and he had to play on Paice's set: "Carmine broke 'em all," Paice laughed, referring to his drum heads.

But if Deep Purple in their infancy loved the Fudge, most had a much more negative response to the Americans at their Finsbury Park appearance. What happened was what usually happens in those circumstances to any band with no sound check, and which is rushed on and off the stage with unfamiliar equipment: it didn't come off well. There was a firestorm of bad press. A depressed Mark went back to the Speakeasy, only to hear people mutter how terrible the band was. Five days later, Vanilla Fudge had to open for the Who at the Saville Theater, but this time, under different circumstances. With their own equipment, including Mark's B-3, and an excellent sound man, a tremendous show unfolded in which the Who's fans stood and cheered the Fudge to an encore. "We owned the stage for a good hour. I don't think the Who were too happy about that," said Mark, because "in the coming days, the press started to favor the Fudge over the Who." Townsend fired back in the press calling the Fudge a "bunch of schizophrenics!" The appearance at the Saville started an animosity between the two bands, and "they never wanted to have anything to do with us," even after the two acts played some shows together in the United States. During one photo shoot with Pete Townsend, Mark recalled an icy encounter, and on another occasion, during a Hendrix concert at Madison Square Garden, Roger Daltry, walking backstage, spotted Mark and "gave me a look as if to say, 'Oh, no, not you again.'" Yet personally, Mark liked the Who's music and ranked them as one of the great bands of the era, noting with fondness their intensity, songwriting, and unique sound.

With the winds of fate blowing in a positive direction for Vanilla Fudge, and London now excited about the Americans, a show was set up for the Speakeasy. Packed with wall to wall people, including the Beatles Mark later heard, the Fudge had a perfect sound, amazing vibe, and matchless energy. Feeling they had something to prove, they put on one of the best shows of their careers. Word of their performances spread throughout Europe, and soon the band found itself in Germany, playing at the infamous Star Club in Hamburg, where the Beatles had cut their teeth On the Reeperbahn, the main boulevard in Hamburg at the center of all the excitement, the Fudge were free to experience all that was legal in Europe and not in America. Then more shows followed in Holland, then back to Bremen, Germany where the Fudge filmed the Beat Club, a popular European television show.

In Bramen, they stayed at a hotel that still bore the scars of

World War II, and on Yom Kippur, the Day of Atonement, Mark suddenly noticed that right outside his window were train tracks—the same tracks that once carried so many Jews to their deaths. He felt sick, calling his sister and talking for over an hour at a time when international phone rates were gold-plated. Scheduled to leave the next morning for London, the boys piled into cars as the hotel manager came screaming for payment of Mark's Lloyds of London-sized bill. Philly pushed everyone into the limos, shouting, "there's no way I'm paying that." Somehow, the band took off without paying the bill and, safely back in London, sporting a new Carnaby Street look and a bounding confidence, they learned the album had broken the top ten. "We celebrated that night," Mark recalled, "by getting drunk as lords. It meant a whole new level of money, more shows, and then a triumphant return to America." The album was nestled just below Diana Ross and the Supremes, the Doors, and Simon and Garfunkel.

From the outset, while never wealthy, the members of Vanilla Fudge had escaped some of the grinding poverty that afflicted some of the other music and movie stars of the age. Soon-to-be guitar legend Tommy Bolin grew up desperately poor; Aerosmith in 1971 was so low on money "we were stealing to survive," admitted Joe Perry.[5]

The band's first management contracts came literally as the members stared at an eviction notice! Perry recalled "We took the contracts back to our apartment, and we sat down . . . with the contracts in one hand and the eviction notice in the other . . . . and shook our heads in disbelief. That's how close it was."[6]

Vanilla Fudge experienced all the other trappings of success as well, perhaps the most important being that they broke into the powerful entertainment medium of television. The Holy Grail of entertainment television was CBS's Ed Sullivan Show, which aired every Sunday night. Sullivan presented a variety of comics, acrobats, ventriloquists, actors, and of course, solo musicians and bands. The show had become one of the most famous in America for presenting Elvis Presley in September 1956 after Sullivan had earlier vowed never to allow him on the show. Sullivan later claimed he had been mis-led on Presley's antics: "the business about rubbing the thighs. He rubbed one hand on his hip to dry off the perspiration from playing his guitar."[7]

Asked about whether Presley's performance on rival Milton Berle's show was vulgar, Sullivan quipped, "I don't know why everybody picked on Presley. I thought the whole show was dirty and vulgar."[8]

The Beatles were no less controversial, and had elevated Sullivan to "the" show that broke the latest hot acts back in 1964. By the time the Fudge appeared, Sullivan had still not relinquished that title.

Rock artists had increased Sullivan's viewership ever since Elvis made his debut—when cameras were only permitted to film him from the waist up due to his sexual gyrations that proved too risque for 1950s tastes. And when the Beatles appeared, even Rev. Billy Graham broke his practice of keeping the television dark on Sundays to tune in. Since the Fab Four, dozens of other rockers had appeared, including the Rolling Stones, the Animals, Herman's Hermits, the Kinks, the Dave Clark Five, and Gerry and the Pacemakers. At one point, it seemed the entire British Invasion of bands performed, along with American groups such as the Doors—who infuriated Sullivan by refusing to change the lyric "Girl we couldn't get much higher"---Jefferson Airplane, and the Rascals. One of the more memorable performances, in March 1969, was that of Sly and the Family Stone, an interracial band whose lead singers, Sly Stone and his sister, Rose, horrified the staid Sullivan audience by racing down into the aisles. Television cameras captured the two having fun and dancing while a mostly white, middle-aged audience of men in suits and women in dresses looked on dumbfounded. Sly would later descend into drug addiction, but at one point his band was considered the most influential black artists in rock. Joel Selvin wrote, "there are two types of black music: black music before Sly Stone, and black music after Sly Stone," and apparently others agreed, inducting the band into the Rock and Roll Hall of Fame in 1993.[9]

In 1968, when the Fudge enjoyed brisk record sales and strong popularity, they got their shot to be on the show. Mark recalled "our families and friends were thrilled—it was a dream come true." For their first appearance, they shared the bill with jazz great Duke Ellington, comedians Flip Wilson and regulars Stiller and Meara, and when the Fudge hit the stage, they performed a shortened version of "You Keep Me Hangin' On." Ironically, up till that point, the men in the control booth really had not been able to get the bottom end and the overall power of any live rock act. Somehow, Bruce Wayne, the band's tour and sound man who had joined them earlier during the first European tour, managed to get into the booth (against union regulations) to do the mixing. Ed Sullivan robotically strode to the stage in his normal manner and announced, "AND NOW FOR ALL YOU TEENAGERS—ONE OF THE HOTTEST GROUPS IN AMERICA—THE VANILLA FUDGE!" (Sullivan put "the" in front of Vanilla Fudge, although the official band name was simply "Vanilla Fudge") Donned in full Carnaby Street attire and makeup ,the band came off great. Right after the show, Mark called his mother and father from a pay phone near the stage as Flip Wilson patted him on the back and said "what a nice kid, calling his folks right after doing the Sullivan show."

So all was rosy in the Fudge camp. The talk was of how strong Vanilla Fudge sounded on live television, thanks to their daring British friend; record sales zoomed in the following weeks because of the exposure and "we were becoming household names." The band appeared on Sullivan a second time a year later performing "Shotgun," and Mark recalled one of his fondest memories was singing backstage with the Temptations, who were also on the bill. It took Mark back to his street corner *acapella* days. Yet all was not perfect. Mark and Vince roomed together and on the evening before the show Vince wandered out into New York City on a date with a woman from the band's public relations firm. There was a rehearsal scheduled for 11 am the following day, but by 3:00 a.m., no Vinny. Mark grew more angry by the minute and was livid by the time Vince showed up at 6:00 . . . the following morning. "How could he jeopardize the show?" Mark asked. It didn't help that Mark was using amphetamines at the time, and he started to scream, then took a swing at Martell, connecting with his fist on Vince's head. That punch landed Mark in the hospital, where x-rays showed he had a hairline fracture of his wrist. "There's no way you can do the show tonight" said the doctor—and indeed, his hand was in a cast. Arriving at the now-delayed rehearsal, Mark had his arm in a sling and was totally mortified. Philly drew him aside: "Look," Basile said, "You gotta find a way to play. We can't cancel this." Behind closed doors, Mike Spina, one of the road crew, helped Mark remove the cast and he did the show, doing the high energy solo on "Shotgun" with his right hand, playing through the pain. When the song ended, Ed Sullivan said "COME ON OUT GUYS. . . SAY HELLO TO AMERICA!" and proceeded to shake Mark's broken hand as Mark blew a kiss to the audience with his left hand. Then the guys ran backstage where the roadies put a cast back on. It took weeks for the hand to heal, but it took much longer for Mark and Vince to repair their relationship and despite numerous apologies, the two drifted apart for years to come.

Another television event involved the "Today Show" with Barbara Walters—which came as a surprise, as few psychedelic bands were invited to appear on such a high brow show. The boys had to be on the set at 5:30 a.m., about the time they would normally be going to bed. Fortified with caffeine, the band listened as the producer explained where they would be at air time. The Fudge went through a few bars of "Moonlight Sonata" from *The Beat Goes On* as their sound check—an arrangement requested by the producers—which proved positive on two fronts. First, the song was an instrumental, which meant the guys didn't have to sing so early in the morning, and it also gave them some

71

redemption from the failed *Beat Goes On* LP, from which "Sonata" was culled. Normally, talk show producers conduct a "pre-interview" to discuss the topics that will be dealt with by the hosts. But no one told Mark anything, and after the band did their song, the host, Barbara Walters, asked "since Vanilla Fudge is supposedly part of the current 'peace movement' how can you correlate the bombastic sounds of your music with peace?" The piece was being taped, Mark had to control his emotions, despite feeling infuriated. He muttered, "the way we play our music is irrelevant to your question. The 'peace movement' doesn't necessarily mean quiet or serene—it's a time for freedom of expression." Baffled, Walters just shook her head, clearly not understanding the answer. Overall, however, Mark knew the show gave the band merit in a medium that was tough to crack.

Another TV show the band did was "The Joey Bishop Show," featuring the popular comedian/actor who became part of the infamous "rat pack" that included Frank Sinatra, Sammy Davis, Jr., Peter Lawford, and Dean Martin. When Bonnie and Clyde was the hottest movie in the country, the Fudge was scheduled on the Joey Bishop Show to appear along with the film's star Warren Beatty. In the "green room" backstage before the show, Mark chatted with Beatty. At the end of the movie, "Clyde" got shot to pieces with endless rounds of machine gun fire, with bullet holes appearing all over him and blood pouring out. Mark asked him how that scene was done, and Beatty replied "my clothes were attached with electric charges and were exploded from a remote on cue." It was one of the first times that special effect was used to capture a graphic scene like that. Bishop's interview with Beatty ran way past the supposed allotted time, and the Fudge didn't make it on. Bishop apologized and promised to have them on again soon. True to his word, Vanilla Fudge was back on a few weeks later, performing "Take Me for a Little While," and no sooner had they started than Mark grabbed the microphone with his right hand and the mike came off the stand. He had to hold it with his left while singing while playing the B-3 with his right. Joey Bishop called Mark over to sit at the panel with Regis Philbin, his sidekick, and Jan Murray, a popular comedian. So the group discussed rock and roll and the lifestyle of musicians while Murray cracked jokes. Little could Mark guess that 30 years later, Regis, teamed with Kathie Lee Gifford, would far surpass in viewership anything Joey Bishop ever attained. Once again, record sales received a boost.

Several months later, the band appeared on the "Dick Cavett Show," which was taped in New York. As the Fudge were headlining the "Schaefer in the Park Concert Series" that night, along with Ultimate Spinach as the opening act, an opportunity appeared for the Fudge to get on Cavett. During the taping of the Cavett show that afternoon, Mark tried to strike up a conversation with singer Jack Jones, who was also appearing, and, as he found with many of the artists of the era who were not rock and rollers, Jones was "cool to the touch." Mark found Cavett much the same—he "seemed full of himself." But it was a good appearance, because both John Lennon and Jimi Hendrix had performed on the show.

Another "song and dance man," Donald O'Connor, also had his own show in the 1960s. While on tour, the Fudge took advantage of a request to appear on his show. The cameras were ready to roll in the morning when Mark, having partied at the Beverly Hills Hotel all night, arrived mentally disheveled. "Carmine was on my case to get it together," he noted, and reminded him "We have a show to do." Retreating to the men's room for his morning constitutional, Mark hears a voice in the next stall talking to himself. He soon identified the voice as belonging to O'Connor. "My mom's not going to believe how we met, Mr. O'Connor!" Mark laughed. They both washed up and Mark went to makeup where the band was introduced to O'Connor's wife and family. After playing "You Keep Me Hangin' On," the group sat on the panel with O'Conner and to Tim's left was the great standup comic Henny Youngman (famous for the line, "Take my wife . . . please.") Tim told O'Connor how wonderful it was meeting his wife and family backstage, and O'Conner asked about how the band developed its style. Then he asked, "So where's your next stop?" Mark turned to his left to Tim, who on cue turned to his left to Youngman, who turned to his left, until it went all the way past the producer to the camera men. With that, Vanilla Fudge showed America they had a comedic touch.

On another popular show, the "Steve Allen Show," Mark described the appearance as "trippy," because it was filmed adjacent to the "Star Trek" set. Mark came out of the makeup room and watched Allen do some of his comedy monologue when he turned around to see "Captain Kirk," William Shatner, in full costume and makeup between takes. "If I was a trekkie," Mark laughed, "I would have fainted on the spot." He had followed Shatner's work on "Twilight Zone," but was not a fan of the space-based television series. The two—both fully in character—stared at each other without saying a word before Mark went on to meet Allen backstage. Allen's show had been one of the top variety shows of its day, featuring Elvis singing "Hound Dog" to a droopy-eyed canine, softening his rebel image enough that it allowed him to cross over into mainstream American society. Vanilla Fudge hoped their appearance on Allen would likewise expose them to a broader audience.

Interspersed amidst the television appearances was a request by

Braniff International Airlines for the Fudge to do a commercial. One by one, the band walked on the plane as the stewardess, as flight attendants were then called, announced "Here Comes the Vanilla Fudge!" (She technically got the name wrong: like Jefferson Airplane, Led Zeppelin, or Moby Grape, there was no "the" in front of the band's name) Mark, the last one on the plane, looked at the camera and said, "IF YOU'VE GOT IT, FLAUNT IT!" which was a popular 60s term for success. The spot ran for six weeks on national television, giving the band still more credibility, despite complaints by some hard-core fans that the band had "sold out." As of this writing, Mark still doesn't know what the band received in revenue for the spot.

Although the Fudge also appeared on "The David Frost Show" and performed "Need Love" from their 1969 Rock & Roll album, it was the popular daytime "Mike Douglas Show" that had became the most significant of the shows in many ways. The famous British actor Richard Harris was on with the band, riding high on the heels of the hit musical "Camelot" as well as enjoying the chart topping hit "MacArthur Park," a song penned by the great songwriter Jimmy Webb. While interviewing the band on camera, host Mike Douglas bluntly asked Mark if it was true that the band's fans smoked pot while listening to their music. Offstage, Harris screamed out "I've got a joint here if anyone wants to indulge!" eliciting rousing laughter from the audience and cushioning an otherwise intense moment. Harris, who enjoyed drinking, had "mooned" the audience during the afternoon rehearsal, and after the show, Mark and Harris, along with several fans, found their way to a back street Philadelphia bar and proceeded to get "blind drunk" together. It was the last they saw of each other.

Meanwhile, a twenty-one-year-old Jersey girl, Patricia Patterson, entered the picture. She worked at Atlantic records in both the sales and the "A&R" (artist and recording) department. A fan of Vanilla Fudge, she had a massive infatuation with a certain bearded lead singer. The rumor was she'd been bragging that one day she'd date Mark Stein and had even said, after seeing him on the Mike Douglas show, that she was going to marry him one day! Whenever the band went to Atlantic for a meeting, Patty would become so anxious that she would run and hide. Upon reflection, Mark never remembered seeing Patty at the record company. Finally, Phil Basile set up a rendezvous between them after he had gotten to know Patty after seeing her from time to time at Atlantic. Patty fed Philly information on advance record sales, a practice that was commonplace, which allowed Basile to make better deals. It provided a sort of leverage. When Philly learned of the crush she had on Mark, he set up the meeting at the Action House out on Long Island.

74

Mark was ready to leave the world of groupiedom: with his ongoing problem with amphetamines and whiskey, deep down he was looking for someone to save him from himself. After a quick hello/goodbye, Patty didn't give up. She managed to meet him again some weeks later, again at the Action House, but this time it was different. They talked, kissed and embraced, then Mark looked into her eyes and deep down knew she was the one who would save him. In fact, Mark Stein was a hair's breadth away from following in the footsteps of so many other rockers who boozed or doped their way into the next life.

But death from drugs was only one dark avenue. Life, addicted, proved a final destination in itself for many. Skip Spence, whom Mark had seen, was one of several musicians whose mental capacities were terminally damaged by LSD. Mark was no stranger to acid, either. His first encounter, when Vanilla Fudge was headlining with Steve Miller at the Fillmore in San Francisco, involved a groupie who came up to Mark and said "Open wide." She dropped an LSD tablet into his mouth. Mark, outfitted in a floor-length blue velvet robe with gold trim around the neck—"spiritual attire for the times in the Haight Ashbury District," as he called it—quickly learned that acid could play on one's emotions, magnifying them into terrific pleasure or insane hell, and that night, it was the latter. The call came out, "20 minutes to show time!" and Mark plunged into an abyss: "voices were echoing off bodies, colors were fading, people started to frighten me and were scattering, unrecognizable." Bruce Wayne smiled and told Mark everything was all right, but Mark saw the devil! Screaming at Vinny to take over, Mark looked into the audience to see Christians being devoured by lions, and yet he knew they, too, were tripping on acid. He screamed for his mother and father over the microphone . . . and the crowd loved it! Finally, during "People Get Ready," an angelic haze came over the audience and white light shone all around and "I thought I saw God." When the show ended, Mark grabbed Carmine and sobbed uncontrollably for ten minutes, having survived his first acid trip.

Now, another acid experience began, starting in 1968 during a West Coast stint with a concert coming up in San Diego with Iron Butterfly. The Fudge had a few days off before the show, and Mark decided to take a short flight from Los Angeles to San Diego—it was only 25 minutes—and when the plane landed crowds buzzed everywhere. When Mark walked into the terminal, news crews were there, filming the arrival of Dr. Martin Luther King, Jr., and Mark had not known he was even on the plane.

(Not long after that, King was assassinated. Later, when the Fudge was playing in New Orleans, Mark dedicated "People Get Ready" to him . . . only to see Molotov cocktails come flying out of the crowd. Philly ran over to Mark: "What are you crazy? Don't you know what city you're in?" However, other members of the crew congratulated Mark, noting it was a kind thing to say.)

While in San Diego, Mark looked forward to several days off with nothing to do but relax. He was poolside at the hotel when two familiar characters approached, Mike Spina and Richard Zimmer, two of the crew guys. Spina said, "Hey, we've got a few days off . . . why don't we all drop some acid and go across the border to Tijuana tonight?" Remembering the Fillmore, Mark resisted, but the crew convinced him the stuff they had was uplifting and positive (which, of course, no one, not even a doctor, could determine). They told Mark they had laughed for hours when they took it before, so Mark gave it another shot.

Early in the evening, the three of them drove to the Mexican border, parked on the American side, took the acid, and walked through customs. On the Tijuana side, they were confronted by vendors, beggars, prostitutes, and were all smiles at first. Some of the locals also started to recognize Mark, and before long a Jeep sped up with the Chief of Police in it. Suddenly, it screeched to a stop and the Chief jumped out and said, "Amigo! I am a big fan of your band. Please, let me show you the town!" So Mark, Mike, and Richard all hopped in with Tijuana's top cop, loaded to the gills with LSD, and it was hysterical. They visited bars, where the Chief bought them beers, then hit local hangouts were Mexican musicians played. At one bar, the Chief insisted Mark get up and play with the band, whom he insisted could play the entire Vanilla Fudge album. Indeed they could—they had the arrangements and harmonies, but in Spanish! Mark played and sang "Take Me For a Little While" in English with the Mexican Fudge—all the while tripping on acid---while the background singers accompanied him in Spanish, and the Chief of Police looked on in amazement. After two songs, Mark shouted "Gracias, mi hermanos!" and vaulted from the stage. The three spent the rest of the night partying, and Mark told his new-found friend from Tijuana that he would return with the whole band after the San Diego gig. Finally, they returned to the American side, still calling each other by their Mexican names (Zimmer now became "Paco"). And several days, later, Mark indeed got Philly and the rest of the band back . . . and sure enough, the Chief of Police was there to chaperone them again.

All acid experiences—indeed, most—hardly turned out so well. Almost all musicians who used LSD had at least one nightmarish experience to go along with their rainbow-filled joy rides. Bad trips did not just come from acid: Carlos Santana played his famous set at Woodstock on mescaline, thinking he had time to "mellow out," when

76

the band was pushed on stage prematurely. Santana, in a "drug-induced haze, looked out and saw 'an ocean of flesh, hair, teeth, and hands.'"[10] Upon starting the set, Santana recalled his guitar "was like a rubberband. The neck was moving around like a duck neck."[11]

Two months later, Santana met Jimi Hendrix in a New York studio where the guitarist was recording. Hendrix appeared fine at first as he ran through what appeared to Santana to be the "umpteenth take" of "Room Full of Mirrors," before "freaking out and playing some 'wild shit' that had nothing to do with the song." The crew "forcibly dragged" him into the engineering booth, "his eyes . . . all bloodshot and he was foaming at the mouth. It was like being in a room with someone who was having an epileptic fit."[12] The experience hardly phased Carlos Santana, who "developed a sort of thing for LSD, mescaline, mushrooms, and stuff like that."[13]

Journalist Gabe Katz at the *San Francisco Oracle* observed "the only way to understand . . . is to turn on. The chemicals are essential."[14] Many musicians and "experts" on the hippie scene began to insist that drugs were the essence of the new music. David Getz, the drummer for Big Brother and the Holding Company, explained that the "whole philosophy of the psychedelic scene was to consciously avoid making anyone the star, focusing more on the interaction between the audience and the band, and trying to create something together."[15]

Grateful Dead guitarist Jerry Garcia recalled "Along came LSD and that was the end of the whole world . . . . It changed everything . . . it freed me [and] the effect was that . . . I suddenly realized that my little attempt at having a straight life and doing that was really a fiction . . . ."[16]

Even promoter Bill Graham, who had obsessively guarded himself against even accidentally ingesting LSD, fell victim to a prank by the Grateful Dead in 1967. "I'd never touch anything they gave me," he recalled. "I'd never hug them," and he refused to kiss their female friends in case someone had acid in their mouths.[17]

Someone had to be in control at the Fillmore, he reasoned. But knowing Graham's precautions, the Grateful Dead put around the mouth area of all the soda cans Graham kept in large ice-filled garbage cans for the crew. After one can of 7-Up, "snap! I started feeling weird. I looked in a mirror and all I saw was green and yellow and blue."[18] "The next thing I knew," said Dead drummer Mickey Hart, "he was hanging over the gong on stage. And he had no mercy. He was beating the gong wildly." That is, until Graham moved to tympani and cowbell! Graham came down, concluding soberly that "Acid is heavy stuff. It's heavy stuff."[19]

But neither acid nor mescaline were Mark's drug of choice:

amphetamines were, and he ingested them to addiction. It not only kept his weight under control, but—when the amphetamine high set in—had effects similar to cocaine wherein the user felt powerful and on top of his game. Each new hit brought with it an ever debilitating come-down, while each high sparked saw growing agitation and impatience. Each musician chased his own different dragon. At the very time Mark struggled with amphetamines, Eric Clapton—by then a guitar legend— had developed a heroin addiction that consumed between $5,000 and $10,000 a week. As Clapton would later admit in his autobiography,

> I just assumed I was in some way immune to it and that I wouldn't get hooked. . . . I also thought I was endorsing the rock 'n' roll lifestyle. In spite of Ahmet [Ertegun's] warnings, I enjoyed the mythology surrounding the lives of the great jazz musicians like Charlie Parker and Ray Charles, and bluesmen like Robert Johnson, and I had a romantic notion of living the kind of life that had led them to create their music. I also wanted to prove that I could do it and come out on the other side alive. I was determined and wanted no help from anybody.[20]

Mark had no such romantic illusions about amphetamines. With him, it was a simple combination of self-consciousness about his weight and the need for energy. He also knew drugs were turning him into a monster. "My habit was getting really bad," he later admitted. "When I'd come down from the amphetamine high, I became an animal, impossible to deal with." The Fudge was imploding and Mark faced the reality that his rock and roll world might fall off a cliff—the same spot many professional ballplayers find themselves in after a career-ending injury or after being released from their "lifelong" team.

As much as the public associates acid or cocaine with rock and roll (the latter coming later in rock's history), the hidden killer among rockers was alcohol. One of the most notorious, John Bonham of Led Zeppelin, had been the perfect drunk in terms of "managing" his addiction so that he never missed a rehearsal nor was ever so blasted that he couldn't play. At all other times, though, he was an alcoholic's alcoholic. In his last days, he downed "two to three double vodkas an hour," and like Clapton, had gotten clean of heroin only to binge on booze.[21]

And, like Clapton, Bonham supplemented his liquor habit with other prescribed medication, dying after a heavy drinking binge in 1980. Ray Manzarek detailed Doors singer Jim Morrison's obsession with booze in his 1998 book *Light My Fire*: they drank "like poets and artists and musicians with cajones. Macho drinking. Drinking to loosen the tongue. Drinking for the sake of alcohol."[22]

Just before his death, Morrison met with the other members of the band and admitted his problem, but he instantly relapsed. Fittingly, his final recording made with a pair of American street musicians in Paris—"drunken gibberish" as Manzarek called it—was a preliminary to a heroin overdose that constituted the immediate cause of death, but in the long run booze killed Jim Morrison as surely as it took John Bonham.

As Eric Clapton put it, "a post-psychedelia drunkenness seemed to sweep over everybody in the entertainment business during the early seventies. To be on the stage, you were almost expected to be drunk."[23]

He admitted to drinking "round the clock;" recalled how he did an entire show "lying down on the stage with the microphone stand lying beside me;" how, drunk and naked at a multi-story Honolulu hotel, he climbed around the ledges connecting the balconies so he could pull a prank on his drummer; and how his reputation became so abysmal that even when genuine technical problems forced the cancellation of a Frankfurt, Germany show, the national papers ran the headline "ERIC CLAPTON—TOO DRUNK TO PLAY."[24]

As with other musicians, Clapton sought to adumbrate and conceal the effects of liquor with a codeine-based sedative, taking up to 50 tablets a day. Alcohol made Clapton relaxed and mellow, while with the drummers Bonham and the Who's Keith Moon, it brought out aggressiveness. Moon had drunk his way through much of the band's impressive earnings in the early 1970s. He would disappear for days, inebriated, "smashed up cars . . . stripped in pubs and restaurants and on the motorways of Western Europe," then would turn up, "remorseful, but still drunk."[25]

The band's biographer Dave Marsh observed that those close to the Who "simply marveled that [Moon] was able to inflict so much varied abuse upon himself and continue to function."[26] "Ups and downs until his eyes crossed," Marsh wrote, "brown ale, champagne, brandy and ginger and no sleep all seemed to leave Moon unscathed . . . ."[27]

Yes keyboardist Rick Wakeman, having already had a heart attack doctors traced to his drinking, was told in 1985 that he had alcoholic hepatitis. Wakeman recalled, "I used to drink port and brandy in pint glasses."[28] When he asked his doctor, "What do you think?" the physician replied, "Six months." "OK, no drink for six months. I can do that." The doctor shook his head, "No, Rick, six months to live."[29]

A shaken Wakeman thought of his pregnant wife, and was told he might not live to see his child born, whereupon he walked out of the clinic, went to the Duke of York Pub, and promptly ordered . . . a tomato juice.

Some paid a physical price for their narcotics habits. Others suffered a much different fate. Ritchie Supa, songwriter for Aerosmith, recalled that "we were all high, living the rock and roll lifestyle," but was unaware that one of his acquaintances was arrested and had "flipped." He handed over Ritchie, setting him up with a phone call that was tapped. Supa was busted for a half kilo of cocaine, and the police seized everything. He had $60,000 in his safe from the band's last road trip, and his whole studio was confiscated. The prosecutors offered him an out: turn in the main target, Steven Tyler and Supa could walk. Supa told the prosecutors, "I may be a scumbag but stick your phone up your ass."[30]

Supa was given a three year sentence. Tyler sent him money "for stuff in jail." When he got out in 1987, the conditions of his parole prohibited him from going near the band. When he finally joined narcotics anonymous and stayed clean for a year, Tyler brought him back in to finish "Amazing."

Supa recalled that "cocaine was built into the invoices on recording budgets as 'multi-track tapes.'" He remembered one incident in which the band was on a yacht to record in a mobile, sea-going studio, and ran out of cocaine in mid-session. "It was somewhere near Catalina," he noted, "and we had a seaplane arrive with drugs." Santana's biographer wrote, "It was a rare day when most of the . . . band was not high on cocaine. . . . The drug became such a big part of the band's daily life that, when they went out on tour, a representative of their entourage had the sole job of always making sure he had an ounce or two available in case anybody in the group ran out."[31]

Perhaps one of the greatest drug and alcohol related ironies involved Ozzy Osbourne, whose band was on tour in 1982. The band's spectacular guitarist, Randy Rhoads, had gone up in a joyride in a Beechcraft Bonanza with the band's tour bus driver, Andrew Aycock and Rhoads' girlfriend Rachel Youngblood. Attempting to buzz the bus, where the rest of the band members were sleeping, Aycock clipped the bus with his wing and plowed into a nearby garage, killing all three. Ozzy, in a drunken state, would later slur to his wife Sharon, "I just don't understand it. . . . I drink myself into bloody oblivion every night, I get stoned out of my mind and abuse myself all these years and the guy who kept his nose clean is the one who buys the bloody farm."[32] Indeed, the toxicology test showed the only drug in Rhoads' system was nicotine.

Regardless of their claims, no rocker was "unscathed" by the drugs or booze. Even if individuals somehow briefly held it together, groups and friendships were sacrificed on the altar of white powder. Don Felder of the Eagles recalled drugs "had always been a feature in our dissension" and "it became increasingly difficult to be in the recording studio with four guys who were snorting so much cocaine.[33]

Hard drugs, he later noted, "corrupt and distort and magnify paranoia and self-doubt. . . . The spiraling use of cocaine caused us to waste incredible amounts of time obsessing over things we couldn't even really hear. It became hard to tell if a note was actually sharp or flat."[34]

Blues guitarist Johnny Winter nearly destroyed his suddenly-blooming career with heroin, recovering and courageously facing the music press in the early 1970s to candidly admit his addiction. Rolling Stones guitarist Brian Jones had become so incapacitated that just before he and the Stones parted, the band would turn off his guitar during rehearsals. Jones died at the bottom of a swimming pool, with a bad heart and liver, courtesy of the bottle and drugs.[35]

No matter how much the other members of the Doors loved Jim Morrison, he too became so erratic and difficult that they found it hard to work with him. Clapton ultimately acknowledged that during his alcoholic addiction his playing suffered badly. Moon was "miserable and isolated and, more than anything, lonesome."[36]

Mark Stein found himself constantly agitated, angry, and edgy as a result of his addiction. Patty relentlessly worked to get Mark off the stuff. At that point, they were living together and finally, after one morning when Mark had promised he was clean, Patty found speed hidden in the kitchen cabinet and exploded, throwing it at Mark and all over the living room. Storming out, she screamed that she was finished and sped back to her apartment in New Jersey. Mark acknowledged it was "the best thing she could have done…at that moment I gave the shit up and I mean for good. I never went near it again." Healing mentally and physically, Mark was able to regain Patty's trust, and were still together after 40-plus years.

Shortly after the Fudge returned from Europe, they were contacted by Steve Weiss, who wanted to set up a tour with a rising star guitarist, Jimi Hendrix. A Hendrix/Fudge double-bill seemed symbiotic, the music business is anything but rational. In the late 1960s, a slate of acts could include such diverse and eclectic mixes of bands and solo performers as the Jefferson Airplane, the Fifth Dimension, Janis Ian, Iron Butterfly, Quicksilver Messenger Service, and the Who. Often, concerts included four or five bands—almost always three—and it was an era in which artists were expected to get on and off stage for 45-minute sets. Promoters strictly enforced schedules, and more than one band had the plug pulled on them. There was little effort made to package a certain "sound" (psychedelic, blues, folk, easy listening, or whatever), or to engage in "target marketing" that would become de rigor years later.

Thus, the business truly was "who you knew" when it came to booking.

Steve Weiss opened the doors for the Fudge to team up with Jimi Hendrix in the fall of 1968. At the legendary Fox Theater in Atlanta, the Fudge was finally billed as the opening act for the Jimi Hendrix Experience, whose album, Are You Experienced? was on the radio non-stop. The guitarist had his first top ten hit, "Purple Haze" (whose lyrics to this day are misunderstood as, "'scuse me while I kiss this guy").[37]

Relaxing in the dressing rooms backstage with Hendrix, Mark recalled he was "jamming with his guitar and . . . was always a pretty cool guy, easy to be around." The Fudge played a great show, which was recorded on a bootleg by a fan, and then the boys sat around the hotel hallway listening to it as "starry eyed fans and groupies were all over the place." Later, Mark read that Hendrix loved the Fudge's first album, and said he played it until the grooves wore out—then someone stole it, and he bought another copy.

At first, the concert tour consisted of Soft Machine, the Eire Apparent, the Fudge, and Hendrix. Playing a concert, the culminating event of a band's activities and the only one the fans ever see, actually constituted one of the last elements of a long and tedious process that fell heavily upon the workers known as "roadies," often washed-up or wanna-be musicians themselves, supervised by the tour managers who had to shepherd both the bands and the road crews. Some, such as the Fudge's tour manager, Tony "Red" Ruffino, were former promoters or agents. Ruffino joined the Fudge at a relatively old age—32—and admitted he "didn't understand a lot of music."[38]

He made all the band's travel arrangements, ensured that they got from one location to the next, and rode herd on the set-up crew. One of Ruffino's most daunting tasks with Vanilla Fudge was not the boys themselves, who tended to be responsible about getting to gigs, but the equipment, particularly the B-3 organ. "Not every town had one," he explained, and shipping one was a big deal. Sometimes I begged Mark to play whatever we could find."[39]

When the band flew to a concert, the organ was particularly difficult to get on the plane, especially public flights. He recalled one set of gigs that went from Canada to the Fillmore in San Francisco where no equipment planes were available. Red rented a private plane—"rusted to shit, with the equipment not bolted down." It didn't even have seats, and was of such questionable airworthiness that the guys had to space out to balance the plane." Upon takeoff, he looked at Mark and said, "We ain't gonna make it," then hugged Mark.[40]

Fortunately, no such excitement accompanied the Fudge's first major tour. Starting in Atlanta, other concert dates included Red Rocks

Park in Denver and San Diego's Balboa Stadium. And while there were four bands on the bill, soon it became obvious that it was not a concert but a battle between two fantastically talented acts for the hearts and minds of the audience, the Fudge and Hendrix. Increasingly, the Fudge left fans chanting "More" and "Vanilla Fudge." At the Hollywood Bowl, tensions grew so strong that one of Hendrix's roadies said "If the Fudge go one second over, pull the bloody power on them."[41]

Mark was furious. He raced back to the Beverly Hills Hotel where the band was staying and he banged on Philly's door and told him what he had overheard, and Basile got on the phone to someone in Hendrix's camp and screamed, "If anyone pulls the power out on my guys, some fucking heads are gonna fly!"

Little did they know that a new group from England—not the Jimi Hendrix Experience—would soon emerge as their most potent competitors. Just before the group started the Hendrix tour, Phil Basile and his associate, Steve Weiss, along with agent Ron Terry, were at Philly's house with the boys when Ron said "Atlantic just signed this new group from England called Led Zeppelin and they'll be opening for you on some dates out on the West Coast." He took out an advance pressing and said, "I'm going to play this and it's going to blow you away." The track, "You Shook Me," blasted through the living room. All it took was Robert Plant's voice, following the downward slide of Jimmy Page's guitar, to excite everyone. Jimmy Page was from the Yardbirds, whom everyone had heard of, but the others—Plant, John Bonham, and John Paul Jones—were unknowns in America. Soon, the Fudge and Led Zeppelin would constitute one of the most powerful concert duos ever to hit the stage.

Atco began clamoring for a new album, as soon as possible. Seeking to ride the momentum of the debut album, Atco wanted the band in the studio in the middle of touring. "There was no time to be creative," Mark said. Enter the group's producer, George "Shadow" Morton, whose musical journey was as unique and odd as could be found. Growing up on Long Island, Morton—who had never written a song in his life—hung out with Jeff Barry, who would soon write the hit, "Da Doo Ron Ron." Through the acquaintance of Ellie Greenwich, Morton got an invitation to visit her at the Brill Building, which was Cadence Records' headquarters. While he conversed with Greenwich, Morton thought that a songwriter (Greenwich's future husband, Jeff Barry) working diligently in his cubicle was being rude by not talking to him. Morton confronted him, and the man said, "Sorry, I was just busy writing a song." Morton said, "You call that a song? I've got better than that." Barry replied, "Really? Let's hear it?" Morton replied that he had samples at home and would bring them next week. In fact, not only had Shadow Morton never written a song, he couldn't even play a musical instrument. He charged back to Long Island, and while sitting in his car all night, Morton came up with "Remember (Walking in the Sand)." That week, he convinced a local girl group, the Shangri-Las, to perform his song (and even got an unknown pianist named Billy Joel to provide keyboards.) Morton played the song for industry honcho Jerry Leiber, then creating Red Bird Records, and it quickly reached #3 on the charts. After writing another teen hit, "The Leader of the Pack," which record executives were reluctant to play because its storyline told of a biker who won the heart of a teen girl before dying in a crash, Morton was de facto a producer. People began bringing him talent, including an attorney who called Morton and said, "I have a girl I want you to hear." Morton grudgingly agreed, and when Janis Ian was brought in, Morton said, "Play me one of your songs." Then he started to read a newspaper so he couldn't see her. An outraged Janis Ian set fire to Morton's paper, and he talked her out of leaving, making her a star with her hit, "Society's Child." As with most things Morton did, that song about interracial love came with controversy, and at first it was too hot for Atlantic Records to handle. It was eventually released on Verve. Morton prided himself on getting hate mail and death threats from both the Ku Klux Klan and the Black Panthers![42]

By the time he got Vanilla Fudge, Morton had worked with the legendary Phil Spector, eventually earning Spector's enmity—a feat common to many who met Spector. On the first Vanilla Fudge album, Morton basically rolled tape on a live performance. "I wanted it real and lots of emotion," he said, "not perfection." Morton later noted that whether it was the Fudge or the Shangri-Las, he heard the finished song in his head, every string, and every note. For Vanilla Fudge, he had wanted raw, psychedelic emotion. But now, as the group sought a direction for the second album, Shadow Morton came up with what he later described as a "stupid fucking move."[43]

"I wanted them to do something totally different," he explained. "With the success of the first album, in retrospect, they could have gone on for 20 years re-creating that formula." It was, he noted an absolute winner. Instead, in an "effort to one-up myself," Morton pushed on the Fudge an idea for a concept album using Sonny Bono's song "The Beat Goes On" as a theme to create a docu-opera project that would be a chronological progression of the 20th century to the present. At the time, it must be noted, the billowing clouds of marijuana made many ideas sound like they had merit, and Mark observed that no one seriously challenged the concept from the Fudge's end. What emerged was, in

Mark's words, "the most pretentious piece of crap ever created." Morton later assumed full responsibility: "it was ego coming from me."

While not absolving himself or his bandmates from the responsibility of making the album, Mark later wondered why the marketing and business people at Atco didn't intervene. It was a monumental blunder! *The Beat Goes On* was indeed ambitious—yet the Beatles had almost a dozen albums under their belts, with a long string of #1 hits, before attempting Sgt. Pepper, which was vastly more commercial. The album worked its way through history using the song, "The Beat Goes On," as the glue, weaving in snippets of news announcements and sound recordings of the times. In some ways, it was more akin to an early version of a BBC history show than a rock album. Having just hooked millions of fans on a psychedelic, hard-rock orchestra sound, the new album greeted them with Mozart, "Old Black Joe" by Stephen Foster, the "12th Street Rag," a small montage of Beatles tunes, and although "Moonlight Sonata" was the only saving grace as it echoed the arranging prowess of the band on the debut LP, everything was interwoven with voices from world leaders in "stoned out psychedelic excursions." It was a soundtrack for a Disneyland exhibit, not a rock album. And stunningly enough, it reached #17 on the charts, indicating the phenomenal level of interest the band's first album had garnered.

That was both good and bad: more people than ever heard *The Beat Goes On*, and more people than ever would be turned off permanently as Fudge fans. "Fans, critics, and most everyone were pissed," Mark noted. "We had just established a base and a forum of respect and it was squashed. . . . Everybody across the board knew it was a major fuck up." On a plane to do a gig in Dallas with English super-band, Cream, drummer Ginger Baker asked Mark, "What's with the new album?" He smirked. When they got off the plane, he refused to shake Mark's hand. Enraged, Mark shouted, "Just for that we're gonna blow you off the stage tonight!" And the Fudge did. (Baker seemed adept at irritating others. Eric Clapton remembered the first time Cream got together in 1966, Baker and Bruce already "rubbed one another the wrong way.") If Baker's jibe about *The Beat Goes On* hit close to home, it bore no connection to the Fudge's live shows, where the band's professionalism and consistency gave them an edge few others had. Ironically, this put them in sharp contrast to Cream, which depended on finding a particular groove in their jams, was hit or miss. As Eric Clapton noted, "We just got together onstage and played and then went our separate ways."[44]

There was no comaradarie, and it's not surprising that the live album Cream released was markedly better than some of their other concerts, later released on live albums—but by then the legend was born. Robert Stigwood, who accompanied Cream on the tour, also would have nothing to do with the Fudge, but whether it was because of his opinion of *The Beat Goes On* or the fact that the Americans had blown away his star band, remains a mystery.

Angry and damaged by the album, Mark and the guys began writing music with a frenzy, turning out a solid third album called *Renaissance*. Aptly named, it implied the band was ready anew to take their place in the musical pantheon of stars, and above all, to write their own material. Except for Donovan's "Season of the Witch," a track that was in the can recorded during the first LP, all songs were written by band members. Mark penned "Where is My Mind," and "That's What Makes a Man," which had probably the most sophisticated and thoughtful of the album's lyrics, and with Carmine wrote "Paradise" and "Faceless People." Vinny added "Thoughts," which was later released as a single in Italy and made the top 10. While maintaining the band's high musicianship, the album retained an operatic sense, and had less rock, than the band's debut album. Melodic and haunting, *Renaissance* lacked the top 40 hit that had initially boosted Vanilla Fudge with "You Keep Me Hangin' On." *Renaissance* reached #20 on the charts, Vanilla Fudge now had three separate albums on the top 50 simultaneously—a remarkable feat for any band not named the Beatles—and live concerts remained breathtaking.

Nothing demonstrated that better than their tour with Led Zeppelin, which began in December 1968. The first show for the Fudge/Zeppelin combination was in Albuquerque, New Mexico. Janis Joplin was also on the bill. Zeppelin for the most part went unnoticed that evening except for an unflattering review where one music critic said they were mediocre, and Plant's voice was nothing special. It was a bit later on the tour, in Seattle, when John Bonham, "like an innocent little cherub," Mark told a BBC interviewer in 2007, "asked if it was ok to come in and meet the band." Of course, he wanted to meet Appice, and Mark introduced them. Doubtless it would be the last time the bombastic Bonham, who increasingly grew abusive and violent when drunk, would be described as a "cherub."

Mark watched Zeppelin's set with interest, and afterward advised Page to get bigger amps and told Plant to move around a little more on stage. Later, he would be astounded by his own gall, but it worked. Page did get larger amplifiers, and Plant did become stronger and more confident on stage. When Led Zeppelin played Boston, Mark took the shuttle from LaGuardia to see the show at the Boston Tea Party, then spent a night drinking with Bonham and Peter Grant, Zeppelin's manager. The following year, while their first LP was nestled high on the charts, the Fudge and Zeppelin, both in the Atlantic Records family, toured again, this time co-headlining and switching lead sets. Zeppelin had started to come into its own, especially at a show in Vancouver, where Mark recalled they "had made great strides, very quickly," and had total command of the audience. Richard Cole, who began as a roadie for the Fudge but had become Zeppelin's tour manager in 1969, looked at Mark, then surveyed the arena, then glanced back as if to say, "Well, you certainly met your match!" Up to that point, Vanilla Fudge was the heavyweights on the tour, blowing away all comers . . . until now. That night, Jimmy Page loaned Mark his famous Sunburst Les Paul—Mark still strummed a little as a hobby—and Mark returned it the next day. Jimmy Page commented to him that he was pleased with the new album the band was recording called *Led Zeppelin II*.

As the tour continued in Salt Lake City, where the Fudge were the headliners, Plant and Page spun the audience into a frenzy, earning several encores. Looking at Cole, Mark asked, "How do you follow that?" He said, "Just go up and play." That night, Mark recalled, we "rocked the shit out of the house. Zep brought out the best in us. What a night for rock fans." A few days later, as both bands were doing press conferences, Mark had commented to Zeppelin's wives and girlfriends, who had accompanied the band on that leg of the tour, that Led Zeppelin was on its way to becoming the biggest rock band on the planet. "Soon," he added, "they'll be drawing more people than Cream." They shouted back, "that's insane," but in fact, Mark's prediction was on target.

Despite the potential for egotism and jealousy, Vanilla Fudge and Led Zeppelin got along famously, often agreeing to alternate sets based on who had the higher ratings in a particular market. The bands had "much in common—working class background, white blues, heavy guitar sounds," as Neil Daniels noted, yet Mark never felt "a sense of competition . . . if anything, we may have been mentors of a sort, but as Zep became stronger, it was a bit discomforting to be de-throned as the best live band in the business." British writer Chris Welch noted "the fudge provided a protective network for Zeppelin, and there were business connections between the bands.[45]

Robert Plant recalled "They were really so kind to us, especially to Bonzo (John Bonham) and myself, because we were like couple of kids." [ibid] Carmine and Bonham developed a competitive, but brotherly, rivalry. When Appice was first introduced to the Brit, he remarked how much he liked Bonham's work with the bass drum triplets on "Good Times Bad Times." Bonham said, "What do you mean? I got it from you. It's on 'Ticket to Ride' . . " Carmine would snap out a roll, or choke off a cymbal, and at the next concert, Bonham would copy the move.

Later, after the Fudge split up, Mark and his drummer, Jimmy Galluzzi from his new band, Boomerang, went to Philadelphia to watch Led Zeppelin play at the Spectrum. During Bonham's solo, Jimmy Page saw Mark sitting on the stage behind a big riser, and ran over, shouting, "Mark, how are you doing?" But there was a precipice between the seats and the stage, and Page almost plunged through it, still clutching his guitar. Mark and Jimmy grabbed him and possibly saved Led Zeppelin right there! "Well, you nearly lost me," an embarrassed Page said. On another occasion, at the Singer Bowl in Flushing in 1969, New York, Jeff Beck was also on the bill with the Fudge and Zeppelin was watching the show. They all hung out in the dressing room when Richard Cole spotted a snotty music critic who had written harsh things about Zeppelin. Nearby was a crate of orange juice pints. Cole shouted, "Let's get that fucker!" and everyone grabbed pints and began stoning him with orange juice! He ran outside into the alley, still being pelted, and ran for his life.

Even though Zeppelin and Vanilla Fudge were friends, however, during the 29-show, 31-day tour that began in April 1969 at the Fillmore West raised tensions. At issue was the length of Zeppelin's stage show, which began at an hour, then expanded to an hour and a half, then grew to two hours. Encores turned that into two and a half hours, and when the new songs the band wrote on the road were plugged in, Led Zeppelin had "wrung a crowd for three and a half hours of nonstop crunch," and the Fudge hadn't even set foot on stage yet.[46]

No matter how good Vanilla Fudge was, after two hours of blasting by Zeppelin, even the most hard-core fans were drained. A different trend was emerging as well. Cream was selling large numbers of albums and with *Wheels of Fire*, a double album, one entire LP was dedicated to live performances, including a 20-minute drum solo by Ginger Baker. Carmine and Tim began to fancy them, and came up with their own solos, becoming America's answer to the Cream rhythm section. Indeed, aside from the Who's Keith Moon and Led Zeppelin's John Bonham, no other drummers were in the ring with Baker or Appice, while Bogert and Bruce pretty much topped the list of exceptional bassists. The Appice-Bogert solos had an impact on Mark and Vinny, who soon developed their own solo concepts, even though, as Mark said, "solos were not in my heart, but I had to keep up." At first, Mark recalled, it was "healthy and brought out some exciting moments, but I believe it was one factor that led to the demise of the band." On the group's fourth album, released in February 1969, called Near the Beginning, the multi-solo effort, now titled "The Break Song," was captured live at the Shrine Auditorium in Los Angeles. (Ritchie Havens was the opening act).

Whatever problems would emerge later, the Shrine Auditorium version of "The Break Song" contained four of the most exciting and musically impressive solos a fan could want. Beginning with a powerhouse groove from Appice's drums and Bogert's fuzz-tone bass, supported by tight accents from Martell's guitar and Stein's Hammond, it was reminiscent of a soundtrack that could have easily been used in a battle scene of a Ghengis Khan movie. The Fudge then magically disappeared into a slow blues groove for guitar and Martell's solo work was more than satisfying, using his Wah-Wah pedal to the utmost. The guitar solo, bridged by the same power chords that connected all the individual parts, gave way to Mark's lightning-fast Jimmy-Smith inspired Hammond solo, only to culminate in a blast of sound effects that pre-dated the synthesizer, then emerge into another blues groove, this time with Mark singing as well as playing. Another set of bridge chords introduced Tim, who plucked his way into a massive fuzz-bass finale, and Carmine played one of the most powerful and exciting drum solos of that era to end the song. At the time, Appice had a unique drum set: in an age when increasingly drummers such as Ginger Baker had not only dual bass drums, but rows of tom-toms, Appice's kit consisted of two massive 26" blond Ludwig bass drums and only one mounted tom-tom and one floor tom-tom. It made his solo all the more impressive.

The audience at the Shrine went wild. Listening to the live recording inside the remote truck after the performance, the band was thrilled. Pressed for time to make the next Atlantic Records convention, the Fudge had the multitracks taken to a nearby studio in Los Angeles and stayed up all night mixing the live recording. They then hopped the first flight back to New York the next morning with the tapes to be ready to be delivered, comprising a perfect complement to the studio songs already recorded for an album called *Near the Beginning*. Among those, a slowed-down version of "Some Velvet Morning," was mixed by Carmine with Eddie Kramer at New York's Record Plant. This arrangement was performed at the International Music Festival in Venice, Italy in 1969 and the Fudge became the first Americans to win the Golden Gondola award. "Shotgun," a cover of the old song by Jr. Walker and the All Stars, an instant high-energy Fudge classic sung by Tim, got the radio play. Like "Break Song," "Shotgun" featured mini-solos by each member, kept within the beat and structure of the song. Mark, with engineer Tony Bongiovi (Jon Bon Jovi's uncle), mixed

"Shotgun" the same week as Carmine worked on "Some Velvet Morning." They put the drums out front, infusing "Shotgun" with even more energy. Mark also noted he wanted "to make Carmine happy." Both Carmine and Mark emerged from the mixing sessions pleased with the other's effort as producers.

Nevertheless, just as the band appeared to be recovering from *The Beat Goes On,* recovering its rock flavor and emerging as a powerhouse, several tensions had started to pull the members in different directions. First and foremost, the recognition Tim and Carmine had drawn as soloists had an effect on Vince, who, constantly being compared unfavorably to Clapton, Hendrix, Beck, and Page, attempted to compensate with increasingly long solos in the "Break Song." He became isolated, and was not getting along well with anyone. Typically, one found Vinny with his earphones on, inaccessible to the world.

Audience comments took their toll on Vince, whose style fit the Fudge perfectly, but who individually was not on the same plane as Clapton, Hendrix, Beck, Jimmy Page, or Ritchie Blackmore, each of whom had introduced radical new sounds and styles. Blackmore, the king of the tremolo bar who proved far better in the studio than live, still churned out impressive solo after impressive solo. (His studio solo on "Highway Star" [1971] remains one of the greatest recorded solos ever). The unpredictable Jeff Beck—called by Clapton the best guitarist of all and labeled by producer Andy Johns "the moodiest bugger I've ever known"—bordered on jazz fusion; Page, an accomplished lead player, had an unmatched work ethic and had begun teasing new sounds out of the studios. By then, Hendrix, his playing already suffering from drug use, released a double-album masterpiece, Electric Ladyland, in 1968. Produced and written by Hendrix—who also played bass and drums on many cuts—Electric Ladyland introduced the studio as an instrument for the guitarist, much the way Pet Sounds had done so for Brian Wilson. Hendrix played Mark the acetates of this recording in the wee hours of a hotel stay in Phoenix after their concert appearance. And Eric Clapton? Throughout England, graffiti proclaimed, simply, "Clapton is God." For Vinny to compete with this pantheon of rock superstars proved an insurmountable burden.

Worse, the guitar, per se, was not the focus of Vanilla Fudge, but rather Mark's Hammond, supported by the powerful rhythm section, and an active guitar line, all featuring the vocal harmonies. Once that style began to deteriorate, so did the Fudge. Ultimately, however, Carmine and Tim simply thought Vince was a weak link and that they could find a guitarist closer to their talent level. Steve Weiss corralled the boys to try and save the band. "What can we do? What is the problem?" he asked.

Tim bluntly pointed at Martell and said, "He stinks!" Tim was abusive to Vince, and even tried to get Jim McCarty, with whom Bogert and Appice would soon form Cactus, into Vanilla Fudge, but even though Mark and Vinny were not getting along, that seemed too radical a step for Mark.

As if the band needed any more pressure, Mark, obsessed with his weight, had begun using amphetamines, which, as he admitted in an understatement, "didn't help." Mark, fully admitting his addiction, nevertheless regretted that there was "never a band meeting" where people offered to help. A much different encounter with drugs nearly left Mark in a Canadian prison. In 1969, when the Fudge played the "Man and World Expo" in Montreal, the event started normal enough—which was to say with frenzied fans. But then Tim asked the audience—which was several thousand strong and being contained by a barrier that was a mere 15 feet from the front of the stage, to "come a bit closer." And closer they came! They smashed down the barrier and were upon the band in a flash. Mark recalled, "We were swarmed with bodies all around us . . . I literally jumped on top of my Hammond to get away from the crowd." Security guards came to the rescue and got the band backstage until the crowd return to their seats, then the Fudge finished the show. Tim was chastised for what he did by both band members and some of the promotion team, but he didn't take it to heart, and actually found it amusing.

But the drama—and danger—had just begun. That evening, Vince and Mark were at their hotel room. Mark had invited some fans in for a smoke and before long, Vince took off with some of them and never returned that night. The next morning Mark awoke to a phone call from Red Ruffino, the tour manager at the time, telling him the band had about two hours to get ready to leave for the airport for a flight back to New York to play a show in the Catskill Mountains.

Mark hopped in the shower and while drying off, there was a bang at the door. He asked who was there, but got no reply. Then came another, louder bang. Thinking it was Tim or Carmine playing a trick— they were in the adjoining suite—Mark moved to open the door when suddenly it came crashing in. He ran to the bathroom thinking it was an intruder, and that he'd be killed. "I had a small piece of hash in the medicine cabinet," he noted, "and that was absconded immediately. There must have been five or six of those bastards on me at once!" They were Canadian Police, who managed to pull Mark back into the room, where they threw him on a bed and told him to "shut the fuck up." One reached down and pulled out a large bag of weed from in between the mattress of Vinny's bed, and said, "What's this?" Mark screamed, "That's bullshit. That was planted there." Hearing the ruckus, Red

91

showed up at the door with the rest of the band, all of them in shock, only to learn that the Canadian police had also busted Paco, one of the band's roadies, as well. "So here I was," Mark lamented, "another rock star led off to jail in handcuffs. Paco and I were hauled away like hardened criminals." The two were booked, fingerprinted, and thrown into separate cells for the arraignment the next morning. Mark found himself in a cell with two counterfeiters and a man accused of raping his 12-year-old daughter. "I thought I was losing my mind," Mark said, "as I looked at images on the walls of men hanging themselves—artwork of former inmates."

During the night, other prisoners began screaming Mark's name as they learned who he was. Arlo Guthrie's 1967 song "Alice's Restaurant," with its "father-stabbers, mother-rapers, and father-rapers" began to spin in Mark's head, without any of Guthrie's humor. When someone said "Stein," the rapist concluded Mark was with Vanilla Fudge and said, "Hey, man, love your music!" Other inmates quickly sought Mark's advice as to where they could hang out if they escaped to America. The following morning, Mark and Paco were taken to the arraignment in shackles when Mark saw Red. He was a "sight for sore eyes," and along with the lawyers, they quickly got Mark and Paco released on bail. The band drove back across the American border for the Catskills gig, when Mark learned that New York radio stations broadcast that he had been busted for an ounce of heroin—"news" that his mother and father heard while driving in their car. (For the record, Mark said unequivocally "I never went near that stuff, not ever"). One time, Mark despondently played a pinball machine when a young fan came up and said, "My mom said you're a criminal." The trial would be postponed again and again, and trying to schedule gigs around it became a "total pain in the ass." Mark traveled to Montreal three times with his lawyer only to find that the trial was delayed again. "It was a major challenge to my nervous system," he noted, "not to mention the paranoia I had every time I was around anyone smoking dope—the band included!"

The trial was set and a few days prior Mark's lawyers had arranged for a meeting with a Canadian law firm, which in turn had him meet with the French-speaking judge who was trying his case. It was to his benefit to have the combined legal teams using all their influence to keep Mark a free man. Charged with the illegal possession of drugs, Mark faced a prosecutor who wanted nothing short of a multi-year incarceration. Suffering through cross-examination, Mark remembered, "Here I was, a twenty-two year old rocker, scared shitless as the prosecutor was in my face trying to intimidate me and break me down . . . it was a nightmare." Confused and afraid, Mark admitted to things that under normal circumstances never would have, but in the end, the judge slammed down the gavel and pronounced him innocent of all charges. He raced from the courtroom, hailed a taxi to the airport, pleaded with the driver to "step on it," and literally had minutes to make the plane. Boarding at the last second, Mark got the last available seat and as the plane took off, he watched Canadian soil drift behind him—along with one of the darkest periods of his life. It was about to get darker.

Chapter Four

Vanilla Fudge had been on the brink of becoming one of the most important rock bands of the era. The tours with Hendrix, Zeppelin, and the growing reputations of the Fudge as individual artists had brought them to a level of stardom few enjoyed. But the fiasco with *The Beat Goes On* had mortally damaged the band. Recovery was possible, but it would take more than one album, and the old saying, "You don't get a second chance to make a first impression," had now become all too real to the Fudge when it came to being a cutting-edge band. *Renaissance* and *Near the Beginning* had merely returned the band to where it was pre-*Beat Goes On*, not elevated it to new heights. And it all came with a great price.

Tim and Carmine—who had grown increasingly isolated as a rhythm section—secretly had opened negotiations with Jeff Beck and his former singer, Rod Stewart, to re-form Beck's original four-piece power trio with Stewart out front. "I was the last to know they were leaving," Mark said. "It was Phil's associate Red Ruffino who told me." Vinny was increasingly isolated, wearing earphones all the time and going off on 20-minute solos in futile attempts to prove to his bandmates that he was worthy. Contractually, the band still had obligations for tours and for one more album. Heading to Europe with the knowledge that the band was breaking up, Mark sank into a funk. The band played the Venice International Music Festival with their rendition of "Some Velvet

Morning," where the band won the coveted Golden Gondola (a European Grammy for a live performance). Mark hoped might keep the group together. It had no impact.

The final European show, in Paris at the Olympiad, ended with Mark going alone to a club as "Here Comes the Sun" by the Beatles came on the juke box. No sun came up for the Fudge. Mark flew back to the USA solo, on a flight that originated in Athens and was "packed like a cattle car." No one spoke English and kids screamed as Mark popped some sleeping pills and downed them with Jack Daniels, anxious to wake up in the United States. He literally kissed the ground when he arrived. But going through customs with a leather coat he purchased in Europe delayed him for an hour as the authorities searched through his luggage, adding to his frustration.

Mark had moved to Long Beach in September 1969, and after a few days, he focused on the next album required by Atco. Adrian Barber, one of the Rascals' producers, would handle the last of the contractually-required sessions. Entitled *Rock and Roll*, the result proved exciting to Fudge fans—who as yet didn't know the band had fractured—and featured, appropriately, two rock songs, including "Need Love" and "Street Walking Woman." It also included a pair of new Mark Stein tunes, "Lord in the Country" and "Church Bells of St Martins," as well as a powerful cover of the Gerry Goffin/Carole King song, "I Can't Make It Alone" and the old Rudy Clark tune, "If You Gotta Make a Fool of Somebody," as well as the Academy Award-winning song in the 1968 film, *The Thomas Crown Affair*, "The Windmills of Your Mind," previously recorded by Dusty Springfield. On several of the songs, one seems to sense the "old" Vanilla Fudge playing together live in the studio, especially on "I Can't Make it Alone," which at times seems to be Mark singing to the other band members. Yet all the tracks were laid down individually: Carmine played his drum track, then Tim arrived late to over-dub the bass parts. In-between, Mark and Vinny put in the keyboards and guitar. Despite attempts by the "suits" to keep the band together, the Fudge disintegrated, playing a final show at the Action House in March 1970 as a disillusioned Mark went through the motions.

That night proved traumatic for more reasons than the unwinding of Vanilla Fudge. When Mark arrived on that chilly March night, lines looped around the block—friends, fans, and family. Everyone wanted to see the final performance of the Fudge. But 90 minutes before showtime, Philly called Mark at his Long Beach apartment. "When are you comin' down? The place is starting to fill up." A desperate Mark replied, "Phil, I'm having a real problem with Patty! She started to bleed—I think she's having a miscarriage. She's screaming that she won't go near any doctor and I can't leave her. I don't know what to do!" Frantically, Philly said, "Jesus, alright, just sit tight. Let me make some calls and I'll get back to you." Soon, the phone rang again and Philly had spoken to someone named "Henry" who could help him. Henry Hill was a member of the infamous Paulie Vario crime group and a close associate of Phil. Mark recalled having a few drinks with him and that he was a "fun guy." On one occasion, Henry drove his car to the rear of the Action House, opened his trunk, and revealed freshly hijacked Revox reel to reel tape recorders and Parisian suits, which he sold to the band for pennies on the dollar.

Henry drove to a nearby hospital, where he used his connections to get an emergency room doctor to go to Mark's apartment and care for Patty while Mark went to his last gig as a Fudgie. On stage, playing "You Keep Me Hangin' On," Bogert displayed a decidedly bored look, letting fans know he couldn't wait for it to end. Someone in the audience screamed, "Fuck you, Bogert! If it wasn't for Diana Ross, you'd still be playin' in bars!" But Tim wasn't fazed. All he cared about was moving on to his new project with Carmine. Meanwhile, Mark gave it his best, but throughout the whole show Patty was on his mind. When it was over, he phoned Henry to learn that everything was all right, and Patty had no complications. He raced home, thanked Henry, and stayed with Patty as she rested comfortably.

Vanilla Fudge's demise, in retrospect, was hardly surprising, and indeed seemed to be afflicting all the major touring acts. Santana was beginning to fracture, the band thinking it was a democracy instead of a star-focused band. The Jeff Beck Group, with Rod Stewart, Ronnie Wood, and Nicky Hopkins, after a pair of highly-praised albums, ripped apart in July 1969 (and would play a central role in the Fudge's own fission); Jimi Hendrix's Experience played its final concerts five months earlier. Cream had preceded both with a November 1968 farewell tour, including the famous concert at the Royal Albert Hall on November 26 of that year and culminating with their Goodbye album. Each band had its own story: Jack Bruce and Ginger Baker, opposites politically (Bruce was a working-class Labourite, Baker more of a Cold War conservative), had long-standing tensions from their days as members of the Graham Bond Organisation, where they clashed musically, erupting in on-stage fights and even the sabotage of each other's instruments. When Baker fired Bruce, the bassist continued to arrive at gigs until the drummer drove him away at knifepoint. Both referred to themselves as jazz musicians; both had massive egos. As their extended jam sessions moved from the sublime to the ridiculous, every song could reached 20 minutes in length—Eric Clapton once noted that he stopped playing during one of the jams and neither Bruce nor Baker noticed.[1]

The Jimi Hendrix Experience, formed by turning guitarist Noel Redding into a bass player, where he was eternally uncomfortable, broke up when Redding announced he wanted to form his own band, Fat Mattress (which Hendrix sarcastically called Thin Pillow), and following some 1969 concerts, Redding's band actually began to open for the Redding-less Experience. Hendrix permanently replaced Redding with his old 101st Airborne buddy, Billy Cox, in April 1969, just as the guitarist began to drift into a series of legal battles and drug busts.

Jeff Beck's breakup, on the other hand, directly affected Vanilla Fudge. During the summer of 1969 Beck and Stewart decided to team up with Bogert and Appice, opening negotiations with them. The Americans went to England in September, just as *Rock and Roll* was released, but the new partnership literally crashed when Beck, in December, had a car accident near Maidstone and fractured his skull. Stewart departed to join Ronnie Wood with the Small Faces, while Bogert and Appice paired up with former Mitch Ryder and the Detroit Wheels guitarist Jim McCarty and singer Rusty Day out of Detroit to form a boogie band called Cactus. In some respects, Cactus was a second-best Jeff Beck group, both driven and limited by the scratchy vocals of Day, who lacked Stewart's suave sex appeal or even his range. But the jam factor of Bogert, Appice, and McCarty made up for it, until, as McCarty later told one of the authors, it got to be competition instead of jamming.

Vanilla Fudge's impending fracture came just as American heavy rock peaked at Woodstock in August 1969. Viewed as a capstone of the Golden Era's musical experience, Woodstock in fact was just the most famous, and largest, of a number of music festivals that year. On July 25, 1969, the Seattle Pop Festival at Gold Creek Park in Woodinville (just northeast of Seattle) drew some of the biggest stars in music. The Doors, the Byrds, Ike and Tina Turner, Santana, Chicago (then going by the name of the Chicago Transit Authority), Led Zeppelin, and Vanilla Fudge. Mark hoped to see many of the acts, but different bands were playing on alternate days to it made it difficult to see them all. He bumped into Tina Turner at a concession stand, and saw the members of Spirit standing around (drummer Jack Cassidy with his shaved, bald head stood out, even among the hippie rockers). The festival had its share of tripping on drugs, but as Mark recalled, there was also a lot of ego tripping, particularly, he felt, from Vince. Unhappy and frustrated with his sound, Martell demanded the road crew double the size of his Marshall stack, to the point of stating he would not go onstage unless his conditions were met. Vanilla Fudge had no choice: extra Marshalls were added. But after calling Phil back in New York, the group was given a solution. Basile said "set 'em up, but don't plug them in." So they did. "I don't think Vinny ever knew the difference," Mark laughed.

The Fudge went on just as the sun set in the West. As they began their closing song, "You Keep Me Hangin' On," Mark reduced the organ note to a whisper. He looked to his right and Jim Morrison stood there, staring at him with an intense look "like he could see right through me." Mark was a big Doors fan, but in truth Jim was checking out the whole band. The Fudge got a great reception and when the set was over, Mark hopped off his B-3 bench and hoped to see Morrison, but he was gone, and would soon die. Meanwhile, nightfall and party time approached, meaning Mark was ripped. Led Zeppelin was up next, and as they got into position, Robert Plant came over to have a word with Mark. But tripping, Mark gave Plant a bear hug and wouldn't let go. Plant "was screaming for me to unleash him," which, finally, Mark did. Zeppelin played an amazing set, then went on to their legendary "mudshark incident" at the Edgewater Hotel—frivolity blown out of proportion by the press, to the point that even Zappa wrote a song about it. The night ended when organist Lee Michaels—another B-3 player— took the stage with only his drummer, Frosty. Supported by a wall of Leslie speaker amplified through dozens of cabinets, Michaels brought down the house.

Another major festival, three months after Woodstock, was the Palm Beach Music & Art Festival, dubbed by the media as "Woodstock South." By that time, the Fudge were limping along and were going through the motions, not even traveling together. Mark flew to Palm Beach on his own and met the others at the Colonnades Hotel on Singer Island. All the major acts stayed there—Janis Joplin, the Stones, Johnny Winter, King Crimson, and Grand Funk Railroad. As at Woodstock, a helicopter transported the musicians to the event. On the afternoon of the show, Mark sat with Grand Funk Railroad near Janis Joplin, who was pounding down the whiskey. Some excited girls came up to her requesting autographs. "Who the fuck do you think you are?" she screamed. "I can't be bothered by a bunch of assholes like ya'll. Now get outta my face." Mark took it as typical Joplin, and was saddened by the story the poor girls would have to tell about one of rock's legends.

On the flight over to the event, the Fudge rode with a nervous Johnny Winter. Bruce Wayne, the Fudge's tour and sound manager, decided to have some fun, and getting a crazed look on his face, suggested the group toss Winter out the door! But it had the effect of calming the guitarist and perhaps eased his fear of flying. He took it with good humor and laughed. The Fudge finally went on at 1:30 in the morning. As they climbed the stairs to the outer stage, it was a cold night in Florida—some said the temperature dropped to 40 degrees. A few songs into the set, Vanilla Fudge was shocked to see a thoroughly boozed Joplin walk on stage and put her bottle in front of Mark, croaking "Have a swig of this shit and let's jam, mother fucker!" Mark took the Southern Comfort from her hands, took a deep drink, and screamed back, "Let's jam then!" Behind her was Johnny Winter, who also came out. So Vanilla Fudge, plus Joplin and Winter played a blues tune in one of the largely ignored moments in rock history. The scene apparently went unrecorded.

Just as few Americans have ever heard about the "Newport Tea Party," but most remember the "Boston Tea Party" (because of the publicity given it by Sam Adams), so too did the other festivals of 1969 go largely unnoticed. Instead, Woodstock—which, by its New York location tended to attract more media, and because of its subsequent motion picture reached a national (as opposed to regional) audience—became the event of 1969. Many name it as the defining moment of that year, forgetting that American's landed on the moon the previous month. Officially billed as the Woodstock Music and Art Fair, unofficially many hoped it would kick off a new "age of Aquarius." The event was touted as "a new stage in the psychic evolution of the world, a mass celebration of what the 1960s was all about," wrote one soon-to-be critic from the Left.[2]

Woodstock's reality was much different than the sanitized film version directed by Michael Wadleigh released the following year. Moochers and freeloaders broke down the chain-link fences and scrambled inside by the thousands for a free concert, turning the festival into "an undeclared disaster area, beset by the shortages of food, water, shelter, and sanitation commonly associated with floods and earthquakes."[3]

Woodstock concluded with Jimi Hendrix playing The Star Spangled Banner as masses of zonked out kids lay in mud and filth. It was a symbolic scene in so many ways. As the curtain came down, Hendrix—the concluding act---was only a year away from his own drug-induced death (joining Janis Joplin, who also performed at Woodstock, and Jim Morrison within a year).

Even as Hendrix's "truly apocalyptic" rendition of the national anthem blasted over a "battlefield, [with] zombies crawling over a field littered with paper cups, plastic wrappers, and half-eaten food, gnawing on corn husks, slobbering over ketchup- and mustard-smeared half-eaten hot dogs rolls, sprinkled with ants," already the loose bond of political revolution and rock had permanently unraveled.[4]

Promoter Bill Graham took a limo and got stuck in mud: "There was nowhere to go. There were no dressing rooms because they had all been turned into hospitals. There was nowhere to eat. . . . It was all very frightening . . . . By the third day, it had become a survival camp."[5] He rightly surmised that Woodstock had become "a camp of people who were in retreat from something."[6]

And it was becoming less "revolutionary" by the minute. Reporter and Hoffman confidant Ellen Sander discovered this when she found herself caught up in the music and ignoring the revolution. She wrote Hoffman a few days later, chiding him for being so "enraptured with the vision of yourself as the latter-day Che . . . that you'll make anything and anyone your enemy . . . . [The] age of politics is over," she advised. "Get it on, dance to the music. . . . Everyone else loved it at Woodstock. The only unhappy people there were the political crazies."[7]

None other than Joan Baez, the queen diva of protest songs, delivered a pragmatic assessment of the event: "it wasn't any fucking revolution. It was a three-day period during which people were decent to each other because . . . if they weren't, they'd all go hungry."[8]

Woodstock (the film) captured a stoned Stephen Stills praising the crowd for its tenacity---"You people have got to be the strongest people I ever saw. Three days, man, three days"—just before Stills left the stage and leaped onto a waiting helicopter to hoist him back to a luxury hotel. When Abbie Hoffman observed that, he snorted in disgust, "There's no morality here. . . . The helicopters bring in champagne for Janis Joplin's band, and people are sick in the field. . . ."[9]

Hoffman and others thought Woodstock would be a natural extension of the Chicago Democratic Convention riots that would advance American society toward a utopian state. But instead of sparking a revolution, Woodstock constituted the petering-out of a movement. Over the next few years, critic Peter Doggett complained, artists "swapped their revolutionary idealism for self-obsession."[10]

An election night party in 1972, when the returns showed Richard Nixon crushing George McGovern, it marked the final collapse of the music/revolution nexus, presided over by weeping from Jerry Rubin, Abbie Hoffman, Allen Ginsberg, and John Lennon. The four screamed at each other, lay "sprawled helplessly on the floor," and finally Lennon ended the night in a tirade about "middle-class Jews," in which he drunkenly bellowed, "Up the revolution."[11]

Having previously himself been suspected by the radical Left of being a CIA plant, Lennon now accused Yippie leader Rubin as working for the Agency! Dejectedly, the guests slipped away, embarrassed to be around Lennon, the "midwife of the revolution, [who] had mutated into its decomposing corpse."[12]

In fact, all along the connection of rock to "revolutionary" politics was tenuous. Jefferson Airplane, whose sound was associated in the popular mind with everything hippie-esque, refused to support any party: "Any statement they wanted to make, any position they wanted to take, could be expressed through their songs and by their . . . lives—not by lending their name to a political horse race."[13]

As the group's biographer later noted, Jefferson Airplane "shied away from lyrics that pointed fingers at the government, the military or other specific targets."[14] Signe (Toly Anderson) Ettlin, the band's first female lead singer before Grace Slick, insisted "There was no fucking message. No matter how much somebody wants to make out now that we were saying something, we weren't saying anything . . . ."[15]

Grace Slick took her place in the band, yet couldn't have been less "hippie-like." A former high school cheerleader who did some modeling, Slick wore makeup and liked nice clothes, was mortified at the notion of communal living, treasured her privacy, and abhorred dirt, especially other people's dirt. Like most in the 1960s, she (and the rest of Jefferson Airplane) became familiar with drugs, producing one of the all-time classic druggie lyrics in "White Rabbit": "One pill makes you larger, and one pill makes you small, and the ones that mother gives you, don't do anything at all. Go ask Alice, when she's ten feet tall." Liberation through pharmaceuticals did not translate into political activism, however, much to the disappointment of radical leftists like Hoffman.

As if to heap dung onto the grave of the revolutionary-rock alliance, 1972's top song was the stunningly boring "First Time Ever I Saw Your Face" by Roberta Flack, and the top ten contained such watered-down wonders as Harry Nilsson's "Without You," "Baby Don't Get Hooked On Me" by Mack Davis, "Alone Again" by Gilbert O'Sullivan, and two Sinatra-era artists, Sammy Davis, Jr. ("Candy Man") and Wayne Newton ("Daddy Don't You Walk So Fast"). American heavy rock remained a powerful influence—one of many, but it was temporarily displaced in "hipness" by a new phenomenon, "disco," named for the discotheque (a dance club with recorded music played by disc jockeys). Neil Bogart of Casablanca Records explained disco's appeal: people, he said, "were tired of guitarists playing to their amplifiers. They wanted to be the stars."[16]

(Others, such as Gloria Gaynor, somewhat condescendingly blamed whites' purported lack of rhythm for the phenomena: "it was kind of hard for white people to get into R&B music because the beat is so sophisticated and hard for the kind of dancing that white people are used to doing"—this comment addressed to a population that had made

101

R&B mainstream by buying black records . . . and dancing to them!)[17]

More likely, Studio 54 co-owner Steve Rubell was correct when he observed that "the theater atmosphere has a lot to do with it. Everybody secretly likes to be on stage and here we give them a huge space to do it all on."[18]

Disco music became a $5 billion industry by the end of the decade, but perhaps disco's peak moment came in 1977, when John Travolta took to the cinematic dance floor in his white suit as the Bee Gees sang in falsetto, the message was clear. Forget protesting: "You Should be Dancin'."

Ironically, much of the media and most of the music intelligentsia missed the real revolution that was at the door. At the very time that American rock was losing some of its revolutionary bite, dividing into numerous sub-streams, including "punk," "soul," "metal," "pop," and so on, the power of western music had already shot out of the West like alien transmissions from deep space. It was headed straight for the Iron Curtain. At the same time the samizdat writers were battling for freedom, probing with their verbal bayonets, rock and roll had already joined the fight. In the material sense, through the form of 45 or 33 rpm vinyl records, western rock found its way into the hands of communist youths. Many heard western music second-hand, with records "distributed on discarded X-ray plates—plastic photographs of bones imprinted with record grooves."[19]

Following the Nagy revolt in Hungary in 1956, the new government under Janos Kadar sought to neutralize the simmering revolution by permitting hundreds of Wurlitzer jukeboxes into the country (causing the generic Hungarian name for a jukebox to be a "Wurlitzer.") Budapest became a hotbed of bloc-rock, as did Sopot, Poland, where an aspiring journalist and club owner, Franciszek Walicki, packed his "Non-Stop Club" with Polish cover bands playing Jerry Lee Lewis, Carl Perkins, and Elvis. He even created the first true Polish rock act in 1958, ultimately named "The Reds and the Blacks." A second band he formed, "the Blues and the Blacks," featured a singer named Czelaw Niemen who eventually sang in Paris and who sang the first rock and roll hit songs in Poland. In Romania, officials decried the music, which aroused "animal instincts" and developed the youths' "cruelty, contempt, and destructive urges."[20]

NATO strategists took notice, observing in the journal Revue *militaire generale* that the obsession with rock 'n' roll was time not spent with Marx or Lenin. Elvis's arrival as a new private in Germany terrified the communists, who saw him as a new weapon in the Cold War.

Germany cracked down on rock in 1958, mandating that 60% of

any music performed had to come from the "peoples' democracies." But when American folk/protest singer Pete Seeger toured the Iron Curtain countries, the Soviets especially saw an opportunity to enlist an American artist in the revolutionary cause. Seeger made 28 appearances in the USSR itself, as well as concert dates in Poland and Czechoslovakia. Yet his Moscow concert demonstrated that by its very nature, revolutionary music was always positioned against "the establishment" when Seeger led the audience in the gospel hymn, "Michael, Row the Boat Ashore," and "We Shall Overcome." What were the Soviet listeners to "overcome" but communism?

While in the West, "protest" music protested the democracies, behind the Iron Curtain, the communist governments were the "man" to be protested. A clear example of this transformation can be seen in German Wolf Biermann, left Hamburg for East Berlin to build a new Communist world, then proceeded to criticize the German communist state. Biermann ridiculed Stalin—an act that only a few years before would have earned him a bullet from the secret police—and even after imprisonment, he continued to record songs that bashed the government. By 1965, Party functionaries denounced his music as "toilet-stall poetry" and "pornography."[21] Within the USSR itself, protest songs were gaining popularity. Stalin was widely, if somewhat subtly, criticized in the 1950s by Alexander Galich.

Then came the Beatles, whose songs, images, and paraphernalia were everywhere from Leipzig to Leningrad. Mop-top hair styles became common, and young people sported Beatle buttons sent to them by relatives in the West. Indeed, the Fab Four were counterculture role models—young, funny, and full of energy, in stark contrast to the aging gargoyles of the Communist elites. Riots occurred in Czechoslovakia after local Beatle look-alike bands performed. One reporter, horrified, wrote of the fan behavior, "They wriggled, they fell off the platform and crawled back onto it . . . . I expected them to bite each other at any minute."[22]

Instantly, a host of copycat Iron Curtain bands appeared, including the Illes in Hungary, Bundaratsite in Bulgaria, the Red Guitars in Poland, Czechoslovakia had Olympic, and the USSR's own Time Machine (formed when the father of the guitar player smuggled home a copy of *A Hard Day's Night*. Before the "Prague Spring," Czechoslovakia even had a rock music magazine, *Melodie*. The freest of the Soviet bloc countries, the Czechs had hundreds of bands with names such as Strangers, Buttons, and Hells' Devils—all, of course, registered with the state. But Beatlemania was everywhere: when the film, *A Hard Day's Night*, opened in Poland in 1965, school absenteeism was described as "rampant" and "the cinemas [were] besieged" as the bitels conquered Warsaw.[23]

Czech schools responded to their absenteeism by offering a six-part series on modern music, including studies of Elvis and Bill Haley and the Comets. The first Iron Curtain hippies were likely Czechs known as the "little Marys" (manicky), but the phenomenon was not confined to any single country. One of East Germany's leading musicians, Horst Kruger, abandoned classical and jazz to only play rock and roll, and when a popular Leipzig band, The Butlers, was forcibly broken up for "damaging art," protests at the high schools had to be dispersed with troops and water cannons. At first, the Soviet hierarchy attempted to ridicule the Beatles, describing Ringo Starr as Tarzan and "a monkey," claiming that the Beatles were "already out of date" in 1964.[24]

Copycat bands proliferated, including Falcon, Guys, Little Red Devils, and dozens of others. Alexander Gradsky, later called "The Old Man of Moscow rock," was a 14-year-old who went "into a state of shock" when he heard the Liverpudlians. Forming the "Slavs" with Mikhail Shokolov, the grandson of the Nobel Prize-winning novelist, Gradsky's band became the top rock act in Moscow. Everywhere, rock caused rebellion. Several western bands played Czechoslovakia and East Germany in 1966, sparking violent scuffles: Hollies' singer Graham Nash saw "all this shooting outside the hotel."[25]

Further tours were stopped by the authorities, and when a Riga concert was cancelled, protestors held a six-hour demonstration with banners proclaiming "Free the Guitars!" Tours resumed in spring 1967, including a Rolling Stones appearance in Warsaw that experienced ticket problems, leading to irate kids storming police barriers, and provoking a police response of tear gas and dogs. Inside the Palace of Culture, the Stones stopped in mid-song when they noticed that the Communist Party elites sat in the front. Keith Richards grabbed drummer Charlie Watts: "stop playing, Charlie." Pointing to the Party members in the first rows, he shouted, "You f–ing lot, get out and let those bastards in the back sit down front."[26] Needless to say, the Stones were not invited back to the Soviet bloc.

Rock was at the center of the "Prague Spring," particularly a band called the "Primitives," one of the earliest Soviet-bloc psychedelic bands. As Alexander Dubcek liberalized Czech society, the likelihood of intervention grew, culminating in the Warsaw Pact invasion of August 20, 1968. Of course, oppression was exactly what protest singers needed. Marta Kubisova, the singer for the Golden Kids, penned the anthem of the Czech resistance with her "Prayer for Marta," which was followed by the shocking self-immolation of Jan Palach in January 1969. Another leading Czech protest song, by Moravian singer Karel Kryl, was "Close the Gate, Little Brother" (1969). It became so popular, Kryl toured Czechoslovakia performing three concerts a day, with no manager, no agent, selling 125,000 copies of his song.

Dubcek was replaced in 1969, whereupon the Beach Boys and the Tremeloes were invited to the annual festival in Bratislava. After a spectacular ascent, the Beach Boys had drifted far behind the Beatles in America, as critics panned them as shallow and unimaginative. Their one-time leader, Brian Wilson and songwriter, battled mental illness and schizophrenia, blasted away by drugs, was unable to travel. His bandmates thus looked at the European tour as a means to regain their momentum, and in turn Czechoslovakia welcomed them as a sign of the return of "Spring." To a packed concert at Lucerna Hall in June, after knocking out their hits "Sloop John B." and "Barbara Ann," the Beach Boys dedicated the song "Break Away"—a song about individuality and freedom---to Dubcek, who was in the crowd. The tour reinvigorated the Californians.

Other western groups played Prague in 1969, including the Nice with Keith Emerson. He recalled the people were "starved and craved Western culture, particularly the new rock music. Records like ours could only be bought at a very high price on the black market, once they'd been smuggled in."[27]

But if "Spring" hardly returned, the communist states were on notice that the juggernaut called rock 'n' roll could not be ignored. As Chuck Negron, the singer for Three Dog Night put it, "the young people behind the Iron Curtain fell in love with our music, then us."[28]

Billy Joel would later have the same experience in Cuba, where he played with Stephen Stills and other pro-Castro rockers. "Stills made a speech" Joel noted. But Billy Joel hadn't come to Cuba to do politics, but music. "I got on stage and said, 'No Habla Espanol,' and launched into 'The Stranger,' and the crowd went crazy," he recalled.[29]

Leslie Mandoki, a Hungarian drummer and student leader, recalled that while rock concerts were banned in his country, fliers would be put up in a single afternoon at the five major university campuses in Hungary for a concert that evening. Usually, he noted, the police would only figure it out by the time the concert was halfway over, at which time they would close it down. Mandoki would later escape to the West and, still later, go on to become the musical director for Audi and Volkswagen, which brought him into the circles to powerful politicians. In that context, he spent considerable time with the then-former Soviet Union's premier, Mikhail Gorbachev and was told, "We could not stop rock and roll."[30]

105

If rock's future was in freeing the captive peoples of Eastern Europe, however, in 1970 Mark was the one who needed liberating. As Carmine and Tim joined Rusty Day and Jim McCarty to form a boogie band, Cactus, Phil insisted Mark and Vinny could keep Vanilla Fudge going with new members. They recruited friends from Poughkeepsie, New York, named Jimmy Galuzzi on drums and Sal D'Onofrio on bass, rehearsing at Breakout Management (Phil's place in Oceanside, Long Island). Immediately, Mark knew it wouldn't work. Vinny soon left to start his own band and Mark took Jimmy and Sal, along with a whiz 15-year-old guitar player named Ricky Ramirez—who reminded Mark of a young Jimmy Page—and Boomerang was born. The band started rehearsals, wrote like crazy, and Ramirez's licks keyed the songs. Within months, Mark recalled, "we were tight and rockin'." Boomerang was less psychedelic, more edgy than the Fudge, with fewer theatrics and more straight-on English-type rock in the vein of Zeppelin and Deep Purple. Phil got the band a deal with RCA, but problems began to emerge quickly.

First, Phil only had enough focus and energy for one band, and to Mark, clearly that band was Cactus. As Mark saw it, the decision was purely business: Carmine and Tim were the hottest rhythm section in the game, and they were paired with two other known rockers (although Rusty Day had a voice that turned off as many fans as the other members' virtuosity attracted). Boomerang, on the other hand, was Mark and three unknowns. Second, Boomerang was hot in the studio, but on stage, the band didn't jell. In live performances, Ramirez, despite having a "swelled head so big there wasn't a hat in Long Island that would fit on it," would retreat next to his amp and barely face the audience. Then there was the issue of living quarters: the band moved in with Mark and Patty! Along the way, Sal was replaced on bass by Jo Casmir, a solid bassist with a screaming high voice who was a great compliment to Mark's vocals.

As Boomerang was forming, Mark and his guitarist, Ricky Ramirez, went to a show at the Fillmore East featuring Jimi Hendrix and his "Band of Gypsies," which included his former paratrooper friend Billy Cox on bass and Buddy Miles on drums. Backstage in the dressing room, Mark sat next to Hendrix, when Buddy Miles, smoking weed, asked Mark "Would you like some coke?" Mark replied, "Sure, that would be great," thinking he was being offered a soft drink. Then the drummer pulled out his coke spoon. After years on tour with Vanilla Fudge, Mark still retained an air of naivete. One of the classic live rock albums, Jimi Hendrix's Band of Gypsies emerged from that evening.

And it would be sadly ironic that on September 18, 1970, while

Stein was at his Long Beach, NY apartment getting ready to leave for Electric Lady Land Studios when Jimmy Galuzzi burst into the room and shouted "You're not gonna believe it! Hendrix is dead!"

Boomerang was on its' way to lay down some tracks with Hendrix's producer, Eddie Kramer at the helm that very day. Shocked and apprehensive the band decided to go anyway. Stein noted that "Kramer was sitting in his office frozen in emotion, eyes swollen.... unable to speak." Most everyone at the studio were in tears, in fact the mood of Greenwich Village that day was crushed under the weight of this tragic news and the potential Boomerang/Kramer collaboration died as well.

Boomerang then did some shows in Canada and opened for Emerson, Lake, and Palmer at the Providence Arena, where Mark was introduced for the first time to the next evolution in keyboards, Keith Emerson's massive synthesizer modules that surrounded his Hammond and his grand piano. Boomerang's set was workmanlike, but ELP was "on another planet." The band managed a second album, but it was never released, and Mark grew more disinterested in the band. He withdrew and took a vacation from music altogether. With Patty and Rich, Mark moved to the north shore of Long Island, rented a house with an acre of land for privacy, and "just disappeared," writing songs and working on melodies.

In 1971, Audrey Lichtner, Phil Basile's secretary, had died in a tragic fire in her home, burning to the ground while she slept. On a cold and rainy day, Mark and Patty attended the funeral. They held hands as family members gathered around the grave. Among the many musicians present Phil had worked with was Kenny Jeremiah from the Soul Survivors, who had a big hit called "Expressway to Your Heart," had been dating Audrey. As the casket was lowered into the ground the immediate family members shoveled dirt on the coffin—an orthodox Jewish custom. Mark recalled the sound of the earth hitting the casket was sobering, and it seemed right out of the dark ages. It gripped everyone with deep intensity.

Soon thereafter, Phil asked Patty to work for him. Over time, she discovered there were two sets of books---one real, the other the dummy—and she brought the real set home one night to show Mark what the group had really made. He had never paid attention to the business end, finding it both confusing and frightening. The band would draw a weekly salary, basically taking as much as needed to support their lifestyle of cars, clothes, wine, women, and song, with the lion's share of the income from record royalties, touring, and other income streams supposedly going into Vanilla Fudge Incorporated (an entity set up and

107

managed by Steve Weiss). When Patty went in early the next morning, Philly was already there waiting for her. He asked what she had in her hands. Quickly, Patty said she needed to get some figures out of the books for the accountant, who needed them for tax purposes. Unconvinced, Phil said, "Patty, I want you to look me in the eye: will you ever reveal to anyone what you saw there?" Wisely she answered, "No, never!"

Phil then fired her, but Patty had already discovered the dark reality of the Fudge finances. Money was misappropriated in so many directions it would take a masterful auditing job to find out just what was going on—Basile was getting a 25% commission right off the top, which was already a hefty sum, but it wasn't until years later that sources revealed that the mob was ingesting a total of 60% off the top! More distressing, Vanilla Fudge was making $7,500 to $12,500 a night in concerts, and had grossed millions in revenue from 1967 through 1970! In reality, though, contracts in the music business were rarely seen by the performers themselves, and the likelihood was that the total "take" was far higher than what the band saw. But in late 1971, when Vanilla Fudge Incorporated was liquidated and final disbursements were paid out, Mark received a grand total of $33,000,out of which he owed $25,000 in taxes! Failing to pay this tax on time almost landed him with tax evasion charges and a possible prison sentence, and only when his sister Sharon intervened---and with the help of several tax lawyers and accountants—that Mark escaped serious trouble. "Management," however, got away with almost everything, as they always seemed to do in the shadowy underworld of rock.

Unaware of these financial manipulations, Philly Basile was like a father to the band. "We loved and trusted him with our lives," Mark said: "that was the confidence game that was played on us and so many naïve musicians back in the day." Along with Steve Weiss, Basile remained in complete control of the Fudge's finances when they were at the top. Nearly 40 years later, Mark sadly observed, "they were in complete control. We simply didn't know any better—how could we?"

Such "arrangements," in fact, were all too common in the world of rock and roll and reflected the rapid, and sometimes radical, rise to riches for musicians used to playing for next to nothing. A typical example is the Jefferson Airplane, who, before they played the Monterey Pop Festival, were lucky to split $1,000 a week six ways after their manager took his cut. Following Monterey, the new visibility of the group saw them commanding several thousand dollars a night and they looked at six figure annual incomes. (During the 1960s, a $100,000 income easily placed a person in the top 5% of all income earners in

America: in essence, the Airplane had joined America's capitalist elites!) Yet these flower children from San Francisco, "rather than enjoying the fruits of their labors, were cooped up in offices, poring over contractual minutiae, debating the relative merits of gigs in Monticello and Colorado Springs."[31]

That was an important part of the music business, too, for it was a business. Eagles' Glenn Frey and Don Henley were serious about longevity in the business and keeping their money. "We had seen a lot of our heroes and predecessors get ripped off and lose everything they had," Henley said. Frey noted "We realized that rock and roll was a war of attrition. The longer you survive, the more you become an institution."[32]

Like the Eagles, the Airplane, reborn as Jefferson Starship, made a career out of music, but the original group was finished. As singer Marty Balin explained, "Fame changes your life. . . . It ruined the band. Everybody became rich and selfish . . . ."[33]

Everybody became rich and selfish" became an oft-told tale in rock, and was particularly ironic given that groups such as the Eagles routinely played fundraisers for liberal political candidates, in large part based on the sense of "social justice" they espoused. Yet when it came to the group's finances, "What's mine is mine and what's yours is negotiable" became the rule of thumb. Don Felder, the guitarist who wrote "Hotel Calilfornia" and joined the Eagles after they already had several hits, such as "Witchy Woman" and "Take It Easy," recalled his first band meeting with Irving Azoff, the group's business manager. Azoff had just set up the Eagles, Ltd. And suggested each of the five members own 20%, but immediately, other members objected as the band had previously been four members.[34]

Twenty years later, the band fired Felder when he began to raise questions about the group's finances—and the split—despite the fact that Felder, Glenn Frey, and Don Henley were co-owners of the name "The Eagles." The Eagles, Ltd. fought Felder, but eventually a settlement was reached, even as Don Henley conducted tours speaking on behalf of . . . artists' rights. Until that time, however, Felder paid almost no attention to money, and wrote that when "Hotel California" came out, "I honestly didn't know how much I had in the bank . . . ."[35]

One of the few to realize early that the business side of music had to be attended to was Madonna (Madonna Louise Ciccone), often portrayed as an "air head," yet who was eventually labeled "America's Smartest Businesswoman" by none other than Forbes magazine. She said "I love meetings with suits. I live for meetings with suits. I love them because I know they had a really boring week and I walk in there with my orange velvet leggings and drop popcorn down my cleavage and then fish it out and eat it. . . ."[36] *Fortune* magazine, not to be outdone by its rival, also wrote a feature article about her business acumen. But such financial and corporate understanding was rare among rockers.

Quite the contrary, almost every star was the uncanny ease with which massive amounts of money slid through their fingers, usually with the help of corrupt management that skimmed—and sometimes ladled—off the top. In the 1980s, Ginger Baker found out his manager was "taking 75 percent of my royalty cheques and giving me the remaining amount."[37]

This was a common story: in the 1970s, Springsteen had a million-selling album, he had a mere $3,000 in his bank account; while the poster-boy of rip-offs, Peter Frampton, made a reported $80 million on his "Frampton Comes Alive" tour and took home less than $150,000! Probably no one—including Frampton---paid as high a price as the aforementioned Moby Grape, who suffered physical and mental side-effects as well as financial devastation in their dealings with Matthew Katz. Astoundingly enough, Katz had a track record for anyone who wanted to examine his past dealings: his arrangements with the Jefferson Airplane should have raised flags for the Grape. Jefferson Airplane had landed its first recording contract with RCA in November 1965 for a solid $25,000, but never saw the final paperwork until the minute it was presented to them to sign. By that time, Katz had attached his own clauses, which took almost 21 years of court wrangling to unravel, and which, when the judicial process ended in 1987, amounted to more than $3 million in contested royalties.[38]

As many of the early rock promoters and managers did, Katz's legal relationship to the team evolved, hovering in a netherworld between booking agent, financial advisor, publicist, and personal manager. Part of the perception that managers consistently "ripped off" artists involved the managers' very real initial outlay on starving musicians—food, clothes, travel money, and above all, musical instruments that constantly needed repair or replacement. Managers saw themselves as "part of the band," yet knew they had no artistic talent in the traditional sense. It was this same tension that gripped Brian Epstein in his relationship with the Beatles, and ultimately, the same concerns that when the manager reaped his "just reward," he got greedy. Often this stemmed from the fact that whatever management contracts existed contained vague and imprecise language about what, exactly, a manager's "personal services" consisted of. In Matthew Katz's dealings with the Jefferson Airplane, he admitted in court that he added a clause to the RCA contract that gave him a cut of Airplane's production money, through a clever contractual phrase in which he was listed as a "co-

110

producer" on the album, even though he did little to actually produce anything. None of the Airplane doubted Katz's role in landing the RCA deal: Jorma Kaukonen, the guitarist, admitted Katz was "very responsible for getting us our first recording contract, for getting people in the industry to take us seriously."[39]

But such genuine and necessary actions on behalf of clients justified keeping contracts and agreements secret, as so many industry managers attempted to do. Marty Balin, the Airplane's singer, "used to ask [Katz] why can't we see the accounts and papers and have copies of the contracts we put our names to?"[40]

Katz kept his managerial contract separate, yet tied to the Airplane's RCA deal, putting the pressure on the band to sign. On the spot, Balin pulled out a typewriter and the band's current singer, Signe Toly Andersen Ettlin, a legal secretary at the time, re-worked Katz's contract and set up percentages for Katz to receive. Katz signed it, as did most of the Airplane except Signe, who was concerned about the clause that gave the manager a share of "any and all artistic endeavors" including those that might unfold after any member left the band.[41]

Such clauses were all too common in rock. Humble Pie, a British group just taking the stage as Vanilla Fudge was fracturing, was a case in point. As a measure of how much larger the paydays were, Jefferson Airplane signed its first deal in 1965 for $25,000. Twelve years later, Humble Pie's guitarist, Peter Frampton played in Philadelphia's JFK Stadium to an audience of 118,000 and Frampton's take alone was $250,000. Dee Anthony, who managed Humble Pie, encouraged the band to set up its own corporation, Owen Development, with himself as the sole officer and the band members astoundingly listed as "employees" (supposedly to reduce their tax exposure).[42]

But among the questionable "investments" made by the "sole officer"were vacation cottages in Nassau. Anthony also pitched the band an idea for a rock documentary such as the film made about Joe Cocker's recent American tour: Humble Pie hit the road for Japan in a chartered Boeing 707, chocked full with 40 passengers that included music journalists, three female backup singers, family members, and Anthony's English chauffeur . . . but no film crew. Forced to hire Japanese crews at over $1000 a day, the band ran up $100,000 in no time and was broke soon. Humble Pie disbanded, which set Frampton upon his own cautionary tale, and the band's other star, Steve Marriott, fell off the scene, dying drunk in his sleep at his home when his lit cigarette started his house on fire in 1991.[43] Frampton, meanwhile, found himself with three solo albums and $175,000 in debt before a stunning, but remarkably brief, turnaround with his hit album *Frampton Comes Alive*.

111

There were some exceptions. Led Zeppelin hooked up with promoter Peter Grant in 1972, who changed the way most rock groups did business. Traditionally, touring bands split their gate receipts with a local promoter, or, if the band was extremely hot, perhaps an act could command 60%. When Grant set up Led Zeppelin's 1972 tour, however, he shocked American promoters by informing them that the band would keep 90% of the gate. Grant himself would handle the promotion and pay the expenses. Local promoters could do some of the detail work and get 10% of a very large gross. Former Fudge roadie, then Zeppelin road manager, Richard Cole, said Grant "just figured that the people go to see the artist and the artist should get the money."[44]

Under Grant's system, Zeppelin raked in the cash: their 1973 tour grossed over $4 million, and put the band on track for earning an incredible $30 million per year. In Tampa, the band broke the Beatles' long-standing largest-grossing show record of $301,000 by hauling in $309,000 (in much inflated dollars, though). The news provoked an angry call from the band's New York lawyer, Steve Weiss, who fumed "From now on, never give out grosses on any Zeppelin dates."[45]

As early as 1971, Zeppelin had outsold the Rolling Stones three to one, but aside from Vanilla Fudge, Zeppelin rarely toured with any other acts. But Zeppelin lacked the Stones' top-tier publicity department, and despite the fact that Zeppelin outdrew the Rolling Stones in most cities, the band fretted that they might not be noticed at all.[46]

Such issues didn't concern, say, the Grateful Dead, with their loyal "dead heads": the band paid little attention to publicity. But increasingly publicity gave the appearance of reality: sold-out concerts were only valuable to the artists if the promoters and record companies knew they were sold out.

One of the best, by all accounts, at handling both the finances and the publicity, was the Brian Epstein, the Beatles' famous manager. Jonathan Gould, whose masterful collective biography of the Beatles remains among the best works on the Fab Four, assessed Epstein's managerial career as professional and trustworthy, quoting EMI executive Ron White as saying the Beatles were "lucky . . . to meet up with a man who was devoted to them so completely and honest to boot."[47]

Unlike so many other managers, Epstein consistently downplayed his own role in the Beatles' success, but the few criticisms of him that surfaced involved deals he didn't make: and there was no indication at all that the Beatles and Epstein were about to part company when he died in 1967. In January of that year, he had just concluded a lucrative deal for the Beatles with Capitol that included a royalty of slightly under 9% and a signing bonus of $2 million, and further sweetening the deal was the fact that the group only had to deliver a specified number of master tracks over the nine-year period, not to a number of albums. This essentially reduced the Beatles' required work load by almost half, and gave the group substantial control over album covers by standardizing the British and American packaging. Criticisms that Epstein was insufficiently aggressive in these negotiations are curious, in that he obtained for the Fab Four a royalty rate nearly double that ever paid to anyone at Capitol (Sinatra had left the company when Capitol refused to pay him more than 3%). This contract, in fact, represented a cutting edge agreement, as very few other deals cut in late 1966 and early 1967 gave artists such latitude.

Lacking a Brian Epstein, then, Vanilla Fudge had become only one band of many to fall victim to the underside of rock and roll accounting. Having made millions, Mark had little money in the bank, plenty of back taxes to be paid, and no band. But he still had a trademark voice, song writing skills, and Patty. And with those advantages, he set out to make a new, post-Fudge life.

A MUSIC CALLING

Mark Stein, Through The Years...

...at age 2, already thinking of a hit

Mark, captured here at an early accordion recital, Jersey City, N.J., circa 1957

AT AGE 11: BORN TO PERFORM

Rockin' with
the house band at
a Brooklyn dance party
MC'd by Neil Scott

Mark signs his first
contract with Neil,
who later became
Neil Bogart, founder of
Casablanca Records

EARLY GIGS

Mark, (bottom), with Rick Martin and the Showmen. They played six nights a week, at New York City hot spots.

Clockwise: Joey Brennan (drums), Joe Grinelli (bass), Rick Martin (guitar and vocals), and Mark (organ),1965

A NEW BAND

The Pigeons

From left:
Mark
(organ),
Tim Bogert
(bass)
Joey Brennan
(drums)
Vince Martell
(guitar)

From left: Tim Bogert (bass), Mark (organ), Vince Martell (guitar)
and Carmine Appice (drums), Newport, RI,1965

NEW TERRITORY
Vanilla Fudge, London 1967

Mark, Carmine Appice, Vince Martell and Tim Bogert

❝ We were pretty much fresh off the plane in London where someone took this photo. (top)
This photo (bottom) was taken perhaps 3 to 4 weeks later. We're all decked out in
Carnaby Street clothes with our hair styled by a salon that tended to pop stars...
All settled in and comfortable in London , England,
waiting to make our triumphant return
to America where our 1st album
broke the top ten! ❞

—Mark

LONDON AND BEYOND

Saville Theater, London

Mark and Carmine
at a promotion event
at Sam Ash Music
in Hempstead,
Long Island, NY,
circa 1967-68

In concert, 1968

"The Ed Sullivan Show," 1969

NICE TO BE RECOGNIZED

Vanilla Fudge wins
Golden Gondola Award,
Venice, Italy 1969

Cashbox Magazine
trade advertisement
for "Some Velvet Morning"
and the LP
"Near The Beginning," 1969

Mark
in Holland,
1968

123

MORE BAND MATES

Playing Around

Norms Jean Bell (sax and vocals), Johnny Bolin (drums), Tommy Bolin (guitar, vocals), Mark (keyboards and vocals), Jimmy Haslip (bass)

Mark with
the Tommy Bolin Band
1975-76
Mile High Stadium
Denver, Colorado

Mark with
Dave Mason
and Jim Krieger
opening for the
Doobie Brothers
at the Del Mar
Racetrack,
1978

AT THE RITZ, NEW YORK CITY

Vanilla Fudge Reunion, 1987

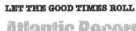

Mark and Patty, 1984   Mark with Michael Douglas

Rehearsing at SIR in New York City for the Atlantic Records 40th Anniversary, 1988

THE ATLANTIC RECORDS 40TH ANNIVERSARY, 1988

Mark with Robert Plant

Back stage and in good company

Mark with Ben E. King

THE ATLANTIC RECORDS 40TH ANNIVERSARY, 1988

A GREAT YEAR FOR VANILLA FUDGE

Live From Long Island, NY, 2006

Vanilla Fu

SATURDAY
OCTOBER 28TH 2006
PRESENTED BY MUSICIAN'S RANGE PRODUCTIONS
LIVE AT THE PATCHOGUE THEATRE

THE ORIGINAL
vanilla
FUDGE

Glen Burtnik   Mind Field

Vanilla Fudge is inducted by
Felix Cavaliere of The Rascals into
The Long Island Music Hall of Fame.
Mark, Carmine and Vince receive
the honor, 2006.

Reunited for a concert at
The Patchogue Theatre,
2006

MARK'S SCRAPBOOK

More Friends Along The Way

Mark with Marilyn McCoo and Florence LaRue of The 5th Dimension, Seattle 1967...
...and with Marilyn McCoo and Billy Davis of The 5th Dimension, 2007

Mark with Glenn Hughes
of Deep Purple, 1986

Mark with Mary Wilson of The Supremes,
American Music Awards, LA,1988

MARK'S SCRAPBOOK: MORE FRIENDS ALONG THE WAY

Patty and Mark with Ian Paice,
drummer for Deep Purple

Mark and Jon Lord renew
an old friendship, Sunrise, Fla., 2005

A special night with old friends: Mark, playing "Smoke On The Water" with Deep Purple (Don Airey, in photo), Pompano Beach, FLA July 14, 2007

Roger Glover, Mark and Steve Morse of Deep Purple

MARK'S SCRAPBOOK: MORE FRIENDS ALONG THE WAY

Mark with Alice Cooper, 2007

Mark and
Steve Van Zandt,
Hard Rock,
Florida, 2007

Mark with
Clarence
Clemons,
2010

BACK ON TOUR

Still Rockin' and On A ROLL

The original
Vanilla Fudge reunite
at The Blender Theater
in New York City, (above):
Mark with Tim Bogert,
Carmine Appice
(shown here)
and Vince Martell,
March 15, 2008

VANILLA FUDGE'S
MARK STEIN & VINCE MARTELL

Let's Pray For Peace TOUR

Mark Stein and Vince Martell of Vanilla Fudge on the "Let's Pray For Peace" tour
with Jimmy Jack (drums) Steve Argy (bass),
Capital One Bank Theatre at Westbury, NY, September 26, 2008

133

BACK ON TOUR: ROCKIN' IN NEW YORK

Mark Stein and Vince Martell of Vanilla Fudge (above), at The Hippie Fest, with Pete Bremy (bass), and Jimmyjack (drums), Brookhaven Amphitheater, Farmingville, NY, August 8, 2009

Photo: Jim Deloge

Mark & former N.Y. Yankee great, Bernie Williams ready to jam with Vanilla Fudge at BB Kings for Little Kids Rock "Right to Rock" benefit, New York City, October 27, 2010

BACK ON TOUR

Carmine Appice,
Vince Martell, and Mark
in their latest promotion
photo

Photo: Jo Lopez
vanillafudge.com

Mark performs
with Vanilla Fudge at the
Boulton Center,
Long Island, NY, 2010

BACK ON TOUR: LEGENDS OF ROCK FESTIVAL, SLUPSK, POLAND, AUGUST 14, 2011

Marekhofman Photography

Mark with Jack Bruce of Cream, at the festival

YOU KEEP ME HANGIN' ON

Chapter Five

For the ex-members of Vanilla Fudge, it seemed like the glory years were fading fast. Despite some success with Cactus and Beck, Bogert & Appice, Tim and Carmine now drifted into solo gigs and played as backup musicians, occasionally without each other. One of the most powerful rhythm sections in rock history seemed to lose its energy. Vinny had retreated to New York, briefly teaching school. For Mark, first Boomerang failed to gain traction, then backup stints with some of rock's big names proved unsuccessful at recapturing the Fudge's stardom. But for all, the nagging feeling of getting old without having grabbed the golden ring was all too present.

Rockers feared being "trapped playing aging music for the aging young."[1] In a medium, as Who biographer Dave Marsh put it, of "hyper accelerated aging," rockers faced careers more fleeting, in some cases, than professional athletes, actors, or even fashion models.[2]

For those who had capitalized on the energy and restlessness of youth to suddenly find that, in fact, their entire cohort had grown up, had families, and slowed down—however slightly—the ethos of "party hardy" became tempered with real-world responsibilities. Those were the same responsibilities that their parents had struggled with in the 1960s, and who were judged guilty of having fallen short. Yet now that the boomers themselves entered the workplace, the civic arena, and the halls of justice, the easy answers of just a half-decade ago no longer fit well. "Burn, Baby, Burn," having been transformed into a call to disco dancing, reflected the growing realization that not only should the structures that had energized the nation for 200 years not be destroyed, but in fact they had to be improved, occasionally renovated, and where necessary, replaced on an individual case-by-case basis.

In short, it dawned on many musicians that the freedom that they had to protest and criticize their own system had never been taken from them; that they had never faced the real, often violent, repression that musicians in other less fortunate nations encountered. The "system," as it turned out, not only had protected them but had seen their cultural talisman, music, dominate every other form of music not just in America but throughout the world.

Rock permeated the advertising industry, and had since the time that Levis jeans convinced Jefferson Airplane to do a commercial (which, they said, they later regretted). Yet the very products that the 60s generation had made popular—music, blue jeans, soft drinks—now needed rock as a means of communication to their consumers. Far from "selling out," rock and roll, like the Borg mother ship, assimilated everything in its path, from politics to pop, from food to faith, from clothing to commercials.

Mark's journey into the world of jingles, then, constituted little more than an affirmation of rock's omnipresence. In late 1979, when Dave Mason was hired to do a Miller Beer TV ad, Mark got the session as well. Producers Gary Sherman and Stanley Kahn ran the session, and thought Mark's voice would sound right for some other projects. Mark, Mason, and the band headed to a college concert in Texas. During a few days' break, Mark flew back to New York to sing the lead on the Miller Beer ad that was slated for half time at the Super Bowl, then flew back to Lake Tahoe at Harrah's to continue the gigs with Mason. On his way to the airport, Mark heard the stunning news from a cabbie that John Lennon had been shot and killed. Dave Mason took the news hard, as he had developed a relationship with Lennon from his days with Traffic.

The Harrah's appearance included an opening act named David Letterman, a comedian becoming famous for his appearances on the "Tonight Show" with Johnny Carson, one of the most popular televisions shows of the decade. Mark and Letterman chatted backstage, before Letterman went on to wow the audience. "I was really taken aback by how he stood by himself in front of an audience and totally controlled a packed house," Mark recalled. Another comedian frequently opened for Mason, an impressionist named Kevin Pollack, later to play a superb supporting role in the Tom Cruise/Jack Nicholson movie, *A Few Good Men*. At the time, however, Pollack did a great Peter Falk impersonation and other impressions, and he always warmed the crowd up well for Mason.

In-between gigs with Dave Mason, Mark called Sherman and

Kahn, asking if they had any more commercial work. The ads paid great, and for Mark this seemed like a fresh, new opportunity. After years of unfulfilled record deals and touring, the notion of making money in the jingle business was very attractive. Sherman and Kahn thought Mark's vocals, arranging, writing, and playing would be beneficial on a number of levels. When one of the key writer/arrangers in the Sherman and Kahn group suddenly died, Mark was invited to go to New York City and join the company. Mark's brother in law, Bob Patterson, lived in New Jersey, not far from the City, so Mark stayed with him.

Before Mark knew it, Sherman and Kahn had him involved in so many projects "my head was spinning." Writing, playing, co-producing, arranging vocals, performing—Mark was doing everything, at one point having perhaps a dozen commercials playing on radio and television, including McDonald's, Coca-Cola, Miller Beer, Scope mouthwash. The residuals were coming in, and it was wonderful getting checks all the time in the mailbox while a run of spots was on the air. That could go on for months, almost every day.

Yet while the pay was good, Mark found it difficult to get into the clique of vocalists who did the majority of the ads. Perhaps a dozen singers split most of the commercial work, including lead and group vocals. All of them came from the "straight" world of sight reading and music theory, and for a rocker like Mark, it "was a hell of a challenge." One morning, at an audition for a malt liquor commercial, Mark showed up to find another singer trying out for the same campaign—a fellow named Luther Vandross, considered one of the hottest voices in the jingle business. They had sung together on some other sessions, and once, while facing each other at the mike, Luther said to Mark, "Man, you're fabulous." Then, realizing Mark was from Vanilla Fudge, he said that Mark was one of the first white cats whose voice really turned him on. Now, they sat on a sofa waiting to get called in for the audition. (Virtually everyone, star or not, had to audition to make sure that the voice was right for the part. Mark recalled sitting in an audition room next to actor Darren McGavin, who was trying out for a Resorts International Casino spot.) Vandross said to Mark, "Man, I just signed a record deal with Epic. I went with them only because they gave me the right to produce my own projects." Mark instantly took a liking to Luther Vandross, in no small part because, like Mark, he also had battled weight problems and asked how Mark kept his weight down.

On that day, neither singer got the job. Indeed, a few months later, Gary Sherman was driving Mark back to New Jersey when Mark brought up Luther. Sherman snorted, "Luther Vandross is over the hill!" The statement took Mark aback, and shortly after that, "Never Too

Much," the first single from Vandross's new album, became an R&B hit right out of the box. Soon, Luther Vandross became a pop superstar, and one of the most talented singer/songwriter/producers in the country. (He died a few years later, in 2005, from a massive stroke.)

Meanwhile, immersed in the jingle business, Mark found that despite his skills he lacked certain fundamentals for the job. Most of the time he faked his way through the charts, confident his ear would rescue him (and it did). In his off time, he studied music theory and practiced reading, although it always felt unnatural. It was a "mental laziness," he noted, that so many rockers shared, and it proved an Achilles Heel. Nevertheless, Mark came within a hair, once again, of catching the "big break."

In 1981, the Sherman-Kahn team had a shot at the next huge Coca-Cola campaign. Three agencies were each assigned a phrase, and Sherman-Kahn got "People Like You Like Coke." "Like mad men, we worked night and day trying to come up with something, and finally landed on "People like you like Coke, Coca-Cola . . . People like you got your own kind of style." They wrote up the charts, assembled the musicians, did the session, and Mark sang lead on the ditty. "I thought it was really good . . . Everybody was really excited," he remembered. They sent the tapes to Billy Davis, the head of advertising at Coke and he said, "It's great . . . but we already got this alternative catch phrase, "Coke is It!" by a competitive agency. That jingle alone would have set up Mark for life.

Then, an opportunity for a shot at the new Gallo Wine national campaign was at hand. Mark and the Sherman/Kahn team had three days to create a spot and deliver it to corporate headquarters in California. Again, they produced a commercial that was warm, melodic, and fit Mark's voice to a "T." Everyone was thrilled with it as the courier came to the office to pick up the tapes that Friday to be delivered no later then twelve o clock, noon on Monday. As fate would have it, the helicopter that was flying to Gallo's headquarters to deliver the project crashed! The pilot survived , but the deadline was missed and the project was lost.

Mark continued in the jingle business for the next two years, on and off, during which time he got a call from Frank Zappa's manager, who asked if Mark would join Zappa's band. Mark passed. Not long afterward, however, Carmine called Mark and asked him to join in a UNICEF benefit at the Savoy Theater in New York City. The other members of the Fudge would be there too, so Mark agreed. A number of top musicians were there, including Greg Allman, who shook Mark's hand and said, "I've got all your albums!" And, an old face was there as well, Fat Frankie who had ditched Mark in Melbourne on the Alice

141

Cooper tour. Drunk and raving, Fat Frankie told anyone who would listen, "We were motherfuckers!" Mark looked him straight in the eyes and said, "I'm still a motherfucker." His expression froze, but Mark wasn't about to let him forget that he had left him in a Melbourne hotel and that subsequently he had been unceremoniously dumped from the Alice Cooper tour.

When it came time for Vanilla Fudge to take the stage, despite having not played together for years, they broke into "Take Me For a Little While" and "You Keep Me Hangin' On," and brought the house down. Phil Basile, the band's old manager, was in the audience with some Atlantic representatives, and he came back stage, threw all the hangers-on out of the room, and said, "Guy's, you're still fucking great. The people still love you. I can get you a new deal. What do you say?" Everyone agreed, they shook hands, and the Fudge was back in business.

Back in California, Mark got a follow-up call from Phil, who wanted to fly the group back to New York for a meeting with Steve Weiss and Ahmet Ertegun. A $3 million deal was on the table! Being cautiously optimistic, Mark, Tim, and Carmine flew to New York to rendezvous with Vinny at Phil's club, Channel 80, formerly the Action House on Long Island. After some handshakes, hugs, and usual ball-busting innuendos, the group was treated to a wonderful night of food and drink. This was all the precursor for the event to follow.

The next day, all were to meet at Steve Weiss's office on Madison Avenue. He wanted to see how the guys' attitudes were toward each other, but there was tension in the air. As Mark put it, "all of us knew deep down that along the way our funds were misappropriated the first time around," but perhaps being older and wiser, they could monitor things better. The conversation turned to what Mark had been doing recently when the issue of the Columbia solo album came up. Phil's face "turned bright red," and Mark sensed its demise was because Rothman had begun poking around in the books. Then Weiss said, "And if you had invested money in Time-Warner stock, you would all be wealthy men today!" It was an outrageous comment, given that he had been the Fudge's business manager and had control of all the money. It was his responsibility to invest on behalf of the members, and, if necessary, in Time-Warner stock! But Mark bit his tongue, aware they were only a phone call away from meeting with Ahmet Ertegun at the behest of Weiss. And indeed, the call was made and the group trundled down to meet Ertegun.

Upon their arrival at Atco, the Fudge were greeted by Ertegun himself, who had summoned all the heads of A&R. Ertegun announced, "Say hello to the Vanilla Fudge [he always inappropriately used the article "the" in front of the group's name]. This will be one of the comeback stories of the year!" It was a nice sequence of events, and soon Mark was on a plane back to California. But he didn't want the Fudge to fall into the "one-trick-pony" routine of rehashing 60s hits. "We wanted to come out with an '80s sound while still keeping the flavor of the band," he recalled. He knew the guys had progressed differently, and had improved as writers. Vocally, Mark was never better. He recalled Frank Zappa's advice back in 1967, and his vow to keep his voice in shape. The band needed a producer who could harness that energy, and it fell into the hands of Spencer Proffer, a journeyman producer who had his own music complex, Pasha Studios in Los Angeles. He had a few modest hits and was plugged into the business. Surrounding himself with public relations people, he was popular with radio representatives, and knew distribution as well. Most important, Proffer was great at selling himself, if not his artists. And he sold himself to the Fudge.

Mark began writing, and the band embarked on what he thought would be a great collaboration. Instead, what unfolded was the ongoing story of how Vanilla Fudge managed to find new and creative ways to implode. Mark had set up a vast array of keyboards at a big room in his Northridge house, and the band had rehearsed there, trying to find a musical direction. Increasingly, Proffer quickly grew to dislike Vinny and insisted that Vince be replaced with a guitarist more suitable to the modern sounds that he foresaw for the Fudge. Vinny refused to budge or modify his sound. While the band waited patiently, hoping it would all click, Martell disappeared into a shell. He went back east for a while, during which time another guitarist, Ron Mancuso (from a band called Modern Design) laid down the guitar tracks. He had a sound similar to Steve Lukather of Toto. That, as Mark recalled, "seemed to be the realm that Spencer was reaching for." Mark came up with a keyboard intro on the Yamaha CS80, loaned to him by Bob Welch of Fleetwood Mac, which became the intro to the Dionne Warwick cover, "Walk On By." Another guitarist who played on the album was Jeff Beck under the nom de plume "J. Toad."

Over the next few months, a buzz began to build about the album, particularly one of Mark's favorite songs, "Golden Age Dreams," which was turning heads by radio people invited by Spencer to the studio. But all the while there was a dark cloud brewing. Vinny wanted to play and sing more, and had retained a lawyer, even though he was getting an equal cut financially. Soon his threats began to unnerve Atlantic.

While recording *Mystery*, Patty learned from Angela Capre, one of her close friends, that Sylvester Stallone, who was directing the movie

Stayin' Alive (the sequel to *Saturday Night Fever*), was coming to Pasha to oversee the music for the movie. In an effort to set up a meeting between Sly and Mark, Patty found out when Sly would be at Pasha, and "arranged" for Mark to be there hangin' out, conveniently when Stallone showed up. Moreover, she got the Mystery tapes loaded up by one of the engineers in Studio B, a small intimate room used mostly for editing or listening. Mark was waiting in the lounge, hoping Stallone would come out for coffee, and when he finally did, Mark stood up and said, "Hey Sly! I'm Mark Stein of Vanilla Fudge!" Stallone immediately sang out, "Set me free, why don't ya babe." With a big smile, he said, "I love Vanilla Fudge. You guys were great!" (To Mark, it was "Rocky" himself speaking to him). Mark replied, "We just did a new album. Want to hear some of the tracks?" Without hesitation, he agreed, and they cued up "Golden Age Dreams." Stallone proceeded to explain to Mark how out of shape John Travolta was, and how they spent months helping him get fit. "Work out six hours a day and don't eat," Stallone said, as a program to get in shape.

Stallone listened to the album for over 45 minutes, and remarked that if synthesizers had been around in the 1960s, Vanilla Fudge would have been trailblazers. (Silently, Mark thought the Fudge were trailblazers, but he kept his mouth shut, not wanting to reprimand Stallone). Mark mentioned that he had hoped to get a shot at singing in *Stayin' Alive*, but Sly pointed out that the music was already finished and it was too late. Just as they were about to leave the room, there was a hammering on the door: Stallone's bodyguards had freaked out, thinking he'd been kidnapped. Everyone had a good laugh, but the frivolity was short lived. Vinny's dark cloud continued to shadow the Fudge.

Beyond the Martell dislocations, each member of the band now had his own manager and lawyer, and adding more confusion to the mix was Phil, who suddenly was facing indictment, being charged with conspiracy to defraud the U.S. government. Basile's connections with the Luchese crime family involved charges that he had offered a no-show job to Henry Hill. (In the film *Goodfellas*, based on the real-life mob, informant Henry Hill is let out of jail early and the mob boss told him, "the only reason I got you out of jail early was that a friend of mine promised you a job." That "friend" was Phil Basile.). When Mark and Patty had dinner with Phil in New York, the stress was written all over his face. At one point, the members of Vanilla Fudge were requested to write letters to the judge proclaiming that Phil was a hard-working, upstanding member of the community. Senator Alfonse D'Amato even got involved, appearing in 1983 as the only character witness at Basile's trial. Absorbed with his legal problems, Phil hired Patty to deal with the band in Los Angeles for him—she had worked for him after she left Atlantic, and he trusted her. But neither the band's good words nor D'Amato's support was sufficient to prevent Basile from eventually being convicted.

Still more chaos was heaped on the band when Ahmet Ertegun came to the Sound City studio personally to intervene in the rehearsal and to talk about "musical direction." Moreover, Proffer was producing another band at the time, Quiet Riot, whose metal sound seemed out of step with the current hit groups (the Police, Toto) but the band's first album shot up to #1 in the world and sold seven million copies in six months. It opened the floodgates for every heavy metal band on the planet. Before its release, Spencer played the album for Mark at his house at top volume, but Mark secretly thought it would bomb. While at Pasha, Mark met the bassist of Quiet Riot, Rudy Sarzo, a Cuban-born American who idolized Tim Bogert.[3]

Sarzo, though, knew the dangers of "throwing yourself into copy stuff," and he deliberately sought out his own style. Rudy and Mark soon got to be friendly enough that Rudy asked Mark to play at his wedding that March.

Proffer continued to push Quiet Riot, especially since the band was signed to Pasha Records, his own label, at the expense of Vanilla Fudge. To Mark it didn't make sense: a rising tide would lift all boats, and they all stood to be successful again if everything came together. Yet Mark, also, had his side interests, producing Modern Design (now also being managed by Patty). They tried to coordinate this Def Leopard-type band's roll out to the Mystery album, but Spencer lured Modern Design away to back one of his other artists, Danny Spanos.

Meanwhile, outwardly, the signs continued to look good for a Vanilla Fudge revival. Atco raved that *Mystery* would be the comeback album of the year, and *Billboard* magazine agreed. But behind the scenes, the Atlantic legal team deemed the album a lame duck because of Martell's threatened lawsuit. The project was in litigation for 18 months, despite the fact that a multi-million dollar deal was on the table. Instead, all money was held back until issues with Vinny were resolved. The momentum vanished. When *Mystery* was finally released, it never made the charts, even after *Billboard* picked the title track to land in the top 20. Adding to the sour taste of *Mystery*'s flop, Proffer's other band, Quiet Riot, raced up the charts with two heavy metal anthems, "Bang Your Head" and "Cum On Feel the Noise." Proffer, who had started the acrimony with his disdain of Vinny, became the hottest producer in the business. All the while, it was Vanilla Fudge that was supposed to be making the comeback album of the year.

The band's relationships quickly waned. Carmine joined Ozzy Osbourne, Tim disappeared into a world of marijuana, and Mark drifted into a funk. Slowly, after some prodding by Patty, he started thinking about putting together yet another band. Heavy metal and hard rock were once again at the forefront of the Los Angeles scene, and with the success of Quiet Riot, record companies were all ears again when it came to the heavier sounds. Bands such as Dio, Poison, Autograph, Ratt, Judas Priest, Def Leppard, and others sold millions of records and brought thousands of fans to concerts. The advent of MTV had also changed the industry yet again, placing more of a premium than ever on thin bodies in spandex suits, pouty lips, and above all, big hair. Gone were "jam" bands; in were slickly produced, television video products that looked good on camera. Moreover, the television series "Miami Vice" had started to feature rock music prominently as an integral part of the show, and Autograph, a band of average talents with clever songs, had nailed a top single called "Turn Up The Radio," which benefitted greatly from its appearance in the show.

Patty insisted to Mark, "With your voice and keyboard chops, you should be able to put together a killer band!" So Mark found a rehearsal space—out of the way so he could explore yet a new musical direction—and began to write again. He laid down grooves with his array of keyboards and auditioned players. Bobby Arechiga, a young drummer hot on the Los Angeles scene, was the first one to play for Mark, and Mark liked him instantly. He played with power and feeling, and had all the earlier rock influences (Fudge, Zeppelin, Deep Purple). They hit it off and soon auditioned bass players, but no one fit. Ultimately Mark laid down the bass groove on a synthesizer and then he got a midi bass module that sampled bass sounds and ran it through a bass amp. His right hand commanded the Hammond and the synthesizer, and his left, Ray Manzarek-style, played the bass, and he somehow had to sing over the top of it. At first it was restricting, but he got used to it as they auditioned more guitarists.

One of the first guitarists was a 16-year-old phenomenon Mark had read about in *Guitar Player* magazine, named Paul Gilbert. Mark contacted the writer of the article, and got word to Gilbert to come down and play. He was terrific, and had amazing knowledge for his age. Gilbert told him that as a kid, he'd draw pictures with crayons of a rock band he was in and the band was called "Stein." Despite his talent, Mark was leery of another teenager after the Boomerang situation. Finally, they let Gilbert go, knowing he'd surface again somewhere (he did, in a band called Mr. Big, with Billy Sheehan on bass). Steve Fister, who played with Foghat, joined the band for a while (and later played with

Lita Ford). So the keyboard power trio called Danger Zone was born.

With the success of Dio, managed by Ronnie James Dio's wife Wendy, Patty and Mark discussed the possibility of having Patty manage the band. Female managers were in vogue, and Mark had grown tired of making calls and sending out pictures and promo kits. "Let's do it ourselves," they said, "from the ground up." The result was Starstruck Management. Patty worked relentlessly to get the band a good showcase, while the band put together a solid hour show filled with mostly new songs and a few standbys from Mark's past. Debuting at the Roxy on the strip in Hollywood, Danger Zone came out to a full house, including recording people and musicians. The band rocked the house, and went next door to the Rainbow to celebrate the night, but soon the fizz was gone when no record deal came along. Fister left and Jimmy Crespo, who played with Aerosmith, came aboard.

Mark loved Danger Zone, and the band played gigs around Los Angeles, but it wasn't taking off. A number of guitarists came and went, including David Jansen, a talented guitarist who joined the band at a show in Window Rock, Arizona at a gig on an Indian Reservation. Another guitarist, Lanny Cordola, worked with the band from time to time and brought his friend, actor John Stamos to rehearsals. But Danger Zone struggled. It failed to get a record deal despite recording several demos, and even with Ronnie James Dio producing, nothing happened. (Ronnie James Dio passed away on May 16, 2010, as this book was written. RIP Ronnie).

Reconciliation and reunions seemed in the air—Carlos Santana, who had seen his album sales dwindle, was lost. "I was thinking very much like a victim," he said, "angry, bitter, disillusioned."[4]

He and keyboardist Greg Rolie, whose split had been every bit as acrimonious as the Fudge's, again joined forces. The power of unemployment and declining record sales tended to act as a cold shower on many rockers who had experienced the peaks of concert performance and the rock lifestyle, and it was no different for Mark, Carmine, and Tim. After about three years without work, a Fudge reunion began to bubble. Carmine had been fired from Ozzie Osbourne's band in a bizarre episode in which he was marketing his own t-shirts and gear at Ozzie's concerts: when Sharon Osbourne heard about it, she instructed a member of Ozzy's crew to go down while the band played and cut the face out of every t-shirt! Carmine received his walking papers soon thereafter.

Tim had drifted from project to project, including an interesting, but unspectacular solo album. That year, 1986, a tour was being formed called the "Back to the Future" tour featuring classic rock acts such as Rare Earth and War. The tour's booking agents contacted Mark to see if

Vanilla Fudge would be interested. While Carmine, Tim, and Mark began to talk yet again, this time Vinny was left out. After the fiasco with the Mystery album, no one wanted him on board this time.

Bogert knew a guitarist named Paul Hanson—younger, looked good, and had been teaching guitar at GIT (the Guitar Institute of Technology) as well as working on film projects. The Fudge brought him in and began to rehearse at Sound City in the valley, and Hanson fit well. Money was on the table, and everyone and their managers got along, yet neither Phil Basile nor Steve Weiss were involved to complicate matters. Rehearsing next door were the Beach Boys, and during a break Al Jardine came over to introduce himself to Mark, telling him he thought the Fudge were one of the most innovative bands of the '60s. The Beach Boys listened to Vanilla Fudge a lot—which gave Mark great satisfaction.

As the "Back to the Future" tour began with shows on the East Coast, at the very first gig Vinny showed up. He had been drinking, and arrived with friends. Everyone was uncomfortable, although they treated him cordially. Instead of focusing on the problems of the last few years, Mark recalled the great times they'd had more than a decade earlier, and went on to play a great show. Suddenly, the weather changed and snows set in, forcing cancellations in the northeast. Here the band sat, waiting for the weather to clear, paying a road crew, sound men, and rental of a lighting system, not to mention hotel bills. (Rockers, it will be recalled, were not particularly thrifty when on the road!) It was bizarre, as if nature herself aligned against a Fudge reunion. Already the band was losing money. Eventually the weather cleared and the tour picked up momentum at the Ritz in New York City, the Capital Theater in New Jersey, the Vic Theater in Chicago, and most of the major city shows were outstanding.

Still, the bus rides proved grueling to the point that Mark occasionally flew solo to some of the gigs, paying his own way. Carmine and Tim were put off by Mark's solo travel, arguing that the band should endure together and stick together. Mark reasoned that they weren't kids anymore and it was more important to keep the lead singer rested with a healthy voice. (During the tour, he never lost his voice once). During one three-day break, he took time to fly back to Los Angeles to take some promo shots with Danger Zone, hoping that after the "Back to the Future" tour ended, the band would find itself. But when he arrived back in Detroit in plenty of time to make the next show, Tim started sarcastically calling him by his last name. "Whaddya know? Stein's back." At the Vic Theater in Chicago, during a live recording for Westwood One, Vanilla Fudge joined Rare Earth, War, and Mark Farner of Grand Funk Railroad who at the time was, according to Mark, doing his "born again Christian thing." He and all the other acts were really good. But while everyone mostly got along, and while they still did "one-off" gigs from time to time, the momentum for a Fudge reunion ceased.

Not only did the tours never seem to take off, the Fudge now seemed trapped in an earlier era of rock, even with the Mystery album. Their longer 1960s songs did not fit the "oldies" formats of most radio stations. Then there was Music Television (MTV), which had completely transformed rock from an aural to a visual medium. MTV began as the brainchild of former Monkee Michael Nesmith who, in 1976, produced a promotional video clip for his song "Rio." The video soon began showing all over Europe and Australia, and then, during a tour of Australia, Nesmith saw several more short music films called "pop clips." Nesmith put together a television pilot show called "Popclips," but found no audience for several years, until, in 1979, he met with John Lack, who was with New York cable channel WASEC (Warner-Amex Satellite Entertainment). Lack turned actual programming over to Robert Pittman, who had hosted a 15 minute music show in the 1970s.[5]

The ideas continued to germinate, and by that time several groups had shot music videos, particularly Queen, which released a pathbreaking version of "Bohemian Rhapsody" on video in 1975. Still, until 1980, most music on television consisted of Midnight Special (NBC), "Don Kirshner's Rock Concert" (syndicated), or single-song performances by groups on "Saturday Night Live." In part, the sharp downturn in the recording industry in 1980 helped push the music business into television. That year proved "disastrous for most labels," when industry revenues declined.[6]

Disco music, which had hit its peak in 1977 and 1978, suddenly was out, and revenues plummeted the following year. Punk and "new wave," popular in England and in the American underground, were ignored by the labels and radio stations. Moreover, while television played a prominent role in the lives of most Americans, teens didn't watch as much. While they had more disposable income than ever, traditional advertising did not reach that age group: they didn't read newspapers or most magazines, nor did television marketing draw them in. The best place to sell to that age group was Saturday Night Live.

Hence, Music Television, or MTV. Launched on cable, the channel had a radically different format than any other. It would play continuous music videos, 24 hours a day. There were no separate programs, with the exception of a Saturday night concert. Suggestions to group music together by artist or band were discarded as unworkable, and the only glue holding the videos together were several young

149

"veejays" (video disc jockeys), recruited in nationwide auditions. MTV drew on the free music videos provided by the record companies (which came only after some tough marketing sells). The channel made a commitment to playing (and premiering) the most recent new music and to give exposure to new artists, and developed a logo that played on the Apollo 11 moon landing with the flag having the MTV logo on it. MTV debuted on August 1, 1981, with a video by the Buggles appropriately enough called "Video Killed the Radio Star," and followed by Pat Benatar's "You Better Run." It was tough sledding at first: only a few thousand people in New Jersey saw the original launch, and nationwide that year less than 25% of the nation's homes had cable television, and advertising companies still didn't "get" the concept.

When finally the idea of a music channel took hold, others followed, though not all with success: Ted Turner's Cable Music Channel, which debuted in 1984, only lasted a month before he sold it to MTV, where it was converted into VH1, a more pop/mainstream music channel. MTV also struggled to include blacks in its format. Michael Jackson, with "Billie Jean," was considered the first true breakthrough African-American artist on the channel, and soon he, Prince, and Janet Jackson found themselves as regulars in the rotation.

At the same time, artists such as Duran Duran, who appreciated the need to look good on camera, attained great success they likely would not have gained had they relied strictly on their music or concerts. Radio stations did not play their dance-oriented pop tunes, at least, that is, until their management hit on the idea of showing "the group as young, sexy, jet-setting playboys, the James Bonds of rock and roll."[7] Duran Duran instantly shot up the charts with not just one, but several songs, and were called by *Rolling Stone* "the first rock band to ride the video wave."[8]

Their song and concurrent video, "The Reflex," won best music video awards and set the standard for production for years to come. Such was their impact that they were invited to write and perform the title song for the next film in the ever-popular James Bond series, *A View to a Kill*. Conversely, bands such as Journey, which had knock-out musicians, never translated well into video. Virtual unknowns such as Men at Work, Def Leppard, or the Stray Cats, who could come up with clever looks or interesting acts on camera, climbed to the top of the charts on the basis of their television appearances.

It was Michael Jackson's "Thriller," one of the slickest-produced and most tightly conceived music videos ever, that forced artists to take seriously the power of television for their products. Jackson's Thriller album sold 10 million copies in America alone and was the most popular album in CBS record history. (The video to "Thriller" was so expensive that CBS and Jackson enlisted MTV as co-producer, and shot a documentary, "Making Michael Jackson's 'Thriller'" to recoup some of its investment). Indeed, by the time director John Landes finished filming the 14-minute "Thriller," it cost $500,000, or almost ten times as much as the average rock video. It was released on December 2, 1983, and Landes premiered it theatrically so that it would be eligible for an Academy Award for best short-subject film. It wouldn't be too much of a stretch to say that more than any other video, "Thriller" made MTV, pushing the Nielsen rating to 1.5. It became the most successful music video ever with sales of over nine million. At the end of the month, Time magazine prophesied that the future of music was video.

Of course, the very premise that "video killed the radio star" meant that now video was exposed to the same scrutiny that radio used to be exposed to. MTV's sexual content, Billy Idol's Nazi salutes, the absence of blacks (the Jacksons and Prince excepted), and the steady "dumbing down" of video imagery. Hollywood directors followed a strict formula, based on age, used to determine the average length of an image that appeared—the younger the viewer, the shorter the attention span was the rationale. Soon, average on-screen time for a given image before the cameras shifted to a new one fell from 15 seconds to two or three.

While male rockers were expected to "look" the part, exceptions could be made for non-lead singers (Leslie West, of Mountain, for example). But all female rockers had to be sexy, particularly in the 1980s, when "glam" rock ascended. The Canadian band Heart, with Ann Wilson and her sister Nancy, out front, became a tragic tale of sexual expectations. Ann, who by many accounts had the best female rock voice in history, was plagued with weight problems. Nancy, the guitarist, had a pleasing but uninspiring voice—but was thinner and sexier. As the industry demanded more and more videos, Ann found herself dressed in what she called "fat clothes," covered from neck to ankle, then given "the talk" by every member of the band, her managers, and the record companies.[9]

It deeply disturbed executives and even some of her fans that Ann couldn't "look like Nancy," or that Nancy couldn't "sing like Ann." (Ultimately, Ann underwent weight-loss surgery with the "gastric band" in 2002, although by 2007 appeared to have regained the weight). Other females—Joan Jett, Pat Benatar, Lita Ford, Kim Carnes, Sheena Easton, Joyce Kennedy, Stevie Nicks, and, of course, Madonna—were expected to sell sex, and were "glammed up" regularly for MTV shots. Some, particularly Madonna, reveled in the outrageous; Benatar made a

151

trademark of her black leather leotard.

Criticisms that music videos were overly sexy or "labored ephemera with heavy imitative association," as Time put it, in fact missed the real destructive element of the genre, which was that by emphasizing everything but the music, it was losing touch with the genuine energy and enthusiasm of rock musicians as they played. Even in staged concerts for the videos, the cameras rarely remained on any player for more than a second or two, and full band shots—where one might see musicians actually interacting—utterly disappeared. Perhaps the "wizards of smart" in the industry (and perhaps even the musicians themselves) thought that this would stimulate an interest in live concerts, but if anything it had the effect of Alice-Cooperizing virtually all rock acts. Few bands, save the Grateful Dead (who virtually never appeared on MTV), could go on the road and match the excitement of a highly-produced music video merely by playing their songs. More than ever, stage shows demanded lights, lasers, massive props: Keith Emerson already had introduced a grand piano that was lifted off the stage and which, strapped in like a pilot, he played as it spun around. Kiss took costuming to the absurd extremes with six-inch platform boots, S&M leather outfits, and white face-paint. Ozzy Osbourne bit the head off a bat that was thrown on stage.[10]

In short, video not only killed the radio star, it went a long way toward destroying live concerts. More than that, MTV may have killed itself. While in 1983 cable advertising revenues rose sevenfold since 1980, to $400 million, and MTV had 20 million subscribers, or 10 times that of two years earlier, it was a short-lasted high.[11]

Industry insiders had already worried that "the burnout rate—the point where the public goes from loving a video to hating it—was shorter for video than radio.[12] Everyone, it seemed, was on MTV, and on way too much. In 1985, 75% of the songs on the Billboard top 100 were backed by videos, which had more than doubled since 1982. By 1986, MTV's Nielsen ratings were fading. Late in 1985, the ratings dropped by one-third from the "Thriller" high. Executives worried that they were becoming "nothing more than an eighties version of the goddamned Nehru jacket."[13]

But by 1988, thanks to Madison Avenue's growing love for cable, earnings from MTV, VH-1, and Nickelodeon soared to $59 million. That proved a misleading trend, reflecting the popularity of cable, not of MTV. Four years later, despite the channel's self-congratulation for helping elect Bill Clinton as president, MTV had indeed become, if not a Nehru jacket, just another nondescript player in an extremely broad spectrum of channels. As its videos got more offensive and outrageous, MTV was less relevant than ever in a medium marked by offensiveness and lack of taste.

In the late 1980s, Patty Stein was working as a personal assistant to Brian Avnet, then managing Frankie Valli. Over time, they had developed a good relationship with Valli, and he told Patty that he wanted to go into the studio to record again. After some thought, she had a brainstorm to put Valli together with legendary producer Phil Spector.

Twenty years earlier, Harvey Philp "Phil" Spector had emerged as one of the best-known (though not necessarily, as Tony Bongiovi pointed out, the most revolutionary) producers.[14] Called by writer Tom Wolfe the "first tycoon of teen,"Spector came from a Jewish Russian immigrant family—first cousins who married, and settled in the Bronx.[15]

As a high school student, he played with Lou Adler in a band before gaining the favor of producer Stan Ross at Gold Star Studios in Hollywood. His band, the Teddy Bears, purchased recording time at the studio and got a deal with Era Records (and its subsidiary, Dore), where they produced a #1 hit "To Know Him is to Love Him." Although no more hits followed, Spector showed a strong interest in production, and he was apprenticed under Jerry Leiber and Mike Stoller in New York. The Lieber/Stoller duo were already influential songwriters who had penned "Jailhouse Rock," "Yakety Yak," "Searchin'," "There Goes My Baby," and "Young Blood." Stoller, who had sailed to France in 1956, returned on the ill-fated *Andrea Doria*. Just outside Nantucket, Massachusetts, the ship collided with the Swedish vessel, the *Stockholm*, and sank. Unlike the tragic story of the *Titanic*, some 1600 passengers and crew escaped the *Andrea Doria* with their lives, including Stoller. When he arrived at the dock after his rescue, Stoller learned that another Lieber/Stoller song, "Hound Dog," had become a hit for Elvis Presley, whereupon Stoller reportedly asked, "Elvis who?"

Just as Hollywood evolved with a distinctive Jewish influence, so too did American pop songwriting. Besides Lieber, Stoller, and Spector, there was the New York Aldon writing house of Don Kirshner (called by Time magazine the "Man with the Golden Ear" for his uncanny ability to pick hits after only listening to a few bars). Aldon Music included 20 young writers—all Jewish—and featured the songwriting teams of Barry Mann and Cynthia Weil, and Gerry Goffin and Carole King. Their music "shaped and reflected the conservative dreams and aspirations of most American teenagers, with their time-honored themes of infatuation and heartbreak, summer romances, the first kiss, dreams of wedding bells and living happily ever after."[16]

Strangely, though, the Goffin-King tandem would write several "love"songs that smacked of sadomasochism, such as "Please Hurt Me,"

"Chains" ("my baby's got me locked up in chains"), and "He Hit Me (and it Felt Like a Kiss)." The all-female group that recorded it, the Crystals, hated the song.

Under Lieber and Stoller, Spector produced and played guitar on such songs as "On Broadway." With Spector, Lieber and Stoller left Atlantic for United Artists, writing "Tell Him," "Love Potion #9," then went on to own Red Bird Records, which served as the production arm for Spector-produced songs by the Dixie Cups ("Chapel of Love"). During that time, Spector co-wrote "Spanish Harlem," then, at Lieber and Stoller's insistence, produced Ray Peterson's "Corrina, Corrina" and Curtis Lee's "Pretty Little Angel Eyes." Establishing himself as a bona fide songwriter and producer, Spector set out on his own with his own label, Phillies Records. But it was producing for other groups that Spector constructed the studio technique for which he was best known, the "Wall of Sound."

As Greg Milner noted in his history of recorded music, Perfecting Sound Forever, "no other producer had so consciously used the studio to bring to life a specific sound that had no counterpart in reality."[17] Spector "actively courted high fidelity," setting out to ensure that—except for drums—no individual instrument would be discernible.[18]

It was new, it was different, and it offended some industry professionals because, as Larry Levine, Spector's engineer at Gold Star observed, "it was not truthful at all. . . ."[19] Rather than simply recording something by duplicating it, Spector enhanced and energized it. Musicians hearing the playback, according to Levine, were "just blown away. They simply could not believe what they were hearing . . . ."[20]

The "Wall of Sound" featured multiple guitars, basses, doubling and tripling most instruments for the sake of fullness. His core musicians, known as the "Wrecking Crew," included Hal Blaine, Leon Russell, and Glen Campbell, while future music greats Jack Nitzsche and Sonny Bono handled arrangements. Far from being wild-eyed rock radicals, the Wrecking Crew were "seasoned professionals who . . . . wore sports jackets and ties, kept up their mortgage repayments, had drinks cabinets at home and relaxed by going bowling."[21]

Their bowling team was called "Spins and Needles"—a play on Jackie DeShannon's hit "Needles and Pins" (written by Sonny Bono and Jack Nietsche). But if the musicians were adult and conservative, the sound was brand new. Spector essentially substituted more of the same instruments for overdubbing in an era when studio machines simply didn't have many tracks. Indeed, he was moving beyond the advantage that Bongiovi and Motown had temporarily achieved with their eight track recording machine. And after laying down multiple guitars, basses, keyboards, he would superimpose chimes, tambourines, and still other instruments, all of it recorded and mixed at earsplitting volume. To say that Spector played the studio was not a misnomer: he wore his musicians out until they lost most of their individuality because it was the "Spector" sound that he wanted. "I knew," Spector later said of his process. "People would make fun of me, the little kid who was producing rock and roll records. But I knew. I would try to tell all of the groups, we're doing something very important."[22]

Noting that "Beethoven was more important than his music, or whoever was playing it," Spector fancied himself a modern Gershwin or Berlin.[23]

Spector may have "known," yet he was also prone to excessive self-mythmaking, creating both stories of persecution and success that no one else could confirm. Suffering from anxiety about his receding hairline (even in his youth), his short stature, and self-consciousness about his overall appearance, Spector colored all his relationships with an attitude of possessiveness and jealousy. His father died young, and his subsequent unhappy childhood left him ravenous for human companionship, to the point that he hated to be alone—as Mark Stein would one day discover. Beverly Ross, a Spector girlfriend and the writer of "Lollipop," later remembered that in his younger days Spector "would talk for hours, as if to delay for as long as possible the moment when he would have to be alone. "He'd have you there until four in the morning even though you had to get up at eight,' she told biographer Mick Brown.[24]

Spector also personally witnessed a mob hit while dining with Doc Pomus at the Spindletop Hotel's restaurant.[25] Many of his acquaintances, including Michael Spencer, described Spector as "emotionally disturbed" and "constantly buggy."Spector apparently agreed by seeing a Park Avenue psychoanalyst.[26]

Meanwhile, by the early 1960s, Phil Spector was learning to "play" the studio through the placement of microphones and the use of echo. In this he was only slightly ahead of his West Coast counterpart, Brian Wilson. Both producers mixed and re-mixed obsessively, obtaining the precise blend of voices, strings, or other instruments. Wilson later said the Spector-produced Darlene Love song, "He's Sure the Boy I Love," "opened up a door of creativity for me."[27] He started working in the same studios Spector used, obsessively hanging around Spector's recording sessions, and began to hire the Wrecking Crew for sessions.[28] Soon, Wilson explicitly was copying his idol, with "Don't Worry Baby" a "virtual homage, complete with Spector's heavy drum and a fat echo on the vocals."[29] (Wilson's biographer, Peter Ames, noted that Brian compulsively played "Be My Baby," to the point of looping it endlessly and blasting out of his home stereo).[30]

While at first no one knew who the boy hanging around the studios was, Spector soon began insulting him at every opportunity. Already suffering from an abusive relationship with his father, the young Wilson ate it up, and only had praise for his mentor. "I never considered [the Beach Boys] to be anything but just a messenger of his music," he said in 1998.[31]

Yet even as Spector reached the pinnacle of his genius, in 1964 with "You've Lost that Lovin' Feelin'," Wilson caught and surpassed him as the master of the studio with "When I Grow Up (to Be a Man)" and the Wrecking Crew were stunned. Spector's drummer, Hal Blaine, "all thought [Wilson] was a fluke at first, but then we realized Brian was writing all these incredible songs," and David Crosby, then of the Byrds, dourly commented, "I thought, 'I give up; I'll never be able to do that . . . .'"[32] A modern textbook history of rock and roll (itself something of an oxymoron!) dedicates more pages to analyzing the sound of the Beach Boys than to Spector, who is mentioned entirely in passing and whose contributions are not discussed.[33]

Wilson would continue to "out-Spector" Spector, layering rich sounds and unique instruments in "Good Vibrations," "Sloop John B." and "Don't Worry, Baby." Tympani, harpsichord, chimes, all interwoven with intricate vocal harmonies made *Pet Sounds* (1966) a tour de force of production.

Sadly and ironically, both men suffered serious mental and emotional difficulties during their later years, with Brian's onset coming sooner than Phil's. In his autobiography, *Wouldn't It Be Nice*, Wilson wrote that he "studied Spector at work in the studio, noticing that like me he was one hundred percent hung up on creating a perfect song." But Wilson also "failed to notice and didn't recognize until many years later, was that his aberrant personality was perhaps his best tool in making records, allowing him to manipulate people into doing exactly what he wanted."[34] It was a trait producer/engineers such as Tony Bon Jovi not only lacked, but one they deliberately avoided.

Even as Brian Wilson reached the same heights as Spector, his idol had perfected the "Wall of Sound" with a crowning musical achievement. Spector signed Bill Medley and Bobby Hatfield, known as the Righteous Brothers, to a Phillies contract in 1964, and the following year he produced their massive hit, "You've Lost that Lovin' Feelin'." That hit constituted the alpha and omega of Spector's production genius. A slow beat soon introduced the baritone of Bill Medley, yielding to a bluesy "Hang On Sloopy" bridge featuring Bobby Hatfield, then concluded with the full Spector-esque Wall of Sound chorus. After Spector lost interest in producing them, the Righteous Brothers replicated the production technique on their 1966 #1 hit, "(You're My) Soul and Inspiration." Tiring of the Righteous Brothers, Spector had moved on, eventually being asked by John Lennon and George Harrison to re-produce the unusable sessions of the album Let It Be. His constant overdubbing of Paul McCartney's "Long and Winding Road" reportedly infuriated the Beatle, and in 2003, McCartney released "Let It Be . . . Naked," without Spector's additions. But Harrison and Lennon liked the work, and Spector produced Harrison's best-selling All Things Must Pass album in 1970 and Lennon's Imagine LP in 1971. Harrison's "My Sweet Lord" and "What is Life" displayed the full power of the "Wall of Sound."[35]

At that point, Spector temporarily disappeared from music, partly due to a near-fatal car crash in Hollywood. Regaining his health—and his industry footing, after some flops with Cher—Spector allied with the Ramones to produce the End of Glory (1980). The Ramones were considered one of the more successful and "mainstream" of the punk bands, thus giving the genre more exposure on AM radio. But his work with the Ramones also revealed a much darker side of Phil Spector: on at least one occasion (and possibly more) he threatened the group with a gun.[36] Two decades later, Spector was convicted and imprisoned for using a firearm in commission of a crime involving the shooting death of actress Lana Clarkson.[37]

In 1987, however, Spector's violence and fondness for firearms was still considered largely a rumor. Now seeking a comeback, Spector agreed to talk to Frankie Valli, Patty, and Brian Avnet. They all met and had a productive afternoon. It seemed that two musical legends from "opposite sides of the glass" were about to join forces. A week later, Spector called Patty and invited her and Mark to a party at his Pasadena mansion. The bizarre episode that followed, which Mark termed "held hostage by Phil Spector," looked much more sinister in light of Spector's criminal conviction later.

After passing out cocktails and talking about John Lennon and the fact that he had slept there and upon awaking sat at his piano and wrote "Imagine" while pointing to Lennon's guitar which rested on a stand and was given to him by Yoko, Spector talked about nothing relevant to the Frankie Valli project. He seemed in an incoherent state and odd to the extreme, disappearing somewhere in the house while leaving his guests confused with nothing much else to do but chat and watch the videos play on a huge screen in the living room. Spector

157

appeared and vanished time and again. Hours went by and somewhere around 3:30 in the morning, Mark recalled, "we all screamed out to Spector that we had to leave." Brian had an early morning tee off and everyone wanted to go home.

That's when the drama started. As everyone all drove their cars to the exit gates, they discovered the gates were locked and Spector had his bodyguards release the Dobermans! The Steins started to get panicky—rumors of Spector's eccentricity were now becoming reality, and his possession of guns was well known. All the guests went back onto the house while Avnet and Stein tried to reason with Spector to let them leave. All he said was that he wanted to have a few more drinks, to talk more, and didn't want to be left alone! Yet Spector disappeared again, infuriating everyone further while Avnet and Stein lost their tempers, screaming and demanding to be let go. Finally, at the crack of dawn the gates were opened and everyone left. Upon hearing about this incident, Frankie Valli would have nothing to do with Phil Spector.

Spector was clearly not the force he was. The music industry had changed dramatically since the "Wall of Sound" days, and music videos had fundamentally altered what rock and roll bands were expected to do. Most of all, it meant that the band itself was no longer the "show"—that a slick, cleverly-produced "show" was the show! This proved particularly and painfully ironic for Vanilla Fudge, which had been one of the most powerful and impressive concert bands of the late 1960s. Yet now, in the video age, even a reunited Fudge would have played catch up to the new polished, tightly-produced, image-heavy videos of the 1980s.

Another event also occurred that threw a Fudge reunion into chaos. In the Spring of 1988, Atlantic Records was having its 40th anniversary to be held at Madison Square Garden in New York City. Hyped as the concert of the year, if not the decade, the event featured every artist on or affiliated with the label since its inception was invited to perform. The Average White Band, the Bee Gees, Foreigner, the Rascals, Crosby Stills & Nash, Phil Collins, Led Zeppelin and Vanilla Fudge! The Manhattan Transfer Company, another Atlantic act were being managed by Brian Avnet was also slated to appear, so Patty fell into the middle of it all yet again. Since the Fudge had no management at the time, she had a direct connection now with the label because of the Transfer and it made sense to her and everyone in the band to coordinate the show.

Still upset over the *Mystery* fiasco with Vinnie, Mark, Carmine, and Tim decided again to use a different guitar player. This time they offered the gig to Lanny Cordola who was intermittently playing with Danger Zone. He was young, cool looking, and carried a positive aura around him. Patty got the budget approved for air travel and hotel accommodations at the Grand Hyatt so off they were to the Big Apple. The Fudge had yet one more opportunity under the big lights! This truly was four days of rock and roll heaven. Mark once again found himself schmoozing with all the bands, checking out each other's rehearsals, running into people that weren't seen in years. Stein recalled running into Felix Cavaliere at the hotel bar and told him what a profound influence he was on him. Cavaliere smiled back in humble appreciation and said "that's so beautiful" Out in the lobby Graham Nash was saying hi to everyone while members of Foreigner mingled with the crowd. One night everyone ventured out to The China Club, a hot spot in the city where we sat at a table and were reunited with Eddie Kramer, the great engineer/producer that worked with both Hendrix and the Fudge.

As Mark turned around, Eddie Brigati, the original front man from the Rascals came by to say hello. It was weird: like Vinny, he hadn't been invited to join his old band. He briefly expressed his sadness over it to Mark, but "that was between him and Felix so I didn't go there." The next night, "we went over to the Beacon Theater where Ted Nugent was headlining with Lita Ford opening." Backstage, Steve Fister, the guitarist with Ford (and briefly was in Danger Zone) spotted me and ran over to say hello. They went to Nugent's dressing room where Ted was just about to go on. He flung his guitar over his shoulder and shouted "Watch This Stein....This Is How It's Done!" It infuriated Mark, who later said "How fucking obnoxious he could be!" Everyone in the room smirked as Mark went to the back of the theater to see the show.

Standing off to the side of the mixing console, Mark thought the bass was low. He shouted to the engineer "More bass! You gotta bring the bass level up a bit!" The lightman turned to Mark in a rage and screamed, "This is the lights! It's the lights." Mortified, Mark ran into the darkness. How could he have been so stupid? He went to the bar and ordered a beer when suddenly an English bloke came over and said, "I can't believe it's Mark Stein!" The voice belonged to Roger Glover, the bassist of Deep Purple, who Mark hadn't seen for years. (Deep Purple, it will be recalled, originally wanted to be the "English Vanilla Fudge"). As the two chatted, Glover said that he was excited to see the Fudge at the Garden.

On the day of the show, everyone arrived in limos to get checked into their dressing rooms with time to enjoy the festivities. While in the dressing room, Bud Prager who was managing Foreigner, came by. As they reminisced, he brought up the Lenny Stogel incident from back in the 70's. (Stogel since had been killed in one of the worst air disasters in American history, the DC-10 crash outside of Chicago/O'Hare). Mark

159

left the dressing room to walk around when Al Kooper came up to get a picture with Mark. Kooper was one of the original group of B-3 players who revolutionized the sound and who popularized the instrument, playing on Bob Dylan's "Like a Rolling Stone" and doing the famous Bloomfield/Kooper album with legendary guitarist Mike Bloomfield. Dan Akroyd was in the middle of all the action milling around when Mark suddenly saw Paul Shaffer. Shaffer called out, "Mark! Where have you been hiding all these years?" For Mark, it was like being "a kid in a candy store surrounded by all levels of wealth and fame." He spotted actor Michael Douglas, who was kind enough to take a photo with him. Then there was Robert Plant being mobbed by the media. Mark said hello, but Plant was puzzled. Then he shouted, "Oh my God! Mark, forgive me, I didn't recognize you—I thought you were a member of the press!" They took some pictures together, and Plant was as warm and friendly as ever. Soon, his bandmate John Paul Jones came by, and the three traded war stories from earlier tours.

Meanwhile, the business at hand dictated by the production manager was for the Fudge to do only one song, "You Keep Me Hangin' On." Because of so many acts, they had to keep it super short. But Patty instructed them, "To hell with that! You didn't come all this way to do just one tune." Instead, they decided to do "Take Me For A Little While," then segue right into "You Keep Me Hangin' On." As they prepared to go on stage, the band was set up behind the curtain with their backs to the audience and when everyone was comfortable on their instruments, at the stage manager's direction, the curtain rose and the stage revolved 180 degrees as the Fudge faced the 40,000 fans and started to play. The sound was great and Vanilla Fudge "kicked ass on both songs, getting a grand response from New York!" As they exited the stage, the first to greet them at the foot of the steps was Ahmet Ertegun who shook Mark's hand and introduced him to former U.S. Secretary of State, Henry Kissinger! Then Phil Collins, watching from stage left came over and said "That Was Great ! I listened to you all the time when I was a boy growing up in England in my room!" Indeed, Mark recalled, "It really was rock & roll heaven."

But even with all the hoopla, all the positive energy that seemed to surround the band, even with the interviews with Kurt Loder on MTV, nothing happened. It all failed to generate any new interest in the Fudge. Months later, Stein was back in Los Angeles with Danger Zone, Carmine had put together a band called Blue Murder, which attracted some attention but which lacked songwriting. And Tim? He was simply hanging out. While matters seemed quiet, a Fudge civil war was about to start, and, ironically, it was a video network that touched off the first shot.

In 1990, with his power trio Danger Zone falling into the twilight zone and dissipating, Rudy Sarzo called Mark and asked if he'd be into playing with Whitesnake, the band formed by the wunderkind singer from a reorganization of Deep Purple, David Coverdale, the group had several hits in the early 1980s, including "Fool For Your Loving" and "Here I Go Again." Briefly, noted guitarist Steve Vai was called in to record parts of the 1989 album Slip of the Tongue (and, later, Rudy Sarzo would briefly play in the band). Excited about the opportunity, and after Coverdale and Vai were pleased with his vocals and keyboard chops on the Danger Zone demo that was sent to them, Stein's attorney had negotiated a $100,000 fee for Stein to play on the upcoming "Slip of the Tongue" tour.

Whitesnake was rehearsing in Lake Tahoe for the tour, and after a short flight from Los Angeles, Mark was picked up by one of the crew and on his way to meet some of the band at a local watering hole. He immediately encountered the former Black Oak Arkansas drummer, Tommy Aldridge, and was shocked at the treatment he received by both Aldridge and the band's tour manager. Mark remembered, "They gave me the cold shoulder." The manager instructed the crew member to take Mark to the hotel and tell him what time he'd be picked up for the rehearsal. The next afternoon, with the town blanketed by snow, Mark arrived at the rehearsal location and no one was around. It seemed like hours before the players strolled in. Guitarist Steve Vai was cordial, as was Adrian Vandenburg, and of course it was great to see Rudy. But Aldridge remained distant and when Coverdale arrived, he summoned Mark in to a private room for a chat. Mark had assumed he was already in the band, but after talking with Coverdale, it was clear that this was little more than a glorified audition.

As Mark remembered the experience, "So here I was set up in a tiny room with these guitar gods with their amps playing at earsplitting volume. I was trying to be cool, feeling like I had to prove myself again, never feeling like I fit in. I mean it really wasn't a band vibe…everyone was into themselves." Coverdale—Spector-esque—would show up a little, then run off. When they actually sang together, it sounded strong. For most of the week, Mark was engaged in learning the tunes, getting sounds, trying to blend. All Aldridge, Vai, and Vandenburg talked about was the endorsements they were receiving. Then, one afternoon, they began to talk about Zeppelin, and they saw the Atlantic 40th Anniversary concert with Jason Bonham playing drums and they made disparaging remarks about the band. It irked Mark, who had experienced Led Zeppelin in their prime. "It was like judging Muhammad Ali by his last

161

fight," he complained. He let the musicians know it.

Early one evening, Coverdale came by with his girlfriend Tawny Kitaen and Rudy made introductions. She refused to shake Mark's hand and turned away. Mark said to Rudy, "What the fuck was that all about?" Sarzo simply shrugged and said he didn't know. Kitaen, who was married to Coverdale from 1989-1991, later ended up in a television show called "Celebrity Rehab with Dr. Drew" for abusing triazolam, a sedative, then made disappeared from public view until 2002 when she was charged with battery of her then-husband, baseball pitcher Chuck Finely.

Her snubbing of Mark alerted him that his Whitesnake gig was in deep trouble. But as badly as he wanted to do the tour, the entire experience was becoming an exercise in futility. Steve Vai finally called Mark back in Los Angeles and the two talked for a long time. "You're a great singer," Vai told Mark, "and you have great organ chops, but Coverdale wants to try another guy out. He's an unknown, but he gets great sounds. . . . We'll see." Mark's response was, "What a relief!" Vai was dumbfounded. "A relief?" Mark unloaded on Vai, telling him how uncomfortable it was, although he noted that he and Coverdale "sounded great together vocally." Vai responded, "Yeah, maybe too good!" At any rate, the new keyboard player was a friend of Tawny Kitaen. As fate would have it Whitesnake went on the road to horrible reviews. One critic called them the "worst band ever." The tour fell apart, and the band broke up.

Meanwhile, the Fudge's short-lived "Back to the Future Tour" had generated a live album—again, without Vinny in the lineup—courtesy of Westwood One. In 1991, Carmine Appice obtained the master tapes, and working with Ron Terry, the Fudge's booking agent from back in the 1960's, he secured a deal with Rhino Records to release the live concert on both traditional records and compact discs (CDs, which had started to replace vinyl records). Mark thought the offer was weak and said to shop it somewhere else. He thought since it was really the only live recording by the band, it should warrant a better offer. Without Mark's permission, Carmine took the tapes to Pasha Studios and removed Mark's lead vocals and replaced him with Derek St. Holmes, Ted Nugent's lead singer. Under the title, The Best of Vanilla Fudge Live, Rhino released the album! Suddenly, sensing perhaps the legal storm that was to come, Tim who briefly aligned himself with Mark because he too had been replaced on the recording, backed out. He feared he was over his head, but more likely it was Carmine that he feared.

Mark and Patty wouldn't take the injustice laying down, and they found an attorney willing to take on the case. After reviewing the

162

facts the lawyer filed a complaint charging Rhino and Carmine with violation of The Lanham Act. A trademark act (title 15, chapter 22 of the United States Code) was a piece of legislation that contained the federal statutes U.S. trademark law. It prohibited a number of activities, including trademark infringement, trademark dilution, and false advertising. After being served with the complaint, Carmine's wife Sarah panicked and drove over to Stein's house banging on the front door and screaming for the whole neighborhood to hear." Mark and Patty, please! You've gotta stop this—we have to talk! This is gonna cost us all a fortune." Her efforts were in vain. The Steins' attorney advised them never to talk to the other side. In the end, Stein was awarded a sum of money along with the master tapes that he could market at his own discretion after waiting one year subsequent to the date of the settlement, and Rhino was ordered to sticker the bogus album stating it was not the original band. All in all, it constituted a major victory for Mark.

While that conflict was being resolved, Carmine was quietly trying to gain control of the trademark another way. He had learned it was expiring, and applied for the Vanilla Fudge trademark under his own name, without the other members of the band. Again, Patty heard of it and convinced Carmine to sign a statement abandoning his position by threatening to report him to federal officials. After Mark and Patty told Tim and Vinny, a document was drafted that said going forward Vanilla Fudge could not record, perform, tour, or sell merchandise unless Mark Stein was performing in the band as the lead singer and keyboardist. Tim came to the Steins' house in Northridge, California after he discussed the document with them and read it a second time, and signed it. Mark did the same, then mailed it to Vinny in New York, who signed it and sent it back. It now had three signatures making the assignment to Mark binding. Everyone felt good about the agreement, especially that Carmine could no longer have carte blanche to engage in fraudulent activities with the Fudge name.

Meanwhile, rock music continued to flow into new and unusual areas. Having detoured dramatically into disco and punk, rock had started to coagulate again in the 1980s around the new visual influence of MTV. The stars of the 1980s still relied heavily on dance hits to break through. Madonna Ciccone, for example, a 23-year-old New Yorker, had debuted with a pathbreaking album (Madonna, 1983) that contained several bona-fide hits, including "Everybody," "Burnin' Up," "Lucky Star," and "Borderline." In 2005, Entertainment Weekly listed the album as #5 on its "Top 100 Best Albums of the Past 25 Years." Heavily electronic, and using Moog bass, synthesizers, and a drum machine, Madonna's songs proved instantly danceable. A year later, her next album, Like a Virgin, included her hits "Dress You Up," "Material Girl," "Over and Over," and, of course, "Like a Virgin." (The 1985 re-release included the hit song from her movie, Desperately Seeking Susan, called "Into the Groove.") In less than three years, Madonna had defined female pop-rock, adding a new raw sexuality that played perfectly into the MTV formats. "Like a Virgin," for example, became a focus of debate on its own for its suggestive lyrics (and cleverly parodied by "'Weird Al' Yankovic's "Like a Surgeon"). "Material Girl" portrayed in a three-minute music video the story of a Hollywood director wooing a Marilyn Monroe-type actress.

What Madonna achieved for female music—soon emulated by Janet Jackson—Michael Jackson surpassed amongst male pop stars. Jackson had exited the Jackson Five in the early 1970s for a solo career, teaming with Quincy Jones to create one of the hottest albums in pop history, Off the Wall (1979) and then Thriller (1982). With Bad in 1987, Jackson had established himself truly as the "king of pop," a label that stuck with him until his death in 2009. Bad sold more than 30 million copies, including eight million in the United States alone, and was the only album in history to have five singles peak on the Billboard Hot 100 consecutively at #1. Jackson's shows and MTV videos constituted production numbers of the highest order.

Mark and Jackson had crossed paths back in 1979 while Mark was recording an album called "Old Crest on a New Wave" with Dave Mason in Hollywood. Michael Jackson was recording an album down the hall in the same studio with his brothers, and during a break—while Mason was away---Mark saw Jackson leaning against a soda machine. Introducing himself, Mark said "We're recording an album here—come on in and listen." Jackson accompanied him to the studio as Ed Thacker, the engineer, rolled up a track called "Save Me." Jackson began to snap his fingers and Mark said "Why don't you just go out on the mike and scat some lines?" With a big smile, Jackson put the headphones on, and began dancing and singing to the song as the tape continued to roll. The result was a one-of-a-kind fusion of Dave Mason, Mark Stein, and Michael Jackson.

Music videos, despite allusions to sex and drugs, still had to get past television censors, which, in the 1980s, were significantly stricter than a decade later. And while acid no longer constituted a favorite of rockers, the drug culture still remained a central part of both the image and lifestyle. Even more than a decade after the "Age of Aquarius," drugs still constituted a destructive and all-too-common component of rockers' lives. Steven Tyler of Aerosmith was so strung out on heroin in 1986 that his own band members—themselves all druggies and addicts—

staged an intervention to save their frontman.[38]

Having tried to get clean on his own, Tyler went on methadone treatments, but failed. He told biographer Stephen Davis, "my manager was giving me a gram of coke every day as a ration to keep me off the streets, and I had a doctor who was giving me pills, and I'm copping bags of dope on the side—'cos when you're a drug addict you don't play with your kids or go work on your art; you go out and try to cop a bag of good Chinese heroin and everything else becomes second."[39]

It was ironic that Mark Stein, who had never used heroin and who became infuriated when, during his Canadian arrest, news reached his parents that he was in jail for the stuff, had written some of the most descriptive and poignant lines about heroin addiction ever in the Boomerang song "The Peddler:"

I hear morn' comin' through the floor

I hear the peddler at my door

I hope he ain't gonna charge me more

Cause his brother beat me many times before

I'm on the tracks of an evil train

And the only price I pay is when I feel the pain

Yet Tyler and Joe Perry had a tone of regret in their words as they recalled their times on heroin. Perry said "When you first fall in love with heroin, it's like discovering God. I started studying the folklore of opium as a sacrament . . . ." Tyler remembered "we'd do thirty takes—forty!—because we were gacked. . . . Today I listen to those albums, some of our best, and all I can hear are the drugs."[40]

Yet Tyler and Perry also noted that they constantly pushed back entire tours because Steven Tyler was slow to write lyrics. Perhaps the genius infused by heroin was not as potent as they thought. Perry described the band as "drug addicts dabbling in music, rather than musicians dabbling in drugs." Before long, Tyler had drifted into dark fatalism, telling a reporter he expected every plane to crash, even to the point of carrying a tape recorder with him on every flight, keeping his finger on the button so that "at least my mom will hear me say good-bye."[41]

If drugs weren't as openly celebrated by rockers as they had been a decade and a half earlier—as reflected in the minimal number of songs about getting high, contrasted with the majority about sex—cocaine use (by then the drug of choice) had started to become as common as wallpaper.

YOU KEEP ME HANGIN' ON

Chapter Six

As rock music ended its second era of ebb and flow—the first being the Elvis years—it did not disappear, nor did it significantly diminish as a cultural force. Rather, it transformed into a cultural touchstone from which almost all other modern music sprang. As music historian Elijah Wald noted, it all came back to the Beatles: "If you are not aware of the Beatles, you cannot hope to understand any music of the 1960s, because they were ubiquitous and affected all the other music. Even if some musicians remained free of their influence, those musicians were still heard by an audience that was acutely conscious of the Beatles. They were the dominant, inescapable sound of the era."[1]

For all intents and purposes, however, the Beatles were gone. In January 1969, they recorded *Let It Be*, which was released after *Abbey Road*, as a "live" album. Recorded on top of the Apple Corps building in London, *Let It Be* involved the novel idea of performing a "live" album (essentially without an audience) of entirely original songs no one had heard before. It proved a difficult, nearly disastrous outing, as the band members were at each other's throats; Yoko Ono never left John Lennon's side (inspiring ridicule and disgust from the others); and George Harrison walked out for a week after criticisms by Lennon and Paul McCartney. For his part, Paul said of the other Beatles, "they were becoming unpleasant people—to themselves as well as to other people."[2]

Between February and August, the band recorded *Abbey Road*, often put together without the four Beatles together in the studio at the

168

same time. In that respect it was reminiscent of the last days of the Fudge, with the *Rock and Roll* album, where the new power and possibilities of the recording studio made it possible for bands to record songs entirely as individuals. This, of course, negated the entire concept of a band. Already, the Beatles in *Sgt. Pepper*, Hendrix in *Electric Ladyland*, and Cream in *Wheels of Fire* had begun to demonstrate the new iteration of the recording studio, where the producer became essentially a member of the group, often contributing conceptually and thematically. In the case of activist producers such as George Martin or Felix Pappalardi, they also played instruments on the tracks themselves. Andy Johns, who had engineered the Rolling Stones' greatest albums, desperately wanted to be a musician himself, and learned his trade simply hanging around studios.[3] George Martin has occasionally been labeled the "fifth Beatle" for his playing in the studio.

Producers' roles, like those of the musicians, had evolved. As Johns recalled, the "60s engineer did as he was told. Boys would bring in whatever they had and he would deal with it."[4] Over time, however, they began to become actively involved. "I took charge," Johns noted. "That's a producer." Johns later discovered a trick some of the best producers used—"change the key when there's a problem!" Tom Dowd, who worked with Rod Stewart, learned early on that a key change could make all the difference in the world in how a song felt.

Studios had evolved into actual instruments, as distinct as drums or guitars: they were creatures to be played, offering sounds to be elicited. Whether it was the booming, end-of-the-world chord at the end of "A Day in the Life," panning right-to-left speaker effects of "Rainy Day, Dream Away," the studio could generate specific effects that were not possible merely with the instrument itself. Phil Spector had glimpsed this with his "Wall of Sound," though Spector was a one-trick pony. (Andy Johns would later observe that as a young engineer he listened to Spector's work "with the bed corners over my head, entranced," but then, as a grown man, hearing Spector's work was "most bloody awful.")[5]

Shadow Morton likewise perceived the possibilities of the studio but failed to remember that without a song, production by itself is worthless. His Vanilla Fudge album, The Beat Goes On, showed that the concept of a rock album without rock and roll was a fool's errand.

Rapidly, early four-track machines gave way to eight, then 16, then in the early 1970s, 32-track recording machines. The most obvious implication of so many tracks was that one could add far more instruments—layers of guitars, horns, more vocals—without having to get it down "live" in the studio. Cream's introductory notes to "White Room" are a classic example, blending a note from a guitar, Eric Clapton

169

and Jack Bruce's vocals, and a single viola note played by Pappalardi, with subsequent live versions of the song sounding stunningly empty. Secondly, each track could be individually manipulated, enhanced, ramped up, toned down, modulated, fuzz-toned, wah-wahed, or wrung through any number of special effects. Third, larger track studios enabled musicians to achieve a certain level of perfection. Play a bad guitar solo? Re-record the solo only. Hit a sour note while singing? You don't have to play the entire song again, merely "punch out" a note. Brian Wilson of the Beach Boys, even more than Martin or Pappalardi, would become the first true musician to play a recording studio (McCartney came close, but still relied heavily on Martin). Wilson, to the chagrin of his bandmates, would labor for hours to layer exactly the right instruments and harmonies, with his crowning glory being "Good Vibrations."

Technology cut both ways. Fans now expected rich, overwhelming sounds and frequently left disappointed when a four- or five-piece band failed to deliver. One of the few touring bands that managed to achieve its massive studio sounds without layers of additional recordings or the accompaniment of small traveling orchestras was Yes, the English jazz-fusion-rock band that featured the talented Rick Wakeman on a blinding array of synthesizers (itself somewhat new to the rock scene). Employing pre-set synthesizer "walls," and the vocals of at least three members of the band, Yes often sounded live as they did in the studio. Some bands, such as Cream before they split up, Led Zeppelin, and the Rolling Stones, gave the musical finger to "sounding like the studio" and instead counted on the energy from their live performances to deliver. This tactic imposed a certain tyranny on the bands, forcing them to do ever more unique and outrageous stage antics to compensate for the lack of the studio's depth. Thus, Hendrix set his guitar on fire, fell on his knees, played with his teeth; Jimmy Page played his guitar with a violin bow; later, David Lee Roth of Van Halen leaped from stacks of amplifiers while doing the splits. Still other hand, individual singers, such as Joe Cocker, now found they were required to tour not just with a five- or six-piece rock band, but with horns and female backup singers. This all emanated from the tyranny of the studio.

Driven by the richness of studio sounds to distract audiences who heard them live, bands frequently "jammed" for extended interims within shorter studio songs. Perhaps the greatest example of this was Iron Butterfly, who took a standard three-minute studio song, "Inna-Gadda-da-Vita," and inserted long guitar and organ solos before giving the drummer the longest solo ever to hit top 40 radio. (According to producer Shadow Morton, the entire "long" version was something of an accident in itself: when the boys couldn't loosen up in the studio, Morton acted like there was a problem in the sound board and told them to play one of their songs when he was actually running tape. Each time the band looked at him, Morton and his engineer motioned to keep going and faked further troubleshooting with the wires.)[6]

Acts such as the Allman Brothers Band, the Who, Joe Cocker, then later, Peter Frampton produced classic live albums that transcended the energy they had in the studio, and for some this proved a detriment. Ten Years' After found it nearly impossible to recreate the feeling of the live Woodstock version of "I'm Comin' Home" in smaller concert venues that did not feature Ang Lee's schizophrenic camera effects. Moreover, audiences who heard one great, spontaneous, live performance that just seemed to capture the best of every player now expected that at every stop on the tour. Led Zeppelin, Vanilla Fudge, and Hendrix, for the most part, had been able to achieve that level of live consistency, and for good reason: live, they eschewed most of the studio tricks and instead relied on the energetic interaction of band mates.

McCartney, especially, realized that the Beatles were long past the time that they could compete in such a live environment. Where they once could hold their own in the Cavern, the industry had changed dramatically, and every new John, Paul, George, and Ringo could play on a technical level everything the Beatles could and more. The Fab Four simply weren't the players on stage that the new generation of musicians were, and, having matured during an era where it was "about the songs," and not about the jams, they had little to offer live except a nostalgic hope that the clock could be turned back to 1964 again. It was during the recording of *Abbey Road* that John Lennon released his single, "Give Peace a Chance," a harbinger of the band's breakup, as it was the first solo work released by any of the Beatles. That August, he announced he was leaving the group, and the August 20 recording of "I Want You (She's So Heavy)" marked the last time the four lads were together in the studio. When the *Let It Be* documentary was released in 1971, the London Sunday Telegraph aptly summed up the film as "touching," about "the breaking apart of this reassuring, geometrically perfect, once apparently ageless family of siblings."[7]

The demise of the Beatles came as no surprise, but it struck rock and roll to the core, as fans longed for the time that the boys would "make up" and the Beatles would again perform live. Instead, an era had passed. As the decade turned, rockers had "transformed teenage dance music into a mature art form."[8]

Tidal waves of social water had passed under the bridge as well: audiences had gone through the Vietnam War, the space race, putting a man on the moon, the sexual revolution, and the widespread exposure to drugs. Singing about wanting to "hold your hand" or "what a day for a daydream" seemed oddly childish, in musical construction as well as lyrics. Added to the mix was the growing wealth (or, at least, income) of many of the rock stars. Bands such as the Jefferson Airplane, who considered themselves radicals and musical bomb-throwers, struggled with the contradictions. In a 1970 Central Park concert, Grace Slick launched into a diatribe against "the audience, the band, and herself" by lecturing the crowd for several minutes:

> You paid $3.50 to come in here and you probably don't have it man, but we do. We can ride in cars that are all closed up and nobody sees us . . . . [We] can smoke all this dope and nobody gives [us] any shit. But they give you shit because you don't have a Cadillac. We do. You know the people you're rising up against? They're right up here on this stage. They're also in the White House but they're also right here. . . . And I'm a jerk 'cause I love it. I love that shrimp shit.[9]

Slick and her "shrimp shit" comment had touched on one of the most difficult contradictions most of the late-1960s and early-1970s rockers had to face, namely their own personal luxury contrasted with calls for revolution and/or solidarity with the poor.

It once again raised the paradox of the freedom rock espoused— and delivered—contrasted with the capitalist wealth that it produced for everyone and, distressingly to some musicians, that it required. The Who, for example, "had no use for the rhetoric of hippie pastoralism that ruled Woodstock . . . . They'd all paid enough dues to have rid themselves of any illusions about the nearness of glamour to squalor."[10]

Like most bands, the Who featured a range of responses to the hippie revolution that ranged from sympathy on the part of Pete Townshend to John Entwhistle, who ignored them, to Keith Moon who "actively hated them."[11]

And like many bands, the Who perpetually overspent, starting each tour between $40,000 and $60,000 in debt. Who biographer Dave Marsh noted that Keith Moon never understood why people found the group's early days so glamorous, then later why people thought they "had a load of money." Of course, the Who did have a "load of money," even if they spent it all—on American cars, on drugs and alcohol, on clothes, replacing the equipment they destroyed every night, and in their all-night binges. Moon "bought a pyramid-shaped home in Chertsey for [$155,000], a pub in Oxfordshire and uncounted cars and gadgets . . . and worked himself as close to bankruptcy as possible," while Townshend often felt "embarrassed" to be so wealthy while "trying to put out spiritual ideas."[12] Reflecting on his physical encounter with Abbie Hoffman at Woodstock, Townshend called it the "most political thing I ever did."[13]

Two decades later, it would afflict personalities such as U-2's Bono, who would fly from continent to continent on a spacious private jet, with an entourage of handlers, so that he could "stand" with the poor. Such comments did not mean the rockers were insincere, or that they lacked a social conscience. It meant that, for the first time, many found themselves in a position where they had to confront one of the two major realities of rock and roll, namely to make money. Obviously, the other was to make music. Yet the drinking/drug ingesting/partying nature of the rock and roll lifestyle demanded cash and lots of it, and it became harder for rockers to champion the lower classes they now sought to escape, or to cry out for revolution—as Grace Slick said—against themselves. In short, rock's widespread popularity in some ways forced rockers to grow up.

Another reality imposed its discipline on the rockers, namely for all their rebellion, most came from middle-class backgrounds. Mark Stein, Jerry Corbetta, Roger Daltrey, Pete Townshend, John Entwhistle, Vinny Martell, Alice Cooper, Glenn Buxton, Jim Morrison, Ray Manzarek, Robby Krieger, John Densmore, Ritchie Blackmore, Grace Slick, Jerry Garcia, and Robert Plant all grew up in middle- to lower-middle class homes. None were dirt poor. Jimmy Page was raised on London suburbs; Alice Cooper in north Phoenix, then an upper-middle class section of town. Brian Wilson and his brothers were certainly children of the 'burbs. Certainly some of the English bands came from hardscrabble origins—the Beatles being the most famous—and most of the truly hard-core bluesmen, such as Johnny Winter, grew up in poverty. Don Felder left a "trailer trash" background; Mexican-born Carlos Santana, whose father was a mariachi violinist, might be considered "lower class," but in Mexico that was not necessarily a position of poverty. Hendrix's father was a soldier, as was Eric Clapton's—in either case, hardly wealthy, but with government benefits in the post-war era, hardly poverty-stricken. The point is, few grew up in extreme poverty, and most had experienced middle-class life at some point. It was, therefore, against type for them to reject money or the comforts that higher incomes brought.

Such was not the case with the new wave of bands in the 1970s, especially in England, where disillusionment led to a new angst, followed by a new wave of rebellion. These new rockers, however, did not rise up against "the Man" or "the government," but against the rock establishment itself. The Sex Pistols, the Clash, the Stranglers, and others— and in taking over the club scenes, they "insulted or derided" the older bands. Since Vanilla Fudge had exited the scene, the newcomers focused their disdain on Led Zeppelin, the Stones, Yes, and Genesis. But Zeppelin and Elton John were "particularly reviled for their success, their wealth, their outmoded vulgarity, and for pandering to America. Worst of all, they were called junkies, drugged-out millionaires who had no relationship or rapport with the kids they were playing for."[14]

Here was another aspect of punk hypocrisy: the punk bands ingested as many drugs as their predecessors—the Ramones, in particular, developed an addiction for sniffing glue—"Anything to get high," Dee Dee Ramone said: "cans of whipped cream . . . and the gas in it . . . . cough medicine, glue, Tuinals, and Seconols."[15]

Iggy Pop checked himself into a hospital, admitting, "I've been addicted for a long time to very heavy drugs . . . . now I'm a fool who uses pills and slobbers a lot . . . ."[16] 'Sex Pistols' Sid Vicious died of a mysterious heroin overdose, by one account administered by his own mother.[17]

It is important, however, to separate the music scene in England at this time from that in the USA. England entered its darkest of decades since the War in the 1970s. British labor-socialism was collapsing, high unemployment and long lines at "the dole" constituted a permanent condition, while at the same time teens who grew up with the prospects of few jobs and even fewer opportunities looked at rock stars with their lavish lifestyles. Punk fed off this resentment, seeing the rockers of the 60s as part of the problem, and punk's answer consisted of sadism, nihilism, perversion, anger, and above all chaos. But, unfortunately, it also consisted of a very real fascination with Nazism, as many of the punkers donned swastikas and German military accessories. Some feebly insisted they meant the whole fraternization with the Nazis as "ironic," but the claim didn't hold water. For many, the only feasible alternative to what existed—either in the free West or the unfree Soviet bloc, was the fascism of years gone by, and consequently, they laughed and ridiculed those who pointed out the baggage of the Nazi symbols they embrace.[18]

Another novel, unexpected, and disgusting element of punk was "gobbing," whereby audiences would swill beer and spit it at the performers, then, when they ran out of beer, simply spit. Richard Hell (a.k.a. Richard Meyers) of the Heartbreakers toured England in 1977 and—in a stunning statement for a punk rocker—found "British audiences were just horrific. Just vile." It may have been "the British way of saying 'We love you'," he noted, "but it got tired quick."[19]

Bob Quine, who played with Richard Hell in the Voidoids, recalled "It was a horrible experience, being covered with spit every night . . . and not necessarily out of admiration. . . . I'm singing my background vocals, and spit's flying in my mouth."[20]

Worse still were the flying unopened cans of beer. In a scene straight out of the Blues Brothers, audiences would hurl full beer cans—"like mortar shells" at the band. Quine, with prolific understatement, noted, "It was pretty demoralizing being hit in the head with unopened cans of beer . . . [although] I was touched by the dedication with which they would willingly sacrifice a full beer in order to really harm members of the band, which they did."[21]

Punk trashed the craft of rock music that so many legendary rockers saw themselves as creating. The Ramones prided themselves on producing an album in a week and spending only $6400, at a time when bands took years to record albums that cost millions to produce. Malcolm McLaren, the manager of the Sex Pistols, rebelled at the philosophy that said "you couldn't do anything without a lot of money . . . we don't care if we can't play and don't have very good instruments, we're still doing it because we think you're all a bunch of cunts."[22] McLaren proceeded, then, to make the same mistake every rebel made, which was to over-generalize, saying, "everybody was desperate to take it back. This was a generation trying to do that."[23]

In fact, the "generation" that was "desperate to take it back" was buying "50 Ways to Leave Your Lover" by Paul Simon, "Bad Blood" by Neil Sedaka, "Ain't No Way to Treat a Lady" by Helen Reddy, "Mandy" by Barry Manilow, "One of these Nights" by the Eagles, "Rhinestone Cowboy" by Glen Campbell, and "SOS" by Abba. Indeed, one has to look hard to find any songs to crack the Top 40 on *Billboard* that even approximated punk. The very same arrogance that afflicted many of the tradition rockers about the quality of their music also characterized the punkers at the other end of the spectrum, where the absence of quality was elevated to a desirable trait of its own. Both ends of the spectrum involved a gnawing fear on the part of most musicians that "something as trivial as 'Louie Louie' might turn out to be more influential and long-lived (and more meaningful and transcendent, too) than the pretensions of the Grateful Dead and other self-conscious music 'artists' . . . ."[24]

Disco music, identified strongly with the Bee Gees and Donna Summer on the performing side and Neil Bogart on the production side, seemed to rise as suddenly as punk and constituted every bit as great a threat as its harsher distant cousin. The first of the disco clubs, the Loft in New York City, which opened in February 1970 by disc jockey David Mancuso, was a members-only private club that focused more on dance expression than relating to music through listening at concerts or tripping. (It was, needless to say, difficult to dance with a partner on a crowded floor if one was blasted on acid or so mellowed out on weed that a nap seemed better than a kick-ball-change.) Music writer Piero Scaruffi described disco as "collective ecstasy.[25]

The music form also constituted a rebellion of its own, reacting to the dominance of the guitar solo. Drawing from the late 1960s and early 1970s funk sounds of Sly and the Family Stone, George Clinton's bands (Funkadelic and Parliament of Funk), and Kool and the Gang, disco took three years to barge into mainstream radio playlists with K.C. and the Sunshine Band, Barry White, and perhaps the first universally-recognized disco dance song in America, Van McCoy's "The Hustle" (1975).

Bogart sensed the change, but also saw that the only way to establish his new label, Casablanca Records, was to take some risks. That involved, on the one hand, signing disco diva Donna Summer and, on the other, the new theatrical-rock metal group KISS. Summer's demo, "Love to Love You Baby," happened to be playing at a party in 1975 when someone bumped into the turntable, resetting the four-minute song back to the beginning, giving birth to the eight-minute disco song. KISS, on the other hand, required radically different marketing techniques: no one quite knew what to do with four guys in makeup, one of whom vomited blood on stage. But in both cases, Bogart pulled it off.[26]

Just as it took an English group, the Beatles, to reintroduce American rockers to the essence of the aural aspects of rock and roll music, so too did an English Beatles wanna-be group, the Bee Gees, spark a sea change in the physical relationship of the audience with music. Australian brothers Barry, Robin, and Maurice Gibb, already known for their well-blended harmonies, had been brought to England by Robert Stigwood and released their first albums on Polydor. Their "New York Mining Disaster 1941," while a grim tale of a mine collapse, nevertheless became a hit in 1967, and their "To Love Somebody," written for Otis Redding, reached the top 20 that year. They soon followed with "Massachusetts" (#11 in the U.S., 1967), "Words" (1968, #15), "I Gotta Get a Message to You" (1968, #8) and "I Started a Joke" (1968, #6) all made the Bee Gees major players in the industry, yet hardly viewed in the same "serious" context as Jefferson Airplane, Vanilla Fudge, or the Who. Managing a few lukewarm hits, they were stuck in never-land by the early 1970s until Arif Mardin, a producer for Atlantic Records, liked the sound of Barry Gibb singing in falsetto, put to a disco beat.

When married to the soundtrack for the smash movie *Saturday Night Fever* with John Travolta as an Italian dance whiz who tears up the disco floors in New York, the Bee Gees entered the realm of superstars.

Their songs on the soundtrack album included "Stayin' Alive," "Night Fever," "How Deep Is Your Love," "More than a Woman," and two previously released singles in the Mardin-Gibb falsetto mode, "Jive Talkin'" and "You Should Be Dancin'." Every one of those songs—save for "More than a Woman" (the Bee Gees' version, as Tavares also did a version on the soundtrack album), which was not released as a single—hit the #1 spot on the top 40 charts. It was truly an astonishing run. *Saturday Night Fever: The Original Movie Sound Track* became a blockbuster, selling over 15 million copies. Another soundtrack song, "Disco Inferno" by the Trammps (1976) only reached #53 before being re-released after the album came out (reaching #11 the second time).

The point was that disco was not an insignificant blip in American music, but a genuine reaction to the excesses of drug-rock and the concert orientation that had taken place for years. Nothing could have been more opposite than a 20-minute Cream jam and the pulsating "four on the floor" beat in which a steady eighth note or even a sixteenth note was played on a high hat, with the cymbal open on the off beats, giving a "tap-shee-yuk-shee-yuk-shee-yuk" rolling feel. Horns, particularly flutes and woodwinds, displaced guitars—whose main function was in the form of a Fender Stratocaster playing a single funky chord line. An overlay of strings fleshed out the sound, eerily reminiscent of Phil Spector.

Arif Mardin may have isolated the Bee Gees' sound, but it was Neil Bogart who tapped into disco's potential. As a singer in the 1960s under the name Neil Scott, Bogart became an executive in Buddah Records in New York, which handled dance groups such as the Ohio Express and, with Kama Sutra Records, distributed the Isley Brothers and Curtis Mayfield. Bogart, having helped pioneer so-called "bubblegum" music (softer rock aimed at young teens with lots of sexual double entendres), started Casablanca Records in 1973 and began to promote Donna Summer. Born LaDonna Adrian Gaines, Donna Summer had a powerful gospel voice. Having backed up a number of rock acts, she came up with the idea for a song called "Love to Love You," which featured her moaning in orgiastic ecstasy. Bogart produced a 20-minute version of the song featuring an abundance of Summer's simulated vocal sex and gaining the singer a place among male listeners equivalent to what Barry White held with females. Summer's next releases struggled until, in 1978, she appeared in the movie Thank God It's Friday and released the single, "Last Dance." She then went on to do "No More Tears (Enough is Enough)" and a disco version of "MacArthur Park"—originally performed by Richard Harris.

For almost four solid years, disco reigned supreme in American music, with hits such as "Rock the Boat" (Hues Corporation), "Love's

Theme" (Barry White), "Rock Your Baby" (George McCrae), "Never Can Say Goodbye" and "Dancin' Machine" (Jackson 5), and "We Are Family" (Sister Sledge). Everything from classical music ("A Fifth of Beethoven," by Walter Murphy) to soulish "Lady Marmalade" by Patty LaBelle to semi-mainstream rock interpretations ("Heart of Glass" by Blondie and Rod Stewart's "Do Ya Think I'm Sexy?") made the charts. But if the Bee Gees gave disco credibility, it was an American band, K.C. and the Sunshine Band, that pushed it into reactionary mode with their string of hits, "Get Down Tonight," "That's the Way (I Like It)," "(Shake, Shake, Shake) Shake Your Booty," "I'm Your Boogie Man," and "Keep It Comin' Love." By the time K.C. had finished, disco was burned out and trivialized, even hated. "Death to disco" and "disco sucks" were common phrases of the late 1970s, and hard rock disc jockeys (for publicity reasons as much as anything) organized mass burnings of disco albums. Critics claimed rock mainstays such as Rod Stewart or David Bowie had "sold out" in their disco songs. On July 12, 1979, a large anti-disco demonstration was organized by rock disc jockeys Steve Dahl and Gary Meier in Chicago between games of a White Sox doubleheader. They exploded disco records and the crowd damaged the field in a riot, causing the White Sox to forfeit their second game.

That week, six disco songs graced the top ten. Less than two months later, not a single disco song made the top ten. A popular television show, WKRP in Cincinnati, repeatedly made disco jokes and the genre was dead. Far from the critics' claims that "homophobia" or "racism" were causes of disco's death---the leading disco icons were John Travolta, a heterosexual married actor and Donna Summer, a black born-again Christian---disco had simply run its course, much the way "good time" pop music as played by Herman's Hermits or Freddie and the Dreamers had run its course. In fact, disco matured just as heavy metal had matured: new electronica music worked its way into clubs, soon married to an aerobics phenomenon that needed extremely high energy, yet non-irritating dance music.

In the 1985 film *Perfect*, Travolta introduced America to yet another craze with his sweaty workouts in an aerobics class led by sexy Jamie Lee Curtis. Demand for workout music led to an entire sub-industry, headed by Power Productions and Muscle Mixes, of specially mixed aerobics and workout tapes that seamlessly blended from one song to the next—all rock, but all tweaked up several beats per minute to raise cardiovascular levels. Narrowly-oriented dance music suddenly found itself with a whole new audience as songs such as "Gloria" (Laura Branigan, 1982), "It's Rainin' Men" (The Weather Girls, 1982), "I'm So

178

Excited" (The Pointer Sisters, 1982), "So Many Men, So Little Time" (Miquel Brown, 1983) and Rick James's "Super Freak" (1981) were all re-mixed into collections meant for runners and gym rats. The punkers hated disco and all its progeny, but it was undeniable that both disco and punk—punk from the anarchy side and disco from the commercial side--represented normal reactions to the predictable direction of rock in the early 1970s.

Nevertheless, the new music styles stunned the now-older rockers. Led Zeppelin's biographer, Stephen Davis complained that "the pop world that Led Zeppelin once knew and dominated no longer existed. . . . Led Zeppelin had been bad-mouthed as gangsters for years, but now the real bullies had their way."[27]

For many befuddled rockers, it was a taste of the medicine they had dished out to LBJ and Richard Nixon for years; indeed, the punkers described the rock establishment as a predictable appendage of Nixon! But punk could no more sustain itself as a never-ending source of criticism than could rock half a decade earlier. There was a reason groups such as the Cowsills and Partridge Family and K. C. and the Sunshine Band scored so many hits: people, even young people, can only absorb so much pessimism and negative "vibes" before looking for a ray of sunshine.

Like the darker, gloomier elements of traditional rock, the only responses to endless pessimism were escapism through drugs (which was already being discarded as a failure), suicide, or conversion, which became the route many chose, essentially joining "the establishment" and turning out songs people would actually listen to. It was one thing for punk rockers to energize a crowd of a thousand in a club, quite another to sell a million records. Groups such as the Clash, who finally signed with CBS in 1977, were virtually forced by the record label to clean up their punk sound, and the result, predictably, were a few hits ("London Calling," and "Train in Vain"). Major record labels avoided punk acts until the late 1990s, and even then the signing of Blink 182, whose single, "Semi-Charmed Life," was the epitome of anti-punk, with its clever lyrics, memorable "doo-doo-doo" chorus, and inoffensive chord progression. Another recent band, supposedly the heir to punk, Green Day, debuted with a song called "Basket Case" that is only Ramones-ish in the most flexible use of the term.

Punk eventually found its way into the market, however. As would occur with the appearance of rap music some 20 years later, however, an army of new record labels assembled to record this new genre. They found what generations before had found, that the only keys to success were to impress existing corporate labels or to work so hard

179

(i.e., by adopting "conventional" and "consumerist" strategies) as to bestow success on an independent label (the route followed by Blink 182 and Green Day). It was, on a small scale, what many so-called Third World countries learned about capitalism, that to share in its wealth, you had to embrace it, and that meant discarding or minimizing parts of your culture antithetical to it. For punk labels to be successful, in short, they had to reject some of the very chaos that made punk a phenomenon in the club scene. Groups such as the Clash soon heard themselves on the very Top 40 radio stations they disdained, and Blink 182 would find themselves confronted by audiences screaming for "Semi-Charmed Life" much the way bluesmen like Eric Clapton would suffer through cries for Cream to play "Sunshine of Your Love." As writer Legs McNeil, a writer who followed the genre, concluded,

> Overnight, punk had become as stupid as anything else. This wonderful vital force that was articulated by the music was really about corrupting every form—it was about advocating kids to not wait to be told what to do, but make life up for themselves . . . it was about not being perfect, it was about saying it was okay to be amateurish and funny, that real creativity came of making a mess . . . .[28]

Punk failed to bring about a revolution on its own, but no doubt was a part of the transformation of rock and roll. And punkers, in a strange, perverted way, saw themselves as carrying the rock torch: McNeil argued, with some legitimacy, that punk had "no political agenda. It was about real freedom, personal freedom. It was also about doing anything that's gonna offend a grown-up."[29]

With Hendrix and Morrison dead, Cream and Vanilla Fudge broken up, Woodstock quickly becoming a memory, and punk in rapid self-destruct mode, rock hardly disappeared. Rather, the monolithic sound of a few years earlier gave way to a spectrum of musical styles, from orchestral rock to reggae, in which punk had its niche. Punk's attempt to break away from the clean sounds of the studios and to transcend even the raucous live concerts of the Golden Age power bands constituted an anti-studio movement, despite the fact that as one critic pointed out, the punk rockers knew their way around a studio as well as anyone. To put it somewhat differently, it took a great deal of musicianship and preparation to sound that bad. It was deliberate. It was raw and purposefully offensive. Iggy Pop would cut himself with glass onstage, the Sex Pistols would scream about anarchy and how Johnny Rotten was "the anti-christ."

Above all, punk was nihilistic and frustrated about the inability of the Left in Britain to deliver on its promises, as the Pistols' John Lydon explained:

> Early Seventies Britain was a very depressing place. It was completely rundown, there was trash on the streets, total unemployment—just about everybody was on strike. Everybody was brought up with an education system that told you point blank that if you came from the wrong side of the tracks...then you had no hope in hell and no career prospects at all. Out of that came pretentious moi and the Sex Pistols and then a whole bunch of copycat wankers after us.[30]

Iggy Pop put it more succinctly, noting that he always thought "Heart Full of Soul," by the Yardbirds was a good song. "What was my heart full of?" he asked. "I decided it was basically full of napalm."[31]

Although they would claim no influence from the American chaos-group, the Ramones, the Sex Pistols were in fact very much a part of the genre. But where in England, with its class structure still intact, such themes connected broadly, in America the punkers became just another subculture variation. To be sure, there were the outrageous (often false) stories of the Fugs defecating on stage, or Frank Zappa stomping on a box of baby chickens, but then there were the quite real antics of Zappa (a supremely talented and demanding musician) putting out sheet music for his band and, without telling them, changing the opening song at every music stand so that when they started playing, there was a cacophony.

Zappa provided key guidance to Mark early in his career. In the winter of 1967, Vanilla Fudge and the Mothers of Invention did some shows in New England. At the time, Mark was used to smoking and drinking daily, and on top of it all, he went without sleep for extremely long periods. "It was the norm," he said. "You were young, your body could handle it, but this raging existence wasn't good for the voice." Zappa and Mark hit it off during their mini-tour, and one night, Mark had completely lost his voice. He couldn't talk, let alone sing. The show was a few hours away. Zappa sat with him backstage and made him hot tea with honey, acting as nurse and psychologist at the same time. He told him to relax, meditate, that he would make it through the show. Somehow, Mark did make it through—though with a rather raspy performance. But it taught him that he had to get his sleep.

Punk's "softer" side, Britain's "glam" rock, originated in 1971 with musicians such as Marc Bolan of T-Rex and David Bowie and the

Spiders from Mars. Glam or glitter rock involved musicians wearing distinctly female clothes (though not to the extent Alice Cooper would soon do so). Their flamboyant costumes, including teased hair, high-platform boots, and lots of makeup, aspired to blend the world of the theater with science fiction. Bowie and T-Rex were soon joined by Mott the Hoople, Lou Reed, and Elton John, but in its original musical form, it often resembled punk with its wildly distorted guitars. Both Bowie and Bolan explored bisexualism in their look (though keeping their sexual proclivities private), and glam's popularity peaked with Bowie's 1972 album, *The Rise and Fall of Ziggy Stardust and the Spiders from Mars.* Yet already in the United States, bands as wholesome as the Osmonds had taken to wearing some makeup—a development soon made more necessary by the advent of music television. But whereas glam appealed to wealthier and upper-middle-class youth with money to spend on clothes and the social freedom to be "strange," pure punk remained lower-class and completely in-your-face angry. Punk was England's middle finger to the world.

"Shock" rock in America took a much different turn, with Vince Furnier of Phoenix, Arizona, donning women's clothes and staging a full-scale operatic production under the name "Alice Cooper." Alice had seen Arthur Brown "set his hair on fire," and bands "smashed guitars," so he reasoned "why can't you turn each song into a story?"[32]

His band in Phoenix, the Earwigs, had a guillotine on stage that they brought from a journalism class, and from that point on, "we always had props on stage." Far from being a musical cross-dresser, Alice Cooper sought to transform rock and roll from a series of individual songs associated with chaotic antics to a full-blown, integrated production. Black Sabbath, which featured singer Ozzie Osborne, was a British band who had just caused a buzz with their "devil worship" debut album. But to Alice, "Ozzie wasn't scary. Insanity is scary. Cutting people's heads off on stage," he noted, "is scary."[33]

Ironically, though, Alice Cooper had taken the Beatles' theme concept albums to the live stage (and certainly was only one of several): when: when Ozzie and Alice toured together, and the two shock rockers discussed how much they had learned from the Beatles! Alice did not see a villain amidst all the punk rockers. Indeed, he was amused by them. But they posed no real threat to the comfort level of the audience. With his character Alice Cooper, however, Vince Furnier "wanted people to step back when Alice walked in." The band was "as much a gang as a band," and he reveled in the "exceptionally negative press" which, of course, helped produce his 14 top 40 hits.[34]

If he had learned to shock from the Beatles' concepts, Alice

Cooper had learned about the power of live performance from Vanilla Fudge, whom he said was the first ever "super band," and, at first, he thought they were so good they must have come from England!

Sounds as radically diverse as shock rock, punk, and disco in fact were all exploring the paths paved for them by the Golden Age rockers, even as some of them denigrated their own roots. Bands as varied as Yes and Black Sabbath toured together; Emerson, Lake, and Palmer ventured into orchestral regions previously explored by Vanilla Fudge, the Moody Blues, and the Electric Light Orchestra; and a veteran band that had yet to have major hits, Pink Floyd, unveiled one of the most influential albums in rock history (*The Dark Side of the Moon*, 1973). Both the Who and Led Zeppelin remained popular touring bands with routine top ten albums, but now such bands constituted a single thread of rock, contrasted with everything from Latino-type sounds of Santana to the forerunners of fusion and jazz-rock such as King Crimson. An army of short-lived "death metal" bands (with a few genuine survivors, such as Metallica, AC/DC, and Dokken) soon appeared taking punk to a much darker level and joining, as Davis put it, "limp English synthesizer bands [and] dreadlocked transvestites," as well as a wave of reggae and new heavier southern rockers such as Black Oak Arkansas and Lynyrd Skynyrd. The Allman Brothers Band, called the "principal architects of southern rock," had been formed at the tail end of the Golden Age of power bands, and in 1971 were hailed by *Rolling Stone* as "the best damn rock and roll band [of] the last five years."[35]

No sooner had the Allman Brothers reached the moutaintop than Duane Allman was killed in a motorcycle accident—soon followed by a similar motorcycle death of bassist Berry Oakley. While the band made several more albums and remained a popular touring act, the reconstituted Allman Brothers only had one more major hit, "Ramblin' Man" (1973).

Four years later, "southern rock" seemed to literally and figuratively flame out when the major part of Lynyrd Skynyrd, including singer Ronnie Van Zant, went down in an airplane crash. Skynyrd's "Free Bird," which reached the national charts, became a standard for all young rockers to master, but it was their southern anthem of defiance, "Sweet Home Alabama" (a response to Neil Young's preachy 1970 "Southern Man") that became a classic, and itself respectfully copied in Kid Rock's 2008 hit "All Summer Long." Perhaps the greatest tribute to Skynyrd came in the 1997 film *Con Air*, where, as convicts on the freshly-captured airplane take off to sounds of "Sweet Home Alabama," the quiet mass-murderer Garland Greene (Steve Buscemi) quips "Define irony. Bunch of idiots dancing on a plane to a song made famous by a band that died in a plane crash."[36]

Amidst this panoply of rock variations, the shattered elements of Vanilla Fudge created two powerful new bands, both under the management of Phil Basile. The first, Mark's Boomerang, had excellent musicians, solid songwriting, but was relegated to second place in Philly's list of acts. The second band, Cactus, emerged as one of America's most powerful boogie bands ever, relegating weaker competitors, such as Canned Heat, to the dust-bin of boogiedom. Along with Carmine and Tim, Rusty Day and Jim McCarty produced a relentless, loud, and driving sound to such boogies as "Let Me Swim," Mose Allison's "Parchman Farm," and Willie Dixon's "You Can't Judge a Book by the Cover." The up-and-coming supergroup "Van Halen," named for brothers Eddie and Alex Van Halen, with singer David Lee Roth, cited Cactus as one of their influences. Many thought Cactus might emerge as an American equivalent of Cream; others pointed out that the songwriting was average and the vocals, painful. But whereas Boomerang proved just one of many excellent hard rock bands, Cactus, by embracing the boogie mantle, won critical praise and carved out a niche. More important to Cactus's success, and Boomerang's eventual failure, was Basile's management. Indeed, when Boomerang opened for Emerson, Lake, and Palmer in 1971, it marked a figurative passing of the mantle from one leading keyboardist to another. Depressed and burned out, Mark and Patty retreated to Long Island.

As Mark concentrated on writing songs, he met a lyricist named Roger Atkins who had penned "It's My Life" for the Animals. With British pop sensation Elton John coming on the scene, the stage was set for Mark to pursue a new direction as a singer-songwriter. He and Atkins worked on a number of songs, coming close to a deal with Don Kirshner, who had developed the Monkees and who conceived of a night-time television rock concert series called "Don Kirshner's Rock Concert that departed from traditional "American Bandstand" formats by having live—not lip-synched—performances. But when the Kirshner deal fell through, Atkins packed up and moved to California, which seemed to be the new center of rock music anyway. Mark and Patty decided they needed to move.

Just two weeks before they were to leave, Mark was on the phone with Patty in a New York coffee shop when he spotted star singer Bette Midler walking down the avenue. He slammed down the phone and ran down the street after her—even though she was trying to be incognito with sunglasses and her hair in a kerchief, Mark knew it was Bette. "Hey Bette, how you doing?" he exclaimed. Midler turned and broke into her large smile. Mark introduced himself and Midler said "What happened to the Fudge?" Explaining the band had broken up, Mark told her how he had been writing material and wanted to get her some songs. She gave him her business manager's number, who was Aaron Russo, former owner of Kinetic Playground in Chicago where the Fudge had performed. (In fact, one of the Fudge shows there had included Muddy Waters, Jethro Tull, and Led Zeppelin). Russo was delighted when Mark called, as they were already acquainted from the 60s Chicago shows at his club. They met at his office in New York City, where Mark handed him a tape of his new tunes. Russo asked Mark if he would be interested in playing keyboards with Bette's band. Incredibly, he turned it down, wanting to stay focused on getting a deal as a singer-songwriter that he believed would be awaiting him when he got to California. Ultimately, Bette didn't use any of his tunes and a singer-piano player in the jingle business named Barry Manilow got the job.

Settling in at Thousand Oaks with the family, Mark began working steadily with Roger, producing plenty of songs and contacting publishers in Los Angeles. The partnership never took off—no one was interested, and the relationship "burned out," only to find a new opportunity with the Fudge was laid back at Mark's door. In 1974, Steven Weiss, the former business manager, called Mark with an offer from CBS Records for a Vanilla Fudge reunion to include two albums for $1 million and options. Carmine and Tim had just come off Beck, Bogert, and Appice, turning out one studio album and a two-record live recording of their Japanese tour. Despite the powerhouse potential, BBA as it was known never jelled anywhere near the level Cactus had, in part because there seemed to be a disconnect between the melodic vocals and the hard-driving sound, and also because Jeff Beck—arguably the greatest guitarist in the world—always performed better with a rhythm guitar or keyboard backup.

Beck had taken a back seat to Jimi Hendrix and Eric Clapton throughout the early years of rock, despite a critically acclaimed first album with Rod Stewart as the Jeff Beck Group. When the car accident prevented a Bogert-Appice-Stewart-Beck band in 1970, Beck formed a new Jeff Beck Group with bassist Clive Chapman, power drummer Cozy Powell, pianist Max Middleton, and singer Alex Ligertwood, who was soon replaced by Bobby Tench. *Rough and Ready*, the band's first album, reached #46 on the charts, which was respectable, but came nowhere close to either of Beck's top 15 rankings for his albums with Stewart, *Truth* or *Beck-Ola*. Moreover, Beck increasingly drifted toward jazz fusion, as was then best characterized by John McLaughlin and the Mahavishnu Orchestra that made its debut in 1971 and featured soon-to-be legendary players Billy Cobham on drums and Jan Hammer on

185

synthesizer. Known for his trademark double-neck guitar, McLaughlin's *Birds of Fire* album (1973) reached #15, an astounding ranking for an all-instrumental LP with no memorable single. While hardly as influential as *Bitches Brew*, trumpeter Miles Davis's double album for Columbia, *Birds of Fire* attracted many in the rock world to jazz and jazz fusion at a time when jazz musicians were still regarded with disdain in many parts of rock-dom. Jeff Beck would soon move heavily in the direction of fusion with a number of all-instrumental albums, most notably *Blow by Blow* (1975) and Wired in 1976 with Jan Hammer.

Thus, the Beck-Bogert-Appice experiment was DOA. For all Appice's skills, he was never a jazz drummer, and Bogert, at his best, played over and around Appice's drum work, much the way (though in a vastly different style) Yes bass man Chris Squire would enhance the drum work of, first, Bill Bruford then later Alan White. The same rhythm section that had turned an average boogie band like Cactus into a freight train seemed in a different studio when undergirding Beck's fanciful and often odd guitar licks. While the demise of BBA wasn't unexpected, it certainly seemed a blessing for Mark and his as-yet unproductive solo career. The boys began speaking to each other again, with Weiss providing the managerial glue to bring them together.

One significant hurdle remained: Weiss wanted Tim and Carmine to get a higher percentage than Vinny and Mark because at the time they were the hotter names. "Of course I resented it," Mark said, "but it was only for the first album and all subsequent recordings would be an equal split." Fresh off serious tax problems, Mark needed the income. By agreeing to the split, however, Mark admitted he made a mistake: "if I had told them to get fucked, it would have been equal from the get go and there was no way they would have blown out the whole deal." As matters unfolded, it was all irrelevant. In New York, Bogert became displeased with Weiss's business dealings and the band never even recorded a single track.

While in New York, however, Mark learned that Sly Stone was getting married at Madison Square Garden and that he and the other guys were invited to a reception at the Waldorf Astoria. All of rock and roll's stars turned out, and a drunken Mark Stein approached a white-haired albino fellow and blurted out, "Johnny Winter!" Instead, the man turned around to him and said, "I'm Edgar. What's up?" Mark "should have been embarrassed but was too drunk to care," waking up at Carmine's house the next day with a massive hangover. Shortly thereafter, Bogert sold his house in Oceanside, New York and moved to California where he began playing with Robin Trower. Mark, meanwhile, got a call from members of Three Dog Night, which had just broken up, and began rehearsals with Floyd Sneed and Michael Allsop. Nothing worked. The band never jelled, and again, Mark found himself without steady work.

Continuing to write, Mark peddled his stuff everywhere in Los Angeles, without success. "It seemed like every time I got close, it disappeared." Convinced that the difficulties had to do with the old Vanilla Fudge management—that he was blacklisted—Mark was referred to a deal maker named Lenny Stogel. A hustler once involved in motorcycle daredevil Evil Kneival's stunt promotions, Stogel became Mark's Manager and hooked him up with Sheldon Talmy, one of the early producers of the Who and a man with a reputation in England as a "big sound" producer. Talmy, believing in Mark's songs, financed his solo album out of his own pocket, confident he would sell it to a major label. So he hired Los Angeles session players and completed the record, but ultimately there were no bites. Stogel, however, arranged for Mark to have a personal audition with the legendary head of Arista Records, Clive Davis. Having heard the Talmy-produced record, Davis wasn't completely sold on Mark, but wanted to hear more tunes at his bungalow at the Beverly Hills Hotel (Boomerang had actually played for Davis in a private studio performance in 1971).

In a rare personal performance, Mark was convinced that his song, "The Best Years of My Life" was a hit. Davis didn't share Mark's enthusiasm. After Mark played it in the bungalow, Davis responded, "Well, you're certainly as good a musician as Barry [Manilow], but I just don't hear the big hit song. I mean, I'm not God, but that's my opinion."[37]

Instead, Davis pulled out a song by a female singer and insisted, "This record we believe is going to be a big hit." Mark wasn't impressed, and told Davis so. The record Davis played for Mark only went to #75 on the charts, leading Mark to conclude, "I might be right some of the time."

So the Stein-Stogel-Talmy team parted ways. ("The Best Years of My Life" was released in England with "The Long and Winding Road" on the B-side several years later on the Phil Spector label). About two months later Mark received a phone call. "Is this Mark Stein?" the voice asked. "Yes, you got him. Who's calling?" "It's Bud Prager and I just wanted to personally call and welcome you to Pyramid Records." Mark was befuddled. "What are you talking about?" Prager shouted, "We are very excited to welcome you aboard and I'm looking forward to meeting with you." A frustrated Mark replied, "Listen, Bud, I really haven't got a clue as to what you're talking about." Prager insisted "This has to be some kind of joke, right?" Then it dawned on Mark that Prager, the owner of the label, must have his signature on some contract. Lenny Stogel had put the deal together, but Prager and Stein suddenly realized that Stogel had forged Mark's name and received a monetary advance that was to be given to Mark less the agent's 15% commission. Both men were aghast, and they both promptly called Stogel—who was, naturally, unreachable. With such a shaky beginning, Prager lost his enthusiasm for the project, then went on to become the manager of Foreigner, one of the great groups of the 1980s.

Again disillusioned and in search of direction, Mark heard from a friend of Patty's that there was a "professor of auras" at UCLA who could help him. Mark made an appointment to see "doctor" Honduras. He asked a few general questions, then asked Mark to sit down at his desk facing him, whereupon he"rested his head into his hands and started to speak." Mark didn't say a word, yet the "professor" unveiled Mark's entire life from childhood to 1974, speaking for perhaps two hours. He told Mark that the people who were surrounding him were not good for his work, that he break the bonds and start playing with other musicians and forget the solo career. "If you do this," Honduras said, "positive things will start to happen."

A few weeks later, Mark made calls to industry people and ran into Reggie McBride, a funky bass player in Stevie Wonder's band, and soon they brought in Bobby Cochran, a guitar player that was playing with Steppenwolf from time to time and was related to Eddie Cochran who wrote "Summertime Blues." They added the up and coming popular drummer Bruce Gary and quickly put together a band before inviting John Kalodner, the head of A&R at Atlantic Records to check the group out. But without income, Reggie soon had the opportunity to play with the rapidly rising guitar star, Tommy Bolin (formerly of Zephyr and Energy, two Colorado bands). Bolin had just come off stints as the guitarist who had replaced Joe Walsh in the James Gang and Ritchie Blackmore in Deep Purple, and had played on drummer Billy Cobham's influential fusion album, Spectrum. His critically-acclaimed album, Teaser, led many to think he was the "next Hendrix."[38]

In fact, Bolin was drifting more toward the Jan Hammer/Jeff Beck/John McLaughlin jazz-fusion sound. When he put together a band to tour, McBride joined and recommended Mark. As Mark told Bolin's biographer, Greg Prato, "I wanted] to go down and play with Tommy— that would be a great way for me to get back on the road, playing with Tommy's band. . . . We played about three times before he said, "O.K., you've got the gig.'"[39]

It was a powerful group, with Narada Michael Walden on drums (Cobham's replacement at the Mahavishnu Orchestra), Norma Jean Bell on sax and vocals, and Mark and Reggie. "It was truly eclectic," Mark recalled, "and had a lot of fire." Bolin was a fan of the B-3, but Mark had already started to enhance his sound with synthesizers, getting a mini-Moog. Walden, however, operated at such a "high level of musicality" that "he would drive me almost like my Dad did when I was a kid." To break the ice before its big debut at the Roxy in Hollywood, the band broke in at La Paloma Theater in San Diego.

At the Roxy show the next night, the audience saw one of the most exciting rock/jazz fusion performances to hit the LA scene. In addition, Bolin's band played a new song penned and sung by Mark called "I Fell in Love," which reflected a strong Ray Charles-influenced arrangement with the band singing background vocals. Tommy had called the background singers the "Sniffettes," a reference to the "Raylettes." The set was graced by sparkling solos by Bolin, Narada Michael-Walden, and Mark, with an added soulful performance by the great singer and saxophone player, Norma Jean Bell.

Almost immediately, however, non-music problems interfered. Bolin had a serious drug problem with both cocaine and whiskey. At the Bottom Line Club in New York City, one of the first shows of the new tour, in front of an audience that included McLaughlin, Stanley Clark, Jan Hammer, and Peter Frampton, Bolin showed up badly impaired, drunk, and blasted from cocaine. He immediately began cursing at the audience. Nat Weiss, the president of Nemperor Records was in the club with other company executives when Bolin spotted him eating. Bolin pointed at him and shouted, "Why don't you just stick those french fries up your ass!" He was immediately dropped from the label.

Picked up by Columbia Records, Bolin and his band recorded a new album, called Private Eyes, at Cherokee Studios in Los Angeles. McBride left shortly after the album came out and Mark recommended a bass player friend named Jimmy Haslip, who "went from playing a biker bar to a gig like this in ten days"). Ironically, Haslip had honed his skills listening to Tim Bogert, as well as the Yes's Chris Squire (another "lead \bass" player), but his favorite was Motown bassist James Jamison).[40]

Haslip later studied with the great and tragic Jaco Pastorius, further refining his jazz influences. Rehearsing at the SIR soundstage, the band prepared for its first gig at Mile High Stadium in Denver, opening for Frampton who was probably the biggest star in the world at the time with his Frampton Comes Alive album (1976) topping the charts. Frampton was already flirting with disaster when it came to drugs, but had nowhere near the addiction that Bolin had. Mark recalled "A lot of people tried to talk to [Bolin], but to no avail. It was a real shame. I told him I would help him up the ladder, but not help him down."[41]

Told by the tour promoter, Barry Fey, to "be the general and keep the band focused," Mark complied—"that always came natural to me." By the time the group reached Denver, Narada had left and was replaced by Tommy's brother, Johnny Bolin.

Working with Bolin became increasingly difficult for Mark, as well as all those around the guitarist. Everyone knew about his addiction, yet no one could stop him. As Mark told Bolin's biographer, "I left the band because I was having a bit of a hard time with Tommy. . . . I felt he was going down a negative path, and I didn't feel like there was anything I could do to get him out of it . . . ."[42]

Quitting before the last tour, Mark returned home to find former Deep Purple bassist Glenn Hughes in his bed. "What's this all about?" he asked Patty. Hughes, who had dated the star of The Exorcist, Linda Blair (herself battling drugs and alcohol), had decided enough was enough with his wild girlfriend and hid out at Mark's house. Mark was a big fan of Glenn's and vice versa. When Hughes finally left, it wouldn't be the last time Mark and Glenn saw each other as they bonded. Glenn stayed with Mark and Patty for several months while he tried to iron out his affairs with Deep Purple. (He referred to them as the "purple people eaters").

Mark wanted to form a band with Hughes in the worst way, sensing their vocal and instrumental prowess could be amazing together, but it never came to pass. Hughes had a solo project waiting in the wings and needed to see it through. While all this was going on, he was seeing Bolin's girlfriend, Karen Ulibarry, who was having a difficult time with Tommy. Both found comfort from one and other and their relationship became strong, despite the demons that Glenn himself often fell prey to. Eventually they married. A short time later, Mark learned that Tommy Bolin had been found dead in a Miami hotel room. "It was a long, gloomy kind of day," Mark recalled. "Early in the evening, I put a call into the Rainbow Bar and Grill, a popular watering hole for rockers located adjacent to the Roxy on the Sunset Strip. A depressed female voice answered, and Mark said, "You really sound down. Is everything ok?" She responded, "We just found out that Tommy Bolin died." It was news that "took my breath away," Mark recalled. "I was shocked, but not surprised. Rumors flew all around relative to his death—that he was left alone to die." But it all boiled down to the same common denominator of drugs and booze that had claimed Hendrix, Joplin, Morrison and others.

The Bolin parents were in poor financial shape, and, as with so many rockers, the royalties and various concert checks seemed to vanish in promoter's pockets and white dust. Mark and Patty organized a benefit for the Bolins at the Roxy Theater in Hollywood featuring a who's who of top rock and fusion artists. The house band that Mark put together was himself on vocals and keyboards, Peter Banks of Yes on guitar, Glenn on bass and vocals, and Carmine on drums. George Duke, the great keyboardist, brought his band to perform a set. The band played songs from the Teaser album. One of the more dramatic moments of the night came when Mark and Glenn sang a duet on a Bolin-penned song called "Dreamer." The packed house also enjoyed killer solos sprinkled with a little psychedelic flavor. But the evening almost turned into a fiasco. Ritchie Blackmore's name was at the top of the marquee, but after promising to be there, he was a no-show. The crowd grew more and more impatient expecting him to perform. Ultimately, Mark had to announce that Blackmore was nowhere to be found, the audience settled down and enjoyed the talent that as there.

Glenn Hughes suffered from an addiction every bit as deadly as Bolin's. He had been recruited into Deep Purple while playing with Trapeze, and at the time was a hot bass player with a terrific rock voice. Ritchie Blackmore, Purple's guitarist, whose distinctive use of the tremolo bar characterized his memorable solos, "had been courting" Hughes since the band saw him at the famed Whiskey a Go Go.[43]

Blackmore asked Hughes to join the band—but as a bassist--- along with a new lead singer, Paul Rogers (formerly of Free). Rogers had perhaps the classic rock voice at the time, made famous by the band's hit "All Right Now." But Blackmore was too late, and Rogers formed Bad Company with Mott the Hoople's Mick Ralphs and King Crimson's Boz Burell. That left Deep Purple to find a new singer, and held auditions via tapes sent in from all over England. One grabbed the members in particular, a thick, breathy voice doing Frank Sinatra and show tunes, belonging to David Coverdale, who had answered an ad in *Melody Maker*. Instantly, the vocal combination of Hughes and Coverdale energized Deep Purple, which had for years been characterized by Ian Gillan's high-pitched screams. The band also suddenly discovered funk, as Hughes settled in with the bass.

Before long, however, Blackmore longed for the power rock sound of earlier years and left Deep Purple, leaving Hughes and Coverdale to invite Tommy Bolin into the band, producing *Come Taste the Band* (1975). A year later, Bolin was gone, forming his own band. Now Hughes and Mark were together for the benefit concert. In part, Hughes saw a mentor figure in Mark Stein: "he had been through the drugs and alcohol phase," Hughes said, and he offered an inspiration. Any strength Hughes thought Mark would supply vanished as Hughes admitted he hadn't yet fallen far enough to deal with his addiction. "I just couldn't get the sobriety that Mark found," he later observed.[44] Carmine Appice, observing Hughes, noted he "was on his way to killing himself, too. But he straightened his act out, thank God—he was an amazing

191

talent."[45]

On the night of the benefit, Hughes, high and boozed up, was backstage with Mark when a young man appeared through the door and said, "Hi, I'm Eddie Money, and I'm such a huge fan of you guys it would be an honor to go onstage and jam with you." Money was in the midst of recording his very first album at the Record Plant in Los Angeles, and had heard about the benefit and came over to help. In a thick English accent, Hughes belligerently asked, "Who are you?" The young man replied, "My name is Eddie Money." According to Mark, Hughes then said, "Take three paces toward me," looking for a fight. Mark quickly intervened, and said, "Hey, Eddie, why don't you take off, and thanks for coming." Money acknowledged the opportunity to escape a possible fight with Hughes, and left. The concert raised about $10,000 for the Bolin family, who were living in Sioux City, Iowa, and they received the check with extreme gratitude. (The evening wasn't the last Mark heard of Eddie Money: soon, while Mark was touring with Dave Mason, Eddie's album became a big hit and he opened the show for Mason at the Universal Amphitheater in Los Angeles, when he came to Mark to thank him for getting him out of the tight spot that night at the Roxy.)

The Bolin affair depressed Mark, although an opportunity arose for him to work with Carmine and Bobby Cochran to form a new band. As suddenly as that appeared, Appice got an offer to play on Rod Stewart's tour. Appice not only had landed with a name artist at the top of his career—Stewart had a string of top-selling albums, and Appice joined for the *Foot Loose & Fancy Free* album (1977) with its hits "You're In My Heart" and "Hot Legs"—but found himself writing with Stewart for the 1978 Blondes Have More Fun . . . or do they? LP when he co-penned "Do Ya Think I'm Sexy?" This "crossover" song moved Stewart into more of a dance/disco sound and the album proved Stewart's last number one album for 25 years. Stewart Mason of *Allmusic* complained that the song marked "the exact point at which it *stopped* being possible to take Rod Stewart seriously," and whined that Stewart was one of the first high-profile old-school rockers to make the leap to disco."[46]

Appice and former Cactus keyboardist Duane Hitchings also combined with Stewart to write "Young Turks" (1981) on the *Tonight I'm Yours* album. But all was not well with the Stewart-Appice relationship: Rod often referred to Carmine as "the dentist—too many fill ins," and looked to replace him on tour. (Fans of Appice would be shocked at Stewart's comments, given how incredibly reserved Appice was on the Stewart recordings!) And Stewart proved remarkably adept as an investor, unlike many rockers, investing his money in oil-lease tax shelters and property. His manager, Billy Gaff, noted "Rod isn't a rock star. He's a growth industry. . . . He doesn't invest in football clubs or crazy music- or record-financing schemes. . . . we stick to art and real estate."[47]

Stewart's transformation from Jeff Beck's frontman to crooner to glam-rocker, soon to include music videos featuring beautiful girls and blindingly rapid camera shots (which declined in total on-screen time from several seconds to fractions of a second) heralded another phase in rock music, namely the transition from something people listened to into something they watched. Certainly musical numbers on television or in the movies were nothing new. Walt Disney's "Silly Symphonies" and Warner Bros.' "Looney Tunes" and "Merrie Melodies" wove in a rich tapestry of show tunes and folk songs. Television shows such as "Hullabaloo" and "The Midnight Special" in America and "Top of the Pops" in England featured "live" rock acts lip synching music, and "The Monkees" television show (1966-1968) had mirrored the Beatles' movies on the small screen. The Beatles themselves had made promotional clips called "filmed inserts" beginning in 1965, employing top professional directors. These promos took on a life of their own, with Queen's "Bohemian Rhapsody" (1975), which appeared on "Top of the Pops," entirely shot and edited on videotape.

With the appearance in 1981 of Music Television (MTV), and the airing of "Video Killed the Radio Star," the music video entered the mainstream. MTV aired 24 hours a day, and on its August 1 debut, MTV played two different videos by Rod Stewart, as well as songs by REO Speedwagon, Pat Benatar, Styx, .38 Special, Stevie Nicks, Phil Collins, the Pretenders, Gerry Rafferty, Iron Maiden, Blondie, and many others.[48]

Rock had ceased to be dance music for kids. It now was a spectacle, complete with flashpots, dancing girls, and special effects. And no one knew special effects better than Alice Cooper. Above all, it had become apparent that rock and roll was not a single "record," but rather an entire production process from songwriter to performer to producer to management and marketing to video. Almost a decade earlier, Pete Townshend of the Who had aptly pointed this out:

> . . . the art does not just lie in the record. It lies in the whole life of the composition, through the record production, what the record says, how people react, what people dance to the record and what the record does at the time. This is what art is, and it won't really be appreciated until you can look at the whole thing in retrospect.[49]

193

In 1977, Mark, after auditioning for Seals & Crofts (who immediately disliked him when "they perched themselves next to me on the piano [and] I started singing "Summer Breeze," their hit) got a call from Bruce Gary. "I hear Alice Cooper is looking for a keyboard player for his Australian tour. I can hook you up with his guitar player, Dick Wagner," Gary said. Mark immediately went to Cherokee Studios where Wagner was laying down guitar overdubs. After a brief introduction and a short exchange, Mark left. A week later, Wagner called to offer him the gig. Mark spent a few weeks learning the "Welcome to My Nightmare" show—and with Alice, it was a show, and not just a concert. There were two separate rehearsals, Alice recalled, one for music and one for production.[50]

Typically, Alice Cooper (the band) was dominated by guitars, but "on the 'Welcome to My Nightmare' show, we had to have a lot of keyboards." Alice had taken his inspiration from Arthur Brown, who set his hair on fire and smashed guitars once a night—but then Cooper thought, "Why can't you take each song and turn each song into a story?"

In March 1977, Patty drove Mark to LAX and after a tearful goodbye, Mark headed off for a tour in the southern hemisphere for a month. Someone else was there to greet Mark at LAX, Alice's tour manager, "Fat Frankie," who said in a self-deprecating way, "I can't make a fuckin' quarter, but I'm still in the business!" They all headed to the VIP lounge, where Alice, his wife Cheryl, and the band (Whitey Glan, the drummer, Prakash John, the bass player, and guitarists Bob Kulick and Dick Wagner) were relaxing, along with the entire entourage of dancers, roadies, and the production manager. Mark was impressed: "this was a serious tour!" Another thought dawned on him: "I'm about to embark on the longest flight of my life." From Los Angeles to Honolulu, to Fiji, to Auckland, then to Sidney and Perth, the total time including stopovers was 36 hours. Throughout the flight, Frankie passed out Quaaludes, but Mark was so wired, he never slept. When he arrived, however, he found that Vanilla Fudge had quite a following in the southern hemisphere and had a big following, even seven years after their breakup. Aside from Alice, Mark was the biggest celebrity on the tour, a fact that Dick Wagner in particular didn't like. (Ironically, Rod Stewart, with Carmine on drums, had just toured Australia and set attendance records across the continent). But Alice's tour eclipsed even those records, playing Perth, Adelaide, Melbourne, Brisbane, Sydney, and Auckland, New Zealand. Abba, the Swedish hit group, followed Alice in several cities, and outside the United States were probably the

194

biggest-selling act in the world. A competition broke out between Alice's fans—waving banners, with their dark eye makeup—and Abba's fans outside the hotels and in the venues.

Mark tried to warm up to Alice on a personal level, but found it impossible. "He was not only the Super Star separating himself from the band," Mark recalled, "but he was going through a difficult time with alcohol." Mark would enter his room to find the shelves lined with bottles of VO: "he was living on beer and whiskey." His weight had plunged, and at times Alice would forget lyrics or lose track of where he was in the show. But the band covered for him and the shows always came off. "The visual effects of 'Welcome to My Nightmare' were awesome," Mark noted, and "the whole performance took you on a journey throughout Alice's Nightmare from start to finish—all coordinated into an extravaganza of madness and mayhem."[51]

Toward the end of the tour, in Melbourne, Mark had fallen asleep before the bus was to take the band to the event. Frankie had not woken him! Mark ran down to the front desk and asked where the band was, and was told they had left. In a panic, Mark hailed a cab and jetted off to the gig, wondering how Frankie could have abandoned him. "I never realized until that moment how much Fat Frankie must have resented me for not sharing the success I had with Vanilla Fudge years earlier. Meanwhile, Mark got to know the manager, Shep Gordon, who seemed to have a great style and hoped Gordon would become his manager. (Gordon, it should be noted, was an amateur photographer who documented the fall of the Soviet empire).

The tour ended, and Mark endured a horrible flight back to the States. He was promised the Alice Cooper tour for the following summer. Back with his family, Mark heard that Wagner had replaced him. Angered and hurt, he called Alive Management to learn what had happened, and he kept getting shunted off to Wagner—who never returned his calls. Mark never got a call from Wagner himself, though he had heard from a drummer friend, Jan Uvena, that Wagner was overheard at the Troubadour Club discussing the upcoming tour, noting that he was sick of the press constantly bringing up Mark's name. Alice had different recollections of the re-shuffling of the band, insisting that the "Welcome to My Nightmare" tour was an anomaly, and that typically he didn't use keyboards in the band, only guitars. But Mark found that reasoning dubious on several levels, including the fact that Alice's drinking frequently kept him from being aware of internal band issues, but also because subsequent tours used keyboardists. Whatever the truth, years later Alice spoke highly of Mark and cited the Fudge as one of his early influences.

In between tours, Mark continued to write, inspired by the new rock fusion music of Jeff Beck's *Blow by Blow* album. Jan Hammer, the master of the mini moog synthesizer, influenced Mark during this time and he practiced intensely on the synthesizer. Of course, by then Keith Emerson, with Emerson, Lake, and Palmer, had taken synthesizer playing to a whole new level, surrounding himself in concert with batteries of electronic keyboards. Mark wrote up a new batch of songs and with the help of the by-then legendary producer Andy Johns, recorded a new demo at Conway Studios in Los Angeles with Jimmy Haslip on bass and Jan Uvena on drums. The owner, "Buddy" Brundo, was so impressed with the sound the band came up with that he used the demo to play for prospective clients, booking a lot of sessions.

Meanwhile, Mark was again looking for employment after the Alice summer show cancellation. He called Les Dudek, a great West Coast guitarist who was signed to Columbia Records and was managed by Jason Cooper Jabre Management, whose stable included Ron Wood and Dave Mason. Mark played the Conway demo for Les, who gave it to Jason. Before Mark knew it, Jason was on the phone, asking for Mark to play the tunes live at his house. When they got together, Mark played a song called "Life is a Ladder" and hadn't finished the third verse before Jason said, "I want to manage you! I'm wired with Columbia, and all I've got to do is make a phone call and you'll have a solo deal!" He proceeded to call Michael Dilbeck, the West Coast A&R man for Columbia, then called Dave Mason and set up a meeting with Mark, explaining Mason needed a keyboard player and had a tour coming up. While Cooper set up the solo deal for Mark, he could play Dave Mason's tour. Literally, within a single day, Mark had a tour with Mason booked and apparently had a solo deal in the works.

He went to the Record Plant, to meet Dave who was in the midst of recording a new album produced by Ron Nevison. They put up a track and asked Mark to lay down an organ part and everything fit. "It was all so natural, they loved it," Mark recalled. Dave asked Mark to come by his house the next day. His home, called "Mariposa De Oro," was nestled in the Malibu hills. Decorated with fine Mexican tiles, with beautiful colors and dynamic archways, which then led to a main room that had ceilings as high as you could see, Mark thought he'd walked into a king's castle. "He had beautiful woodwork, rugs from Persia, velvet couches, tapestries, and window treatments to die for," Mark observed. "Best of all as a nine-foot Steinway Grand Piano and set up on the far wall was the biggest JBL sound system you ever saw." Mason wanted Mark to tour with him, and even though that particular tour was heavily acoustic, Mason told Mark to enhance the sound with organ, piano, and synthesizer.

Also on the tour, Jerry Williams, a talented singer-songwriter from Texas, had written a few tunes on the new album and was himself poised to get a solo deal. Jason Cooper was behind him, so Williams and Stein became the backup duo—"sweet musically," as Mark noted, but "a bit strange." Mark had to cover the bass with his left hand, and it "crimped my style" a little, he recalled. Before long, tension built between Mark and Williams, with his "backwoods Texas crap" coming out, mixed with cynicism and hostility. Moreover, he and Mason were tied through their songwriting and through their cocaine use. The band shared the stage for perhaps a dozen shows with Kenny Loggins and his band—always a "cool customer, a great performer, and a respectful guy." Loggins's guitarist knew all the Vinny Martell licks from Vanilla Fudge and got a kick out of playing them at the sound checks. Nevertheless, by the time the tour ended, Mark and Mason were not on the best of terms, convincing Mark it was again time to pursue a solo career.

Back in Reseda, he worked on new material with Jason, when a call came from Dave Mason's tour manager, "Skinny" (Jim Marcott). Mason was preparing a new show, and again wanted Mark in the band—but this act was a six-piece rockin' band which fit Mark to a "T". This time, a close relationship developed between Mark and Dave Mason, and several tours followed over the next two years.

During one tour, while in New York, Mason and Mark were at a popular night club called Tracks, where all the rockers used to hang out. Meat Loaf came over to the table and told the group that he had just gotten a record deal and was going to record his album. Paul Stanley from KISS looked on from an adjacent table. Sitting across the table from Mark was a familiar face, but Mark couldn't place it. "Where do I know you from?" Mark asked. "You look really familiar." The person scowled back at Mark, and Mark repeatedly questioned him, saying, "Did we go to school together or something?" Finally, in a huff, the young man got up and stalked away. Mason turned to Mark, asking, "What the hell is the matter with you? That's John Belushi!" A mortified, embarrassed—and drunk—Mark Stein didn't know what to do. But a short time later, Mason and Mark jammed on stage playing "Feelin' Alright" (which Mason wrote), with Belushi doing his famous Joe Cocker impression that he popularized on "Saturday Night Live," and all ended well.

Dave Mason and Mark also collaborated on several tunes, and Mark's keyboards and vocals are clear on Mason's exceptional rendition of Carole King's song, "Will You Still Love Me Tomorrow?" At nights,

Mark hung out with Mason and the "Malibu Colony Crowd," actor Ryan O'Neal and his future wife Farah Fawcett, Dan ("Grizzly Adams") Haggerty and his wife, Diane. Moreover, eventually Mark made his solo record with Dave Mason producing it. Columbia put up $175,000 for the budget and gave Mark a $50,000 advance—still good money at the time. He hired great players, including Les Dudek, Bill Meeker on drums, and Reggie McBride on bass, cutting the recording at the Record Plant. Jimmy Haslip also showed up to do some bass tracks, and saxophonist Tom Scott and Steve Cropper of Stax fame both laid down tracks. But Mason continued his hard partying, often showing up late for sessions until Mark finally lost his temper and chewed him out. To his astonishment, Mason replied to Mark, "I've been waiting a long time for you to say that to me!"

During the recording period, Dave Mason played a show at the Greek Theater in Los Angeles, and had Mark's record played over the house PA system as people filed in. That night, Mason featured Mark on a few songs, including "I Fell In Love," a Ray Charles-influenced blues tune that he played with Tommy Bolin and was now on his Columbia solo LP (which was not yet released). The song featured female backup singers accompanying Mark as he sang at the grand piano. Steven Stills even jumped on stage and joined in on "I Fell In Love." Mark was again on top of the world.

It was the summer of 1978 and life was good. The tours with Dave Mason continued, the band was rockin', and had great vocals. They played scores of college concerts throughout the spring, but with summer upon them, they played outdoors. Racking up thousands of miles on the private plane, a four-engine Viscount with the interior set up like a living room, complete with bar and a VCR, the band was livin' it up. Moreover, they never had to worry about being at an airport at a certain time to catch a flight. Instead, they traveled at their own convenience. Occasionally, they took a bus, as Mark recalled, "across the glorious United States of America." When they played Central Park in New York City, their home was the Plaza Hotel. Mason treated his band with great generosity. Each member had his own limo if he wanted; the pay was great, the per diems were good, and half the time Mason picked up the tab anyway if the band was eating together. "We Just Disagree" was a top five single for Mason, and his albums sold well. In those days, Columbia and all the major labels spent wads of money on promotion and tour support for artists and, like the LP "Let It Flow,"so did the blow! Pablo Escobar, the most powerful drug lord of the decade, had sold his cocaine via Columbia to North America in a big way, and it infiltrated the recording industry from artists to executives across the board. The stuff was everywhere!

One balmy afternoon at Belmont Racetrack, Mason and the band played to thousands. Mark had a few days off, so after the concert, he planned to go over to Bayonne to spend an evening with his parents. His cousins Linda and Barry Wiener came to the show and they offered to give Mark a ride. Barry drove a Cadillac Coupe De Ville and, fifteen minutes into the trip on the Long Island Expressway, they got a flat tire. Barry pulled the car over to the shoulder of the highway and Mark jumped out. "I'll fix it," he said. "Used to do this all the time growin' up!" The flat was on the left rear tire and Mark grabbed the jack out of the trunk and hoisted the car up. What was about to happen was an incident he never forgot. After loosening the lug nuts, he began to pull the tire off and the jack slipped! His left arm was caught in between the top of the tire and the wheel well. The weight of the monster resting on his forearm was unbearable, and he screamed in agony as his cousins looked on in horror! The pain was excruciating. Desperately, Barry and Linda tried to lift the back of the Cadillac up to relieve some of the pressure, but to no avail. "This is the end," Mark thought. "I'm going to lose my arm. My playing days are over!"

As cars whizzed by, Mark's arm went numb, but just as he was about to pass out, an oil truck pulled over behind them and the driver jumped out, grabbed his jack, and by the grace of God lifted the back of the car up and got Mark out. The man helped Mark to the side and asked if he was alright. In a daze, Mark looked at his arm and it was dented in just over the ulna or forearm bone, the one to the right that leads straight to the wrist. Before Mark could thank the Samaritan, he was back in his truck pulling onto the expressway and was gone in a flash. Like the "Lone Ranger," the trucker was Mark's angel. Barry drove Mark directly to the Bayonne Hospital where his arm was x-rayed and, incredibly enough, showed no break. He had sustained nothing more than a bad bruise. After spending the day with his parents, Mark was back on the road and played the next show without missing a beat. He was amazed at how lucky he had been that day.

Yet it was all about to come apart again. Barry Rothman, Mark's attorney who negotiated the Columbia deal as well as a big potential publishing deal with April Blackwood, brought up the fact that he found $100,000 for bassist Noel Redding of the Jimi Hendrix Experience. Rothman thought he could do the same for Mark, as Vanilla Fudge had been a part of that same management group 10 years earlier. Mark reluctantly approved it, knowing it might mean eventually tying back in with the mob. After the Greek Theater gig, Jason told Mark he and Dave were heading for New York to meet with Jack Craigo, the head of A&R

199

at Columbia to pick the first single from Mark's album. A week later, Jason called to say there would not be a single, and that Columbia wasn't going to release anything at all, deciding to scrap the whole project. This stunned Mark: Columbia had already spent a quarter of a million dollars and had added money to the artwork budget. "My gut reaction," Mark dourly noted, "was that it had something to do with Rothman trying to find those possible hidden funds." In fact, Mark learned that Craigo listened to the album and had nothing positive to say, but that Mason stood up for Mark, telling Craigo he had "cloth ears," but to no avail. A week later, Mark opened Billboard to see Craigo and former Fudge business manager Steve Weiss shaking hands on a new deal they were putting together. Whether that had anything to do with axing Mark was never determined, but Mark remained convinced that something had occurred.

The Malibu that Mark Stein encountered with Dave Mason and his movie star friends reflected another new reality, not just in music, but throughout entertainment: cocaine had replaced both the "lighter" drug, marijuana, and the heavier drug, heroin, as the pharmaceutical of choice. While there had been some horror stories associated with coke, its dangers as a powerfully addictive drug were often still ignored or downplayed among the gliteratti. Crack cocaine remained a slavemaster of the lower classes—although from time to time one heard desperate tales of rich kids who destroyed their lives with the drug.

Even that part of rock and roll, however, had begun to change. The "holy trinity" of sex, drugs, and rock and roll was under assault from . . . life. Widespread, indiscriminate sex now had to deal with the AIDs virus and the epidemic of sexually-transmitted diseases, not to mention the explosion in illegitimate children. Veterans of drug use struggled to get clean and sober. Pete Townshend found that "instead of a night's lovely planeing out, nice colorful images," what followed was "a week of trying to replace your ego [and] remember who you were . . . ."[52]

The corpses of Hendrix, Morrison, Joplin, and the leftover shells of musicians such as Skip Spence constituted flashing red warning signs that, in fact, drug use came with severe consequences. Mark had learned this lesson the hard way—not as hard as many, but not without pain, either. As Grace Slick said, by the 1980s, "you couldn't go screw everybody, unless of course you're brain-dead and you want to die. And you can't go around taking a lot of drugs: it's not cool. People think you're a jerk. And both of those things are a lot of fun to do. I'm glad I had that opportunity. I enjoyed it thoroughly."[53]

Yet Slick herself had to battle for sobriety, and often the fond memories survivors had were just that—fond memories by those who had not paid as high a price as others. Clapton was already fighting alcoholism; Mark had weaned himself from amphetamines; and one was as likely to find a rock star in a rehab center in the late 1970s and early 1980s as on a concert stage. Pete Townshend, once an avid pot proselytizer, expressed his moment of self-awareness with drugs as a betrayal, when he "found I could give it up just like that [snapping his fingers]. When I realized that everything I'd been crediting to pot was nothing at all to do with it, the fact that I could write a song or play guitar or have a good time at a party or enjoy a satisfying sexual relationship [without it]."[54] It bothered him that "everybody credited everything innovative and exciting to drugs."

The Airplane experienced another, different new reality facing the Golden Age rockers when they played in Germany in 1978, Slick had food poisoning and refused to perform. At first, when the musicians explained that there would be no show, the fans seemed resigned. But when the promoters came to the stage, a riot ensued. The crowd stormed the stage, one person had an axe and began chopping up the drums, another poured gas over the shattered drum set and started it on fire, then when firemen showed up, the mob threw bricks at the firemen. This shook the Airplane: "in the '60s and early '70s, Jefferson Airplane had been no stranger to unruly audiences. But now the band—not the police, not the government—was the intended target [and the Airplane itself] had become the pigs."[55]

This itself proved unsettling, but more disconcerting was the awareness that it had been a decade since some of the rockers had their greatest hits, and while they continued to attract their similarly-aging audiences, "the kids" often wanted something new and different. Athletes' career spans were adumbrated—National Football League running backs have an average career of less than three years, and "old" in the NFL is 30—but for rockers, a 26-year-old could easily be a has-been. It did not frustrate all of them: Townshend insisted "I'm very old-fashioned. I've seen and done it all in a lot of ways, and I've come back full circle to being right in the middle of the road. And that's not as boring as it sounds. It's terribly exciting, like a revelation, to find that there is a middle of the road."[56]

One could almost hear the screams of hair follicles being torn out of Abbie Hoffman's head! More amazing still, Townshend said this in the early 1970s, before many of the rockers would reach the same conclusions.

Part of the transformation could be blamed on the evolution of rock itself. With the need for more Alice Cooper-type shows, with Keith Emerson mounting a grand piano that was lifted off the stage and spun around, or Pink Floyd deliberately shaping their musical stories, stage lights, and effects to enhance the experience of someone on drugs, audiences grew more passive. As Dave Marsh, the Who's biographer put it, rock had "deliberately incapacitated itself."[57]

Traditional expressions of appreciation for groups that had done something exceptional—the standing ovation, kids rushing the stage—became de rigeur, to the point that seats in concert settings became entirely useless. In one sense, it constituted a form of returning the rock experience to a dance experience, and this was nowhere more true than in the punk clubs, where teens bopped up and down for hours, with bands almost irrelevant. The bigger the show, the less involved the audience was. But the less involved the audience, the more the performers lamented that they "couldn't connect," or that rock had become "too commercial." In the early 1970s, the response had been to record a live album, which captured the energy and audience interaction of the concert. But the 1980s had a "been there, done that" approach to live albums.

As rock changed yet again, Mark Stein had concluded that perhaps his time as a rocker had ended, and he entered an entirely new, and different, world of music: writing and performing commercial ads. A decade earlier, he would have been labeled a "sell-out," but as many of the Golden Age performers found, staying in the business demanded flexibility. More important, the sound of rock—even if watered down and temporized into the "pop" tunes that many rockers had blown off as "bubble gum" music earlier—was integrating itself into the culture as no music in history ever had before. And Mark's flirtation with jingle writing would in fact demonstrate the incredible triumph of rock over all other music forms in America . . . and the world.

YOU KEEP ME HANGIN' ON

Chapter Seven

Even as the "big-hair" metal of 1980s rock wound down, fundamental and massive changes were occurring in American music—not just in the performance and style of music, but in the marketing and selling of the product. Those changes would affect the industry for the next 20 years and beyond, and possible even end the modern record business as it existed in the 1980s. For the first time in his rock career, Mark Stein sat out many of these changes. Efforts to re-form Vanilla Fudge had shipwrecked, his solo career had stagnated, his attempts to form new bands or join existing ones had not borne fruit, and his experience in the jingle business was ultimately short-lived.

After practically a lifetime of touring, recording, collaborating, and jingle-writing, Mark decided to take a sabbatical. He wanted time to renew and recharge, and figure out his next career steps, to the point that he went into seclusion. Hardly had he dreamed that this hiatus would last a decade. During that time, he was introduced to philanthropic efforts, raising money for community efforts through newspapers that represented Jewish, African-American, Latin and even environmental groups. Mark learned to sell advertising space, garnering corporate ad support for the papers. He found he was "really good at it—I learned the corporate structures of the Fortune 500 and became very comfortable talking to marketing executives up and down the food chain." Mark sold to CEOs, marketing communications managers, human resource directors, even calling public relations directors at major colleges and universities.[1]

With a rising economy, Mark earned huge commissions while keeping the presses rolling. As the technology boomed, he set up an office in his home. This was becoming a common occurrence in the business world, enabled by advances in computers, phones, and fax machines. Invoices, letters, bills, and musical scores could all be transmitted in minutes. Processing power of computers soared as their prices plummeted. Indeed, by the mid-1990s, microprocessor chips cost a fraction of a cent, and both the computer and the internet spread to one-quarter of the American population faster than any other technology in history until the cellular telephone.[2]

(Intel alone knocked out a series of chip improvements that improved processing power by 1000 percent in less than seven years!)[3] By 1996, with the "Pentium" chip, processors ran at quadruple the speed of the previous chip. It took the computer only 16 years to spread to one-quarter of all Americans; the internet, seven.[4]

Mark took full advantage of the new digital age and best of all, he was all over the phone and incognito. Little did those on the other end of the line know they were talking to a 60s rock legend! As Mark put it, "I put my life as a singer/musician on the back burner but became a director of community relations and advertising, helping to keep corporate America at the forefront of philanthropic efforts." With his new (stable!) income, and confronted with the realities of money management, Mark started to learn first-hand about finance and investing. He diversified his portfolio and rode the booming stock market, which had continued to soar through the Clinton years, both on the back of the Reagan tax cuts and on the opening of new markets in the former Soviet bloc—a bloc that rock helped break up. And for once, Mark was no longer at the mercy of promoters, agents, or managers. Patty had taken over some of his management, and with her knowledge of the law, could read a contract as well as anyone. Repeatedly, offers came to Mark to tour and to become involved in music, but he passed. That didn't mean he didn't keep his skills up, practicing several times a week, arranging, and writing. But it was only for his own pleasure and that of his family and friends.

Reflecting on his beginnings in music, he observed "That's how the whole damn thing got started," playing for the pure joy of playing. Everyone in the Pigeons all fantasized about being rich and famous, but "as young rockers, we didn't have the financial pressures that come with 'growing up.' It was really for the joy of playing. . . . And that's what promoters, managers, and agents all preyed upon."

While Mark retreated into seclusion, the music industry—on the

205

surface—entered a golden age of sales that seemed endless. Instead, American rock music was heading for a cliff in a kayak, and only the shrewdest and most talented performers and executives would be around to talk about it 15 years later. No fewer than eight major changes hit the music business in a single decade.

First came massive format changes. The recording industry, like television, had survived critical format changes. By the 1980s, 33 1/3 rpm "long play" record albums, which were already being edged out by cassette tapes, now had a new competitive format, the compact discs (CDs). Cassettes had not harmed the music industry, even though it was possible to make a copy of a cassette and share it free with another person. Nevertheless, many predicted CDs would "kill" the industry. For one thing, CDs did not scratch easily and were quite durable, whereas the old LPs warped quickly in the sun, seemed to scratch at the drop of a hat, and slid out of their jacket sleeves all too easily. As the phrase implied, compact discs were, well, compact: they fit in a 5" x 4" plastic container called a "jewel case," which flipped open at one end and which sealed itself reliably. Album artwork—which much condensed (often to the point of needing a magnifying glass to read the print)—still remained a marketing feature, and was tucked inside the plastic case. Suddenly, the space needed to house walls of albums could be consolidated into a couple of CD "towers," plastic stands that could hold 50, 100, or several hundred CDs; or the discs could be crammed en masse into traditional bookshelves. And contrary to early warnings, CDs actually touched off a boom in the recording industry. From a peak of $4.13 billion in sales in 1978, the record industry experienced declines to only $3.81 billion by 1983, despite price hikes, MTV, and the phenomenal success of Michael Jackson.[5]

While the CDs brought inherent advantages in reduced shipping, storage, and shelf costs, and in durability, their smaller size and plastic containers diminished the tactile and visual satisfaction of flipping through albums and admiring the artwork. Albums, once a package of which the record itself was a part—the most important part, but nevertheless not the entire consumed item—gave way to jewel boxes that had far less collector appeal. (Few people mounted autographed CD jewel cases in wall displays, for example). As to the cost efficiencies, consumers never saw any savings. Quite the contrary, record companies charged anywhere from $12 to $16 for a typical CD, well above the cost of an old-fashioned album. Profits for the record companies rose in the 1990s, pointing to rosy times ahead (see Figure 1, "Record Industry Statistics in the 1990s").

Fig. 1, Record Industry Statistics in the 1990s

Year	Total Dollars (millions)	New Releases	Dollars per release (thousands)
1992	9024	18400	490
1993	10046	20300	495
1994	12068	36600	330
1995	12320	30200	408
1996	12533	30200	415
1997	12236.8	33700	363
1998	13723	33100	414
1999	14651	38900	376
2000	14404	27000	533
2001	13700	27000	507

Source: Recording Industry Association of America, various years)

While total sales rose—then stagnated---the number of new releases, which hit 36,000 by mid-decade, sharply dropped, recovering only once again in 1999 before fall by 30% in 2000 and 2001. The threat of 'ripping" or pirating music still substantially lay in the future, but in the early 1990s, CD sales concealed important self-inflicted wounds on the record industry. Indeed, by 1992, the recording industry had the highest rate of pretax operating income growth in the communications industry.[6]

Along with the demise of the album cover as an enhanced part of the product, another crucial loss for the industry in the transition from vinyl records to cassettes and CDs was the disappearance of the 45 rpm single, which served as an introduction to music for many youths. "That's the entry-level purchase everyone makes; when I was young, you could buy two singles for a dollar." said Joe Kvidra, GM of Tower Records store in Chicago.[7]

Yet singles were ditched without serious strategic planning by industry execs, and the industry was only saved by accident when individual downloads and pirated music led to listeners purchasing entire albums.

A second major change, which constituted a larger ongoing problem than the shift to CDs was likewise not widely appreciated even by experts on the history of the record industry, involved major changes in what would appear to be an unrelated entertainment medium, children's cartoons. Classic Bugs Bunny, Daffy Duck, other Warner Brothers cartoons, as well as some other animated works, incessantly employed the music of Tin Pan Alley from generations before. Every child heard Bugs Bunny sing, "I dream of Jeannie, she's a light brown hare," or Daffy croon "When the swallows come back to Capistrano." Music of the 1930s, '40s, and '50s thus made a transition to kids of the

'60s and '70s. But as the studios sought to contain costs, they began to drop the song references; and with the politically correct movement of the 1980s, traditional and classic songs that might have been deemed offensive or racist were likewise torn from the process of passing along those parts of the nation's music history. Where show tunes and "easy listening" hits of earlier years were internalized by the kids of the 1960s, rock and roll missed an opportunity to sell itself to the kids born after 1970 in the same way.

Still another transformation—a third important shift under way since the 1960s—involved the way in which professional songwriters were replaced by artist/performers, was nearly complete. Major recording companies of the 1950s worked with a stable of songwriters whose job was to write songs that people liked, not necessarily songs that came from their soul.[8]

Beginning with the sheet music business of the late 1800s, the song industry had employed "pluggers" to sing the company's latest works in public places such as theaters or parks—and sing them, and sing them. Music critics complained that the music companies thus concocted and controlled music, and that it "really didn't come from the people." In fact, very few people have original song ideas, which is precisely why, when someone comes up with a catchy tune or interesting riff, it catches on like wildfire. Far from brainwashing people into accepting songs they didn't want, the music industry introduced people to music they could not create themselves because they lacked the talent.

Professional songwriters, usually instructed to write their tunes for men and women, and without particular emphasis on age, produced some of the most lasting music in American history. Virtually all of the "easy listening" hits of the 1950s, including the top songs of Frank Sinatra, Dean Martin, Tony Bennett, Rosemary Clooney, Patty Page, Perry Como, Bing Crosby, and many others, were penned by the pros at Tin Pan Alley. These songs then became a part of popular culture because of their easy access to everyone—then were spread throughout society via cartoons, advertisements, television, and movies. While many of the hits of the crooners invited slow dancing, the songs were perfectly fitted to become "elevator music," or piped instrumental music used as background in elevators, shopping malls, grocery stores, and offices.

The idea originated with an artilleryman, Major General George Squier, in the 1920s, and he received several patents for the transmission of information signals over electrical lines. Seeing the potential to deliver music without the radio, Squier lacked the capital to fund a project himself, so he teamed with North American Company and created Wired Radio as an affiliate. In the process, he coined the term

"Muzak" (combining music and Kodak cameras). It took a decade to get the technology on the market and test it. A trial run in Lakeland, Ohio revealed that for-pay music would have a tough time competing in the general market with music that came free over the radio, so Wired Radio shifted gears and sold its service to restaurants and hotels. A New York City restaurant received the first Muzak system in 1936, relying on a host of record players spinning vinyl records at a central office. After World War II, William Benton purchased the company and began to experiment with "stimulus progression," or the use of music to improve productivity in the workplace.[9]

Some studies showed that "stimulus progression" lowered blood pressure and heightened productivity through deliberate increases in the intensity level of the music. But in the 1950s, some accused the company of using music to brainwash people, and several unsuccessful legal actions were brought against Muzak.[10]

Developing a style that was deliberately bland and unobtrusive, so as to enhance shoppers' or diners' experience without diverting their attention, Muzak was nearly invisible everywhere except on elevators (where there was nothing else to listen to, hence, "elevator music"). By the 1980s, some 80 million people heard Muzak in one form or another every day, and Muzak was even piped aboard the Apollo XI spacecraft that took Neil Armstrong to the moon.

To rockers like Mark Stein, Muzak was an abomination. He called it a "homogenized" performance of songs "to the point of silliness. If an artist wanted to delete the soul and energy from their work, simply put in the hands of Muzak or more appropriately termed soundtracks for bored elevator riders." Strangely enough, though, Muzak constituted a critical litmus test for the longevity of songs. Rock and roll was both a physical (dance) and aural (listening) music form, and young people experienced it in both contexts. Some bands (Pink Floyd, King Crimson) were "experience" bands, meant to be absorbed with good weed in darkened rooms. A few, such as the Grateful Dead, provided low-key rock that stoned listeners could move to without the threat of harming themselves. Others—Sly and the Family Stone, Kool and the Gang, Bruce Springsteen, K.C. and the Sunshine Band—overwhelmingly were "dance" acts, meant to get people up and moving. Most bands of the '60s, '70s, and '80s had sought a happy medium, mixing high-energy dance numbers with ballads or "message" music. (It greatly bothered hard rockers Aerosmith that "Angel," their 1988 song, was their highest rated single to that date at #3, was a ballad). No one wanted to sink too far into the drug-music genre, for an audience wasn't always going to have marijuana (or something harder) handy; and no one wanted to blast,

blast, blast all the time.

But what the rockers discovered, beginning with some of the earliest hits of the Beatles, was that songs that had clearly identifiable melodies were suddenly showing up in elevators! Depressing as that may have been to many '60s and '70s rock and rollers, in truth it constituted a major achievement, because it meant that their music had made the transition from dance music to plain old music. One no longer move to the tunes---and as the fans of the 1960s aged, many could no longer move to the groove. Sly Stone's famous admonition to "dance to the music" in some cases could only generate a little stationary wiggling and energetic toe-tapping. The souls were willing but . . . .

And yet even without the cartoon-crossover process, the popularity and even the dominance of the 1960s, 1970s and early 1980s rock songs was increasing as the Baby Boomers aged. This was due to a fourth transformative factor: where children's cartoons once transmitted music of one generation to the next, now Madison Avenue perpetuated the songs of the Golden Age of rock through its commercials. Often, advertisers used the performance of the original artist for these classics. Perhaps no one proved more identifiable in this new medium than rocker Bob Seeger, whose song "Like a Rock" became the anthem for Chevrolet pickups. But beginning in the 1990s, songs such as "Don't Stop Believin'" by Journey, "Major Tom," by the Shiny Toy Guns, Madonna's "Ray of Light" were used to hawk products. As early as 1985, Burger King used Aretha Franklin's "Freeway of Love," and in 1987, Nike employed the Beatles' "Revolution" to sell food and shoes. Phillips Electronics also used the Beatles' "Getting Better" for its electronics, and H&R Block employed the groups' "Taxman" (an attack on the government) to identify the tax preparation fellow as the "taxman." Microsoft (the Rolling Stones' "Start Me Up"), Apple (U2's "Vertigo"), Toyota ("Let Your Love Flow" by the Bellamy Brothers), State Farm Insurance ("Point of No Return," by Kansas), Nissan (Nazareth's "Love Hurts"), the New York Stock Exchange ("Right Here, Right Now," the Fatboy Slim version), and Volkswagen (Styx's "Mr. Roboto"). Kentucky Fried Chicken sold drumsticks to Lynyrd Skynrd's "Sweet Home Alabama," and televisions were marketed by Best Buy to Cheryl Crow's "Soak up the Sun." Autos, especially, seemed a perfect fit for rock music, with General Motors selling Cadillacs to Led Zeppelin's "Rock and Roll," and Nissan promoting its Maxima to the Who's "We Won't Get Fooled Again."

Critics sometimes complained that the songs' lyrics or the songwriters' intentions actually clashed with the products they marketed—Iggy Pop's "Lust for Life," about shooting heroin, was used to advertise Royal Caribbean Cruise Lines, whose largest stash of drugs is in the ship's dispensary. Wrangler jeans used Creedence Clearwater Revival's anti-war "Fortunate Son" to sell bluejeans—waving against the backdrop of an American flag, no less. And one of the classic, mismatches, but effective commercials, was Mercedes Benz employing the Janis Joplin song "Mercedes Benz," which was a critique of materialism. Yet the critics miss the some obvious conclusions: as noted earlier, "protest music" often was popular in spite of the lyrics, and studies showed that often kids didn't have a clue what the songs were actually about. More important, advertisers knew that music, which came into the human body via the ear—an "organ conditioned first and foremost by emotional response"—found that they could achieve instant emotional connections by harkening back to the music of the Baby Boomer's teen years.[11]

Thus critics essentially were whining that the music they had once celebrated as being so effective, precisely because "back then" it appealed to raw emotion, was still effective and for the same reasons. Indeed, the Golden Age rock music continued to provide a lift to the industry as a whole.

The aging Baby Boom generation, which continued not only to consume music at higher rates than past 40-, 50-, and 60-year-olds, but who passed that music along to their children. The result was an astounding revival of "classic rock" to a generation of kids who had never heard the songs. Classic rock stations provided one of the few successful music competitors to talk radio. When Capitol released a three-double CD collection of Beatles' songs, called *Anthology*, 40% of the sales were to teens and young adults not even alive when the Beatles first recorded their songs. The album sold five million copies.[12]

Taking advantage of the demand for classic/Golden Age rock, entrepreneurs found another new medium in the field of direct marketing through Home Shopping Network and QVC. Mark's old acquaintance, Denny Somach, pioneered the direct marketing of music in 1989 when he produced a music infomercial for Golden Age classics, hiring famous deejay Wolfman Jack to pitch the 50,000 copies. It was so successful, he produced a second one with Don Kirshner.[13]

If these had been the only changes in rock music, they alone would have constituted a transformation greater than anything since the arrival of the Beatles. But there were still other major shifts occurring in modern rock music, none more important than the fifth development, the consolidation of the recording industry into five major conglomerates. By the late 1990s, these five dominated the $14.6 billion-a-year record industry, accounting for 62% of the gross revenue in the $10 billion commercial radio business.[14]

Strangely, however, the larger the music companies got, the more invisible they became, continuing a trend that started with the sheet music publishing business. Virtually no one bought a CD because it was on Columbia or Reprise.[15]

Contrary to popular perceptions, payola had never really ended. Instead, the record companies worked their hit-making magic through "independent promoters," who got paid directly from the label and who dispensed goodies such as concert tickets or artist gear to the deejays. As music columnist Greg Kot wrote, an "independent promoter got paid an additional $2,500 from the label [if a song made the top 40 and] if it went top 10, that ratcheted up the price to $5,500. Even something as trivial as boosting a song's profile by adding five to seven spins a week could cost the label an additional $500 per station."[16]

Eventually, the pressed record executives begged Congress for relief from their own sins. Clear Channel president and CEO Mark Mays noted the irony: "For years the record companies . . . have complained about paying the promoters but have also refused to stop paying them. Instead of disciplining themselves to break the pattern, they are asking Congress to do it for them."[17]

One researcher stated that it was common for a label to spend more than $1 million in promotion costs for a single by a major artist, and "marketing expenses—including radio promotion money—for multiplatinum albums by singers such as Alicia Keys and Jennifer Lopez could range upward of $14 million."[18]

Before Congress could act, New York's publicity-seeking attorney general, Eliot Spitzer, started high-profile investigations of payola in the Empire State that resulted in the major music companies admitting they slipped cash to programmers and agreed to pay fines of $31 million. Three years later, Clear Channel, CBS Radio, and Citadel also paid $12.5 million in fines and to allow closer scrutiny of their labels.[19]

The consolidation of radio, combined with the listening habits of Americans, led to a sixth industry change. AM radio, which in the 1960s and 1970s had dominated music listening, and which had provided the primary way in which record companies introduced new acts to the public, had faced a decline in listenership since the advent of FM radio, with its freer formats. The availability of FM radios, both hand-held versions and in cars, ended AM's dominance and was viewed as "edgier." But both formats had to compete with television, where MTV was now not just supplementing the record business, but in some ways competing with it. AM radio lost its clout, and began desperately searching for new audiences. As the Boomers got older, they took more of an interest in politics, and "talk radio." The so-called "Fairness Doctrine," which had required radio shows to provide equal air time for all views, was repealed in 1987, but its ability to control on-air opinions was already fading.

Into the breach stepped people such as Morton Downey, Jr., who pioneered an aggressive and often abrasive talk format in Sacramento, California. Fired in 1983, he was replaced by Rush Limbaugh, who would go on to have the most popular radio show in history. Meanwhile, talk formats began to spread and rock was bumped. Rock music stations slowly disappeared. Clear Channel Communications began to purchase stations across the country, further shifting to talk formats. By the late 1990s, Clear Channel owned 1200 radio stations that covered 247 of the top 250 markets in the country. It attracted massive new audiences in the 25-50 age group, but teen listenership fell by 11% in the decade and the 18-24 age group fell by 14%.[20]

When Clear Channel acquired SFX Entertainment, the largest concert-touring firm in the nation, the cost of CDs spiked to $19 from $14, and concert tickets rose by and average of $10 to $44.

Yet the sad fact was that AM radio's time had passed when it came to music. The top 40 format had failed to capture a burst of new bands, and had ignored another major event in American popular music, the advent of "rap" or "hip-hop." This was the seventh fundamental change in the industry during the 1990s. Emerging from black dance deejays and rhymers, rap constituted a street music that required little, well, actual music. Perhaps the first rap hits to reach mainstream audiences were the Sugarhill Gang's 1979 "Rapper's Delight," or Kurtis Blow's "The Breaks." Ironically, though, it was white acts that gave rap credibility with the larger part of the listening public and introduced it to AM radio. Blondie, whose 1981 "Rapture" (later mixed together with the Doors' "Riders on the Storm" in a phenomenal grafting) contained several bars of Deborah Harry rapping toward the end. The first rap album to take off, the Beastie Boys 1989 Paul's Boutique, married hard rock and rap.

Sandwiched between these two, however, was the song that truly legitimized rap among rockers, Aerosmith's "Walk this Way," performed jointly in a re-mix with rappers Run-D.M.C. Aerosmith was involved in the middle of legal battles (what else was new for rockers?) When Tim Collins, Aerosmith's manager, was handed a new rendition of the group's hit song. "This is a rap version of 'Walk This Way,'" he was told by Rick Rubin, the deejay of the Beastie Boys. "Um, Rick," Collins replied, "what is rap?"[21]

A Queens, New York, group---Joseph "Run" Simmons, Jason "Jam Master Jay" Mizell, and Darryl "DMC" McDaniels—known as Run D.M.C.—had been cutting "Walk This Way's" drum patterns and adding rhymes for years, rapping the lyrics. They contacted Aerosmith and offered to do the song together. In the classic music video, Steve Tyler and Aerosmith alternate singing the song on one side of a wall on a giant stage, and Run D.M.C. rap it on the other side. Eventually, they kick down the wall between them, and the song greatly enhanced Aerosmith with a group of younger listeners, while exposing the traditional rockers to rap.

Rapping entailed much more than clever rhymes, though, for what gave it its musical grounding (such that it was) was a process called "sampling," in which the deejay recorded a drum beat or bass line from an existing song for the rapper to rhyme over it. Before long, deejays were not just sampling drum or bass lines, but entire (well-known) musical riffs and even full songs. In 1991, rapper Biz Markie lifted some of Gilbert O'Sullivan's 1972 hit, "Alone Again (Naturally)," without authorization and was sued. All copies of Markie's album had to be yanked from the stores. Suddenly, record companies found they had to clear new sample-based music, leading to a boom in sample-based infringement suits.[22]

In 2001, a Belgian duo called 2 Many DJ's put together "a Frankenstein hybrid" of *acapella* tracks and instrumentals of different and unrelated songs, such as Christina Aguilera's "Genie in a Bottle" with the guitars of the Strokes' "Hard to Explain, followed by Danger Mouse's *The Grey Album* in 2005.[23]

Rap, though, may have further accelerated the death of the music industry from a number of perspectives. As Shadow Morton noted, rap was "cheap to produce." It cost record companies very little—there were no massive orchestras and sparse arranging, although sampling costs could be significant. But to record executives, it was an inexpensive product with large markets, including high percentages of suburban white kids with plenty of money. Record companies leaped headlong into the rap phenomena, downplaying or ignoring other genres. Because it was so easy to produce, it was easy to copy or steal—not with downloads, but with actual theft of lyrics or ideas. Yet because it lacked a great deal of musical (though not lyrical) creativity, it became a genre that virtually anyone could imitate. Street kids without a musical bone in their bodies could write lyrics that rhymed. This enhanced rap's popularity as a music form: instead of artists being looked up to because they possessed talent average people did not have, a reversal occurred in which rappers were admired because they did what everyone else did, and not even necessarily better.

Rap's use of sampling embodied the eighth significant element in American rock music's transformation—one which may have contained the seeds of the music industry's destruction. Sampling laid the groundwork both morally and technically for "ripping" entire songs through illegal downloading and file sharing. Biz Markie may have been the first to be targeted by the law, but hardly the last. While to some in the early 1990s, downloading of files seemed just another typical copyright infringement issue, others perceptively warned that it was different in kind, and that this was an order of magnitude threat that could only be co-opted, not defeated.

To understand the thread to the traditional record industry posed by downloading, it is important to realize the fundamental differences between CD technology and the new MP3 technology. Although MP3 file codes had existed since 1987, the low level of computer sophistication and internet transmission capabilities made it less useful or even inaccessible to many consumers for another decade. But by the late 1990s, when more powerful microprocessors made it possible to extract files in seconds—rather than hours—and when cable modems and fiber optic wire allowed instantaneous transmission and receiving of high-density information packs, suddenly downloading MP3 files, storing them, and even sharing them via e-mail not only became possible but became popular. MP3 files could be downloaded from a personal computer and burned onto a CD, allowing people to mix their own albums and democratizing the product. More important, and worse from the record company's perspective, once someone had burned a CD from other music, it could be shared with others who, if they had a CD burner themselves, could acquire the music free, depriving the artist (and, of course, the record company) of their due rewards. At first, the cost and difficulty of this process—a person had to have CD burner software on his computer, and know how to work it—limited the amount of shared music. But with the continued, often geometric, increases in computer processing capabilities, by the end of the decade people equipped with a good computer and a cable connection could transfer MP3 files over the internet in minutes, if not sooner.

Within short order, "music sharing" sites appeared, in which people would post their songs and others could log in and download what they wanted. Record industry executives had once scoffed at the idea, thinking they could crush music sharing with appeals to moralism, then, if those failed, threats of legal action. Slowly and quietly, kids ignored both and music sharing boomed. Suddenly, the challenge posed by file sharing, which execs dismissed as insignificant, crashed in like a tidal wave. Striking back, the record companies targeted Napster.

Founded in 1999 by an 18-year-old, Shawn Fanning, Napster consisted of an internet site using a new file sharing code that proved extremely user-friendly. The site quickly acquired some 50 million visitors and 26 million registered users, all sucking music off the internet at no cost, becoming essentially a free Tower Records. A few accountants at Columbia, Reprise, and other labels punched in the numbers and discovered that the companies were losing millions in publishing royalties. Oh, yeah, they added: the artists were also taking a hit. While the artists and the recording companies could not go after every teenager downloading songs, they could shut down internet sites that encouraged piracy. Slapping a copyright violation lawsuit on Napster, they concluded, would nip downloading in the bud. Almost overnight, Napster became the underdog: its visitorship soared ten-fold.[24]

Joining the suit were artists such as hip-hop producer Dr. Dre and metal band Metallica. To many youths, the hypocrisy was stunning: Metallica was a group of multimillionaires, "the epitome of rich rock stars living in mansions who could afford multimillion-dollar art collections, Serbian hunting trips, and a $40,000-a-month 'performance enhancement coach' in the recording studio . . ."[25]

Napster knew it couldn't win, offering to settle for a $1 billion compromise in which it would become a subscription service charging customers $2.95-$9.95 a month, pay the labels $150 million a year and set aside $50 million to pay the independent labels. But the majors thought Napster was dead and declined the deal. At that point the record industry missed its best chance to co-op the inevitable and ensure a revenue stream based on downloading. Epic Records Mike Tierney said, "It's embarrassing . . . . The way we're doing it is definitely not the future."[26]

Attempting to stem the tide, Apple Computers introduced its portable, computerized MP3 player, the iPod, in late 2001. This portable media player used a miniature hard drive not only to store and play the music, but to offer playlists (that the user programmed in) or to "shuffle" the songs, randomly generating the next song. But the key to Apple's attempt to plug the download dike involved the creation of iTunes, a proprietary media application that worked with Apple's iTunes Store, where users could purchase a song for $.99 and download it onto their iPods. Originally, the Store had a "digital rights management" (DRM) feature that protected songs purchased on iTunes in such a way that they could only be played on up to five computers at one time that had iTunes accounts, and could not be played on any non-iTunes computers. But staring at the inevitability of consumer demand, in 2009 Apple announced it would make all its songs DRM free. (At the same time, newer songs saw their prices rise to $1.29.) Perhaps the most ingenious feature of all was called "Genius," a computer program that used a "collaborative filtering" software consisting of algorithms that determined the similarity of songs that the user hadn't purchased to songs already in the playlist. "Genius" therefore exposed the listener to up to hundreds of perhaps obscure artists or songs. Most important, while Apple hoped that users would purchase most of their music from the Store, realistically the executives knew that many songs would be pirated, or added from listeners' existing CD collections. Their willingness to allow outside music to be imported constituted a remarkable theoretical compromise from the original Macintosh stand-alone philosophy.

Paul McGuinness, U2's manager, referred to iTunes as the "penicillin for the recorded music industry," in his 2008 keynote speech at the MIDEM music conference in Cannes, France.[27]

On the surface, his claims appeared valid. Downloads on iTunes rose from 70 million in 2004 to 300 million in 2005 and soon iTunes became the nation's #1 music retailer, surpassing Wal-Mart. By 2007, Apple still represented about 70% of the digital music business.[28]

Some of iTunes' success came from the 2005 ruling against file-sharing site Grokster. Like Napster, Grokster was a file sharing company, and found itself sued by MGM Studios for copyright infringement. Essentially, MGM wanted to make the site liable for the actions of the users' copyright infringements. A year earlier, in the case of *Sony Corporation v. Universal Studios*, VCR manufacturers were protected from contributory infringements. But the Supreme Court saw Grokster differently, mainly because VCRs had other legal uses, while Justice David Souter, writing for the majority, noted that "one who distributes a device with the object of promoting its use to infringe copyrights [as opposed to other uses, as with the VCR], as shown by clear expression or other affirmative steps taken to foster infringement, is liable for the resulting acts of infringement by third parties."[29]

In other words, the only reason for Grokster's existence was to encourage illegal acts. Grokster quickly announced it would no longer offer file sharing, placed a clear notice on the website that such activity was illegal, and had to pay a $50 million fine to the music and recording industries. The site even posted a message on its website in May 2009, "Your IP [internet protocol] address . . . has been logged. Don't think you can't get caught. You are not anonymous."[30]

Meanwhile, in 2005, despite the surge in paid downloads, industry executives estimated that for every song downloaded and paid for, seven were being pirated; and by 2008 the ratio had exploded to a 40:1 pirated-to-paid download ratio. The recording industry moved from suing sharing sites to going after individuals, with the most eye-popping case being Jammie Thomas, a 39-year-old mother with an annual income of $36,000. The Recording Industry Artists of America (RIAA) brought a suit against her for uploading 24 songs and making them available on the peer-to-peer site Kazaa. Sony said she was stealing music and asked for a fine of $150,000 per song. A jury agreed with Sony and awarded the RIAA just over $9000 per song, for a total of $222,000. Even though the judge later had second thoughts about the decision and said she deserved a new trial, there was no doubt she knew she was breaking the law when she shared the music.[31]

Piracy seemed impervious to moralizing, and hackers seemed to defeat every new security code the recording industry concocted. That left only prosecution of the end-users. Law professor Lawrence Lessig said that such actions represented a bias against a generational change in music: "We've never used the law to block the next generation's form of creativity, but that's what we're doing in this case in particular."[32]

Others, such as Sandy Pearlman, a McGill University professor, said in 2008 that a portable database containing all the music ever recorded was imminent, and "Once this paradise of infinite storage is entered . . . it will represent the end of all intellectual property rights."[33]

Before long, even rappers—whose entire "gansta" image revolved around lawlessness—complained about piracy. In 2007, rapper Ghostface Killah put out a You Tube video in which he said,

> Ya'll don't want to go cop our CD, you'd rather download our shit. . . . So I got 115,000 friends on MySpace, and then get 30,000 [sales] in the first week, that's not good. I know a lot of you got my shit, but you just download it. I'm asking you to go to the store and buy that, man. . . . Snap out of it. This is real talk. I think it's gonna make me leave the game. . . .[34]

Undaunted, one "friend" issued the irreverent reply, "Dear Ghostface, Being a MySpace 'friend' does not actually mean we are 'friends' . . . . I sincerely doubt you would come over for brunch, help me move, or lend me money. MySpace friendship doesn't obligate me to purchase your album. Also, people don't really buy records anymore, fyi."[35]

Some prophesied that piracy would destroy the industry entirely. Producer Tony Bongiovi argued that because concentrated airplay as a barometer of what was actually popular, it became impossible "to pay for

218

the next Billy Joel. You pick local markets to play records and test the reaction."[36] Yet some data suggested that the impact wasn't as dire as Bongiovi Jovi suggested. One study by the Pew Foundation discovered that 37% of musicians said free downloading hadn't made a difference in their careers, and 35% said it helped.[37]

Another survey by the Leading Question research team in 2005 found that downloaders purchased over four times as much music as the average fan.[38] Aram Sinnreich, an analyst for Jupiter Media Metrix, said "it is safe to say that active usage of online music content is one of the best predictors of increased consumer purchasing."[39]

Nevertheless, sales continued to decline, falling by almost one-third between 1999 and 2003, and whatever happened with total sales, Bon Jovi was right in that the dynamic of funding groups or artists to develop new music was all but gone. Record companies could not pour money into the development of groups—which in the past had allowed bands (even the Beatles) to mature and improve their sound. The Beatles, it will be recalled, had several recording sessions before they turned out their hit album With the Beatles. Likewise, virtually no self-funded band—regardless of how popular in selected local markets—could fund a long-term, major theme album such as Sgt. Pepper or Born To Run, Bruce Springsteen's epic that took 14 months to complete. There were exceptions: the Hives, a band, in 2000, produced a poor-selling album. Reprise picked it up and revived it in 2002 and pumped $100,000 into radio stations in the new payola, making the band a hit.[40]

Thus, despite the constant refrain from critics that record companies were unnecessary, the Hives and other acts like them offered evidence to the contrary. Another band that managed to cut through the noise without major industry support was Death Cab for Cutie, an underground act that managed to get mentioned in the "hip" dialogue for the television show, "The O.C." Within two years, Death Cab's relatively unknown album sold 325,000 copies and in 2007 went gold, generating the "O.C. effect." If a band could get your music into movies or on television, it was possible to break through the crowded field of internet-posted music. Bands could also get national attention through Pitchfork, an internet website founded in 2005 that did fan reviews of new music and which came to dominate cutting-edge music with 240,000 readers by 2007.

All of these changes had occurred while Mark Stein was substantially out of the limelight. Ironically, Vanilla Fudge did not even benefit from the massive revival of "oldies" and "classic rock." The Fudge's music proved incompatible with the programming formats: it was too long, and too psychedelic. This wasn't unusual. Virtually no stations played anything from *Wheels of Fire* or anything by the Grateful Dead; "Inna-Gadda-da-Vita" never found its way into rotations because of its length. Occasionally one of Hendrix's earlier tunes—"Purple Haze" or "Foxy Lady" would get airplay, but material from his *Electric Ladyland* album was delegated to movie soundtracks or radio talk-show bumper music. In short, "classic rock" meant only the top 40 "pop" songs, and really ignored the meat of what was, at the time, Golden Age rock and roll. While this wasn't unusual behavior for station executives, it nevertheless constituted a cultural distortion of the highest order about what music was important for an era. It wasn't so much that the formats sanitized Golden Age rock—after all, "Purple Haze" was purely a druggie song—but that it removed the essence of what rock was for the era: revolutionary, different, subversive, challenging, expansive, experimental. Moreover, where in many ways the top hits of the 1950s perfectly captured the essence of rock at the time in their two-minute, catchy 45 rpm moments, classic rock constituted only a tiny sliver of what rock was, and what it meant to people, in the period 1965-1980.

Thus, while some artists lived quite well on royalties from airplay two decades later, Mark and the members of Vanilla Fudge could only rely on their loyal and aging fan base to attend reunion concerts. And while playing with Dave Mason and Alice Cooper had paid the bills for Mark, it provided no stream of residuals to him for songs that others had written. And in 2000, it was about to get worse.

In the late 1990s, after *Best of Vanilla Fudge Live* fiasco, Mark began to get calls from friends and family members that Vanilla Fudge was being advertised to appear on several venues scattered along the East Coast. After checking it out, Mark found it was true. Of course, he was upset. He was never formally asked to rejoin the band to play on these dates and he recalled the agreement signed by Vinny, Tim, and himself that said that the group couldn't use the trademark name unless Mark was in the band. He became more infuriated by the day, and contacted an attorney. After the lawyer read the agreement, he stated that if Mark wanted to send cease and desist letters to the promoters of the upcoming events, he was within his rights, and Mark did so. Most of the shows were cancelled and for a brief time Mark felt justified. But in fact he had awakened a financial giant that would nearly destroy him and Patty.

The subsequent lawsuit consumed their lives for the next two years. Ironically, it was probably the all time biggest fan of the band, Randy Pratt, son of Edmund Pratt (Chairman and CEO of Pfizer Pharmaceuticals, who was instrumental in making it a multinational corporation), and who had befriended Tim, Vinny, and Carmine and had a recording studio built in the basement of his Manhasset, Long Island,

220

home where he hung out and recorded with Mark's old friends. Pratt had retained Rubin Baum, one of the most powerful law firms in New York, located in Rockefeller Plaza.

Mark was charged with fraud and unlawful conduct in a complaint that stated that the agreement was phoney and which said that the signatures on the agreement were forged. He now had to find a litigation lawyer in New York to represent him. Living in Ft. Lauderdale, Florida, Mark and Patty began to research legal firms through their close friend, Janice Ginsberg, who at the time was dating Joe Serling, a New York entertainment attorney. He recommended Jim Cinque of Cinque and Cinque who had represented Whitney Houston, Bob Dylan, and others in litigation. After speaking with Mark and Patty and reviewing the complaint, he took the case. Of course, Mark had to pay him a retainer. Cinque thought after speaking with the Howard Weller, who represented Pratt, Martell, Bogert, and Appice that the whole issue would be settled quickly, especially after he saw the agreement they had signed.

Instead, the nightmare was just beginning. Mark was ordered to appear at a deposition and had to fly to New York City where, for the first time, he had to meet the band along with Weller. The day before, Mark and Patty met their counsel face to face for the first time, and the following day they entered the offices of Rubin Baum. The mere size of this legal juggernaut took Mark's breath away. Weller saw them and said, "Ah, They're all here!" He led Mark, Patty, and Cinque to a conference room that overlooked what seemed to be all of Manhattan. Vinny and Carmine were there while Tim had stayed in California. Mark asked that all lawyers leave, as he thought perhaps he could smooth things out with the band on a personal basis, and his request was granted. But his efforts were fruitless. Weller made phone calls to Pratt and after about an hour of the other side conferring, any pre-deposition settlement was denied.

The deposition began with Cinque at Mark's side, and Patty ordered to leave the room. Mark was deposed for hours while Vince and Carmine looked on. Vinny was cordial but Carmine was like ice. At times, Mark gave answers as he looked them directly in the eyes, and occasionally Vinny would shake his head from time to time as though he wanted to call the whole thing off. But on and on it went. Frightful, arduous, long hours of intimidation interrupted by Cinque's objections were met by Weller's threats to have conferences with the magistrate if Mark refused to answer certain questions. Every word was taken down by a court reporter. There was a moment when it seemed surreal—Mark thought, as if "this was a movie, where the beginning scene started with this deposition, then fading back, back, all the way to the mid-1960s where the story began."

The depositions frustrated and angered Mark. Vinny and Tim had signed the Vanilla Fudge trademark over to him in June 1993 because they sensed that he would go out on a limb to protect the name and to prevent any further damage to the brand after the infamous lawsuit against Carmine and Rhino Records involving the fraudulent live CD.

In the weeks that followed, the plaintiffs hired a forensic handwriting analyst who showed up at Cinque's law offices to examine the document. Mark and Patty were staying at the home of her brother, Bob Patterson, in New Jersey when Mark called Cinque to see how the meeting went. Cinque dropped a bombshell on Mark: the other side was going to challenge the document. The analyst believed that the signatures were forged and now they were considering adding Patty to the lawsuit for fraud and misconduct. Cinque had thought that once the analyst looked at the document, the case would be settled. Now Mark's legal fees would escalate. Sensing Cinque's insecurity, Mark felt the blood drain from his face. He knew that Pratt had very deep pockets, and coupled with the obvious vengeance of Mark's former bandmates and the large law firm foaming at the mouth to take advantage of the situation, it spelled bankruptcy for the Steins and who knew what else if they couldn't stop the suit.

Mark and Patty had returned to Florida where the process server banged on their door. He flashed a badge to the security personnel and they had no choice but to let him in the building. Although he pounded on the door incessantly, the Steins refused to answer, but to no avail. When they finally opened the door, the process server was gone, but the complaint was taped to the door. They looked at each other with fear in their eyes—"these fuckers are really out to get us!" he recalled saying. But in the coming months, the Pratt/Weller group would find that adding Patty to the lawsuit was their biggest mistake.

First, Mark had to find his own handwriting expert. On the advice of Cinque, he hired Paul Osborn in New Jersey, who headed his family owned company. Undoubtedly, the company's most famous case had been the Lindbergh kidnapping trial (State of New Jersey v. Hauptman) in 1935. After reviewing the document, Osborn stated that in his opinion, the signatures were indeed authentic and would so testify in court if the suit went to trial. That was good news, but the bad news was that the legal fees skyrocketed. Cinque attempted to go to war with paper storms of documentation in an attempt to cause the plaintiffs to incur more costs than they wanted to bear, but the tactic didn't work. More depositions followed—the band, friends, witnesses—going on for months. Pratt was apparently prepared to spend a half-million dollars in legal fees. At one point, the other members offered to drop the case if Mark paid them $150,000 in restitution along with an agreement that he would relinquish his rights to the Vanilla Fudge trademark along with other demands Mark called "insane." "Naturally," he said, "I told them to get fucked." But more threatening letters followed, as they realized they had the full support of Pratt's bank account.

Finally, a conference call with Cinque, Patty, and Mark took place in which Cinque told them the suit didn't look like it would end any time soon. Mark and Patty decided to release their counsel and represent themselves, going pro se. "Talk about being scared shitless," Mark noted. Here was a rock and roller and his wife, neither of whom had been anywhere near a law school, going against one of the largest firms in New York. They had to notify the magistrate and the U.S. District Court for the Southern District of New York, and soon the opposition learned of it too. It came as a shock to everyone. Mark and Patty learned through the process that a court usually has considerably more lenience and patience with pro se litigants, and the plaintiffs learned that as well.

So Patty had now embarked on what ultimately would be her finest hour. Through all the fear, all the intimidation, she did a quick study on all she could about the law, reading all she could, talking to the court which was incredibly helpful, and getting advice from every possible source she could muster , while Mark looked on in amazement. It was now their turn to depose the other side, and Mark had to help organize all necessary documentation and questions for the upcoming depositions. Tim Bogert was ordered to fly in from LA to be deposed, while Patty and Mark had to fly back up to New York , again leaving the serenity of their ocean front condo. Mark had personally prepared long lists of questions for the deposition, in fact they were so well organized that even Weller was impressed. Along the way, as Mark handed out documents to the court reporter from their exhibits and to Weller and as Patty rendered her summations, Weller made a remark to the extent of "Stein and Stein "are very impressive!"

Bogert was, needless to say, uncomfortable as Patty swore him in. He was now under oath and for several hours answered questions from both Mark and Patty. At one point, both Mark and Tim shook their heads at each other, knowing the whole mess had gotten way too big, out of control, and even at the close of business, Weller commented on the closeness they still had for each other. When his deposition was over, Bogert walked to the end of the conference table to Mark and gave him a big bear hug. That didn't mean he had relinquished his rights in a settlement, but only that he was glad his part was over and perhaps it would reach finality without too much more pain.

Then came Pratt's turn to be deposed. As Mark was in the hallway, Pratt approached him with pictures of Mark on stage during some high-energy performances, smiling in admiration. It was bizarre, how this fan of all fans was trying to destroy him. Pratt's deposition, Mark recalled, was "crazy." During a break, off the record, he'd make kind, almost innocent, remarks to the Steins and Mark replied, "It would be so much better if you spent all this money on something positive." Pratt stared back, not knowing what to say. Mark hoped his position had begun to soften, as he wasn't anywhere near the great evil that Weller had portrayed Mark to be.

Momentum had suddenly come to their side. When Weller saw that the Steins' position was firm, and they would not give in to any of his demands, he blinked. He made an offer to reduce the $150,000 demand. He asked, "what if we reduced the sum to something far less?" Mark barked back that he intended not to relinquish $1! Weller became flushed, and for the first time lost his overconfident swagger. Patty was now having talks with the magistrate and the court and was really getting the swing of things. There were times when the magistrate would order Weller to supply hours of documentation and he requested Mark and Patty to let him off the hook but Patty would never weaken. NEVER! She literally looked into the belly of the beast and said "Go to hell! Come and get me!" Weller threatened to sanction them. At the start of proceedings, Mark later noted, the sanctions "would have scared the shit out of us," but in the end it was all legal posturing. Patty wanted to go to court! She believed they would win. She wanted Mark to get ownership of the Vanilla Fudge trademark and have them all convicted of perjury. Tim and Vince knew all too well that they signed the paper—now everyone's nerves were frayed.

The other side now sought a settlement—after all Pratt now had to field the outrageous legal fees! But Patty was livid over the fact that they added her to the lawsuit, and was out for vengeance! She couldn't forget the day that she herself was deposed for over 12 hours by Weller and some other female lawyer from his firm. They tried to break her, to bust her, but nothing worked. Years later, Mark would insist that "through this ordeal was born the most courageous woman I ever saw." Everyone involved, on both sides were taken back by her, the magistrate included. Weller finally called her while they were home in Florida. "All right!," he said. You've brought us to our knees! We want to settle this thing." Over the next month or so, back and forth they worked to get the settlement finished.

Finally the lawsuit was settled. The band got to tour and use the name with another singer as Mark's replacement, paying him 10% of every gig and after a year he was free by law to rejoin the band if he desired. Somewhere in their thinking, apparently, Vinny, Carmine, and Tim thought there would be a broad, new career awaiting them. But the fact was, after a few scattered gigs, the lineup could barely get arrested. Promoters pined for the original band, with Mark. Soon, the phrase "time heals all wounds" became the group's motto and they began to talk again.

Then came something that showed how minuscule their disagreements were. Shockingly and suddenly, the world of all Americans was shattered on September 11, when Muslim terrorists flew planes into the World Trade Center and the Pentagon, killing 3,000. Islamic terrorism, which had been ignored and explained away, now confronted the nation as never before. Mark and Patty, horrified, watched the images and over the subsequent days heard the stories of the recovery efforts. In particular, Mark was struck by the important work of the rescue dogs that were combing ground zero for any possible signs of life. He saw pictures of the wonderful canines back at their stations, panting, scarred, burned, and bleeding, even given intravenous fluids to replenish them. Those animals had been trained to locate human bodies buried under rubble. Some became so depressed at not finding a living person that the firefighters had to "play dead" and let the dogs occasionally have success at finding a "survivor."

Hoards of money was being donated to victims' families, and every day new committees were set up to organize the funds coming in and to organize the distribution of resources to the appropriate recipients. Before long, as always is the case, the clouds of doubt started to darken the legitimacy of this effort. In the end, some families were helped, some weren't, and to this day no one knows for sure where every dollar ended up. Patty suggested that Mark record his version of "America the Beautiful." "Put it up on your website and raise money for the dogs! It doesn't seem like anyone gives much of a damn about them!" During the Fudge days, during the sound checks Mark used to enjoy doing his Ray Charles-inspired version of the song. The crew and sound guys used to dig it and always said he should record it. Here was a perfect opportunity.

Patty suggested Mark call Randy Pratt. She sensed now that the lawsuit fiasco was over, he might in retrospect have felt bad about the whole thing and maybe now might help him organize the project. Reluctantly, Mark made the call and she was right. He was friendly and offered Mark his studio to record in and told him to organize the band. In fact, he told Mark to get any players he wanted and Pratt would fund the whole project! Mark couldn't believe his ears. Immediately, Mark called upon his old friend Jimmy Haslip to see if he'd be into it. Not only was he, he offered to recruit players for the session. The band was John McCurry (guitarist who played with John Wait), Bobby Rondinelli (drummer who at the time was in Blue Oyster Cult), Jim Campagnola (a hell of a sax player that did sessions with Natalie Cole and Eric Clapton), Jimmy Haslip (now the highly-demanded session bassist and longtime member of the Yellowjackets) and Mark on grand piano and vocals.

So as the leaves had fallen in the late fall of 2001, they all met at Randy's house in Manhasset, New York. Everyone was excited, the band played great together and "America the Beautiful" was born, along with a new, positive relationship with Pratt. During the course of the session, he invited Patty and Mark out to dinner and made Mark an offer he couldn't refuse. Randy asked Mark if he'd like to do a solo album! He would fund the project from top to bottom—the use of his studio, his engineers, and pay for the band. It was bizarre in light of the recent hostilities, but maybe that was his way of making up for all the aggravation he put Patty and Mark through. Naturally, Mark accepted. "America the Beautiful" raised some money as a five dollar download on his website, all the proceeds going to the American Veterinary Medical Foundation. Even Mark's neighbor in Florida, Baseball Hall of Fame Yankee pitcher Whitey Ford donated to the cause, and Mark was flattered when, after Patty sent a CD to the White House, President George W. Bush replied with a signed certificate thanking Mark for his efforts during this time of crisis.

Mark started writing new songs and new arrangements. His vision was to create an album that reflected the singer/songwriter side of him. "I was on a mission," he said. "I was into the Springsteen sound and especially loved Clarence Clemons and I always loved the R&B pop sounds of Luther Vandross not to mention Billy Joel and his great songwriting." With this trio of influence, White Magik was created. But as noted, times had changed. Unless you were a young female vocalist, like Brittany Spears, or Springsteen himself, it was difficult to get a label deal. Most artists in Mark's situation sold their wares online. Initially, the response was great. My fans were into "The American Dream" and "Shame On Humanity," two of the more popular songs off the CD. White Magik got some critical acclaim and was actually getting airplay in Australia, of all places. Alice Cooper had Mark on his syndicated radio show and also played some of the CD .But there were those that were disappointed because the album lacked the heavy rock psychedelic sounds Mark was known for in the past. But he loved all kinds of music and at the time, that's what he enjoyed. Was there yet another chance for

Mark to return to the spotlight? It seemed yet another comeback was on the horizon.

Chapter Eight

It was the winter of 2004, while Mark was recovering from spinal fusion surgery, when there was a message left on his mail from Tom Vitorino. He said he was managing The Doors and requested a call back to see if Mark would be interested in him managing Vanilla Fudge. At first Mark thought it was just another one of those crank calls that seem to come with someone promising the world, and he didn't respond. Even if there was credence to the deal, it would be crazy to even entertain the thought of getting back with the band after all that happened. Several days later, he called and left another message. Patty called him back to check it out.

She told Mark that it really sounded like Vitorino was serious about getting the original band back together to tour with the Doors. He felt the time was right and was talking about good money. Mark relented, and called Vitorino and the spirits really flew. "You guys are all still alive and should be touring and making money instead of suing each other," he instructed Mark. His offer was really attractive, but it was up to Mark to break the ice with Carmine. He called Carmine and they buried the hatchet. It was good to talk about what we could do as a band. Tom wanted to get us back on a higher level again, where we should've been. Vinny and I were already on good speaking terms. He and Peg had even contributed some great backing vocals on the *White Magik* CD. When Mark called to tell him about this new proposition, Vinny was a bit taken back at first, because after all that had occurred he was surprised that Mark would forgive and forget. But as Mark noted, "life

228

sometimes takes us on unexpected journeys and what was being laid down for the future could make it well worth it to try and forgive the past." The promise of touring, recording and actually having a replenished career just sounded too good to pass up at this juncture of their lives.

Tom wanted to set up a meeting among them all, he didn't care where, but it had to be done so they could all face each other, say whatever needed to be said so the air would be cleared. This he said was essential in order for the Fudge as a band to move forward in a new and positive direction. He had wonderful ideas, filled with promise. At the time, Mark was still recovering from back surgery, and he requested everyone come to Ft Lauderdale because he wasn't yet able to travel. When everyone agreed, Mark knew it was serious! Tim and Carmine flew in from Los Angeles while Vinny flew down from New Jersey. He stayed with Mark a few days before the meeting which was set at The Fort Lauderdale Hilton.

Mark was still wearing his back brace when he entered the conference room with Vinny and Patty. Tim came over to him with open arms and a quick hug. Mark greeted Tom Vitorino with a hug as well as Carmine walked into a room filled with good cheer. Tom got right into the fact that he loved the music of Vanilla Fudge and believed if they could let bygones be bygones he could manage the band and get them back to a great career again with extensive touring and even new recordings with some exciting ideas for merchandising. He envisioned packaging the Fudge with The Doors of the 21st Century, Pat Travers, and The Yardbirds for an upcoming 2005 summer tour as his first offering. It paid well, and offered a shot at a VH1 TV rock special to be shot at The Trump Taj Mahal in Atlantic City. This was the best offer since the old days, really, but now it was time for the shouting matches. We all got it out of our systems. Everything was said that needed to be, agreements were made on how to solve some past monetary disputes. Mark found it "very healthy." With that over, they were all honestly happy being back together as a band. Down to the Tiki Bar they all went for a few beers and a few toasts."Here's to never saying never!" rang out as both relief and laughter ensued. Some of the patrons upon discovering who they were and that they were playing again got excited, which added to the flavor of the night.

June came quickly, with Mark recovering nicely from his surgery after months of therapy. Randy Pratt shipped him a Hammond and Leslie speaker which Mark stored at Vince Waslewski's studio, "Other World " in Ft. Lauderdale. Vince and Mark met when Mark was searching for a studio in 2002. Waslewski was excited when he found out it was Mark Stein of Vanilla Fudge, being a fan and having once played in a rock band himself. Mike Kovins; the president of Korg Keyboards shipped Mark a Triton Extreme, as Mark was an endorsee for years and with the reunion of the band, the Korg/Stein relationship was re-energized. Mark was energized learning the new instrument. Orchestral sounds, special effects and a great sampled grand piano sounds abounded from this great new machine! He got comfortable integrating these sounds with the Hammond and started to come up with new approaches and updated arrangements for the new tour. All this occurred about three weeks before full band rehearsals which happened to be right in Fort Lauderdale in Mark's own back yard. The tour bus company, oddly enough, was also based in Lauderdale and since the very first show was in Tampa, Florida. Patty had worked out a good deal with owner of the bus company and they designed a lower bunk for Mark that would buffer the stress on his back for long trips.

Rehearsals went well. With the hope of a resurgence, the energy was great and the band played and sang with passion. Joe Lopez, who had worked with Clarence Clemons on some of Bruce Sprnearingsteen's tours was hired as tour manager and worked a lot with Patty ironing out lots of details. Tom's job was made a lot easier because of it. Joe was a really great guy who was also a pro photographer, and he shot some killer new promo pictures of the Fudge. Tim and Mark were at ease with one another after all these years and all of them seemed to be having fun with each other again.

So off went the Fudge, back on the road. The shows were going really well. People were happy to see the original band and they were getting excellent reviews. The one common remark from critics was that they could feel the fun the band was having on stage and it was reflecting in their music. Our vocal harmonies were still in tact after all this time and all the acts on the tour always remarked about that, in fact, a cool comaraderie developed between the Doors and the Fudge. There were times when Robby Krieger would come on stage and jam; Carmine would play with the Doors, and one evening in Montreal, Mark played "Riders on the Storm" while Ray Manzarek sat behind him offering total support. It all led up to the VH1 special that was being filmed in Atlantic City at the Trump Taj Mahal.

The show was called VH1 Classic Decades/Rock Live. It was projected to be a weekly TV show that featured bands from the 60's to the present on stage and with introspectives. Certainly this was the vehicle that could put Vanilla Fudge back on the map. On the bill was Macy Gray, Perry Farrel, Pat Travers, Antigone Rising (an up and coming female rock outfit) and of course, starring the Doors of the 21st

Century. Vanilla Fudge's job was to create their own special arrangements to a few Doors tunes, with the idea being to pay homage to this great American band. Patty asked Mark, "Why don't you try turning 'Love Her Madly' into a ballad ?" During a break in the action, back at home Mark sat at the piano and the arrangement flew out of him as if it was already written. Excited, Mark called Carmine and Tom and played and sang it over the phone and they were blown away! Another idea came to him for "The Changeling" in the guise of a mid-tempo rock R&B groove with a sort of Lou Graham, Foreigner-style keyboard and vocal. Mark called Vinny and played that one over the phone to him. Vinny said the piano reminded him of "Dr. John.".Tim and Carmine came up with a great rhythm track when the band got back together in Vancouver, British Columbia at rehearsals, prior to the Canadian leg of the tour.

Krieger was impressed when the Fudge played the tunes at sound check—at one point; he said it might be cool if the Fudge did an album of all his songs. It was August 5, 2005 and the Trump Taj Mahal was buzzing. Pictures of the all the acts were flashing on screens all over the hotel and casino. Tom Vitorino was in charge of producing the music and coordinating all the scheduling for the acts. At one point, Lovin' Spoonful's John Sebastian showed up and was supposed to sing "Summer in the City" with the Fudge backing him. At sound check they tried to make it happen for him but somehow it wasn't jelling. Mark thought a few more run-throughs might have brought it together, but Vitorino suddenly bolted up to the stage and started screaming "Stop! Stop! This just isn't makin' it!" Sebastian stormed off the stage, never to be heard from again! Mark was taken aback by it all, especially since he had been a Spoonful fan.

During the afternoon, interviews were taking place on camera on a cool set that was created for the special. Vinny, Carmine and Mark were excited to be a part of it, happy for the exposure. Then Tim came down from his room in one of his sullen moods. The band was being shot on camera for what was to be a wonderful TV special, the chance to be seen again in a positive light in the modern era and Tim acted like a complete asshole in front of the director of the show! He made remarks to the extent that he really could care less if he was there or not. The director would ask him questions about the band: "isn't it great to be back playing and touring again?" to which Tim would look away from the camera without a comment. Or he would just sneer and make some negative off-color remark that pissed off the director and freaked out the other band members. Carmine and Mark desperately tried to keep things positive and draw the attention away from him, but the damage was done. A heavy anchor like that would tend to sink most ships. So it was just like old times. The Fudge shot themselves in the foot yet again.

Nightfall came and it was getting close to showtime. The afternoon debacle was put on the back burner; the Fudge had a show to do. In the dressing room, they were getting makeup while the lights and cameras were getting ready to roll and the audience was filing in to the Decades Rock Arena. Vitorino spent some quiet time with them getting them mentally prepared for what could be the band's shining moment. He wanted Mark to speak on camera and to the audience and to harken back to the Seattle Pop Festival in '69 when the Fudge were performing "You Keep Me Hangin' On," and Jim Morrison was standing and staring at Mark just a few feet from his Hammond. The moment came as the band was announced and they hit the stage. Over the mike and looking to the crowd Mark prefaced the show by thanking the Doors for the opportunity to open for them on this tour and told the story of yesteryear and said "and if we all just close our eyes and wish hard enough, maybe Jim will return and be with us one more time tonight."

"The Changeling" rocked the house and "Love Her Madly" was mesmerizing. The sound was great and the audience which was filled with fans, young and old, were swingin' and swayin' to the music. Then, suddenly, as they were closing the set with "Hangin' On," lightning struck the building and somehow obliterated the sound on the taping. The soul, the vibe—all the great textures that they had painted were washed away. It was incredible! The sound folks said that this never, ever happened before. So since it was a taping for television, the band had to try and recreate the whole scenario again. Back to the stage they went, and again played the songs. Mark tried to recreate the moment but the natural spontaneity was gone. Afterwards, Ray Manzarek came over and said "that's what you get for conjuring up Morrison." The whole thing was so bizarre that no one could believe what had happened. Word spread all over the place, and a new rock legend from beyond was born.

When morning came, Patty and Peg Pearl, Vinny's wife said their goodbyes as Vitorino gave everyone hugs and said that in spite of all the mishaps, the camera shots of Mark and the band were great and it looked like with some good editing, the television special was going to be a success. Vanilla Fudge boarded the bus for the last show of the tour which was to be in Portsmouth, Virginia.

A few weeks later, while back home in Florida relaxing, Mark received a call from Vitorino. Mark answered with anticipation, thinking he would learn of upcoming Fudge dates. Instead, Vitorino had bad news, telling him Tim Bogert had just been in a motorcycle accident, and while he had no permanent damage, his shoulder and arms were badly hurt and he wouldn't be playing any time soon. Mark felt a wave of frustration come over him. "With all we had going, you would've thought he could've entertained a safer hobby, but Tim just loved to ride, something he did for so many years, and with out incident until that moment." Mark called him, learning Tim was at home filled with pain killers. Vitorino was less depressed than upset: he had a number of irons in the fire—corporate dates, more shows, and lots of money, but they all wanted the original Vanilla Fudge. As time passed, and it was apparent that Tim wasn't recovering, the other members argued for a replacement and when he was ready to return, Tim would step back in, but Vitorino was adamant about the resurgence including all original members. Mark and Vinny kept trying to reason with Vitorino, arguing that most classic rock bands no longer featured original members and were out working—why should it be different for the Fudge? But he insisted that everything was predicated and promoted on the original lineup, without it, buyers would start dropping the price and all that was being built would fall apart.

Then, in the midst of all this, came more great news. Six weeks earlier, while in Vancouver BC, the Doors were hit with a lawsuit from John Densmore, the original drummer. It all had to do with using the name without proper approval, the same difficulties that had cropped up with the Fudge over the years, just painted a different color. The judge in the case apparently ordered all merchandising with the Doors name on it to be immediately removed from all vendors at the Canadian shows. Vitorino and his staff was scurrying to meet the demands handed down from the court, meanwhile, Manzarek and Krieger were all over CNN being interviewed about the lawsuit. Vitorino worked the phones for hours trying to negotiate a settlement. Although the Doors were allowed to use the name for the remainder of the tour, Densmore received compensation. Everyone thought the VH1 special would not be affected.

Apparently, whatever agreement made between Vitorino and Densmore was not in writing. Densmore's camp made waves that reached the shores of VH1's legal department and the whole show was cancelled, never to be aired. The director and producers of the special were furious. The cost for a single day, paying the Doors, Vanilla Fudge and all the acts on the bill, not to mention the other production costs ballooned to over a million dollars, all of which were completely lost. Vitorino took flak from all sides, but in Mark's view, he had earned some of the blame. Mark's own legal issues had taught him "you have to get it in writing!"

Nine months of unemployment followed before the band was offered a new record deal from Escapi Records, a Dutch label. In the interim since the Doors fiasco, Carmine had the idea for the band to create an album entirely made up of the Fudge doing Led Zeppelin songs. He spoke to Vitorino about it, and the manager liked the idea. After all, Vanilla Fudge was really the only band to tour with Zeppelin in the early days; there was a history there and it could serve as a hook to get interest and publicity. Vitorino thought he could pitch this concept to promoters. Mark wasn't thrilled with the concept, but when Escapi made an offer, he went along with it. By then, Tim was healed up enough to work again and the band all got down to the business of picking songs for the project. They consciously refused to do some of the best-known Zeppelin songs, including "Stairway to Heaven." "Why re-write the Bible?" as Mark put it. "Babe I'm Gonna Leave You "was one of Mark's favorites. He worked up an Elton John style piano vocal arrangement, as well as developing some ideas for "Dazed and Confused." Vinny, by then back in New Jersey, came up with a beautiful acoustic guitar version of "Black Mountain Side" and decided he wanted to sing and rock out on "Rock and Roll." Mark recalled "Our aim [was] to keep the emotion and the power."[1]

The band members all gathered in Los Angeles in the summer of 2006 to rehearse and record the album there. Vitorino had set up a show for them on the same bill with the reconstituted "Jefferson Airplane," now "Jefferson Starship"at the Pan Pacific Amphitheater, so it made sense for everyone to be in California. Patty stayed in Florida with the Stein's grandson of 10 months, Kristopher Ian, while Mark was gone for a month.

Rehearsals went really well and the recording went like clockwork. Vinnie and Mark stayed about a half hour from the studio in North Hollywood . The band came up with some cool Fudge versions of "Your Time Is Gonna Come," "Ramble On,"and did a spectacular job on "The Immigrant Song." Although Tim was supposed to sing lead on that song, Mark ended up doing it back in Florida at Other World Studio with Vince Waslewski engineering both that and "Ramble On." The sessions in Los Angeles were produced by Carmine, who had been instrumental in putting the deal together. Since he wanted the responsibility of getting the studio together and organizing the project, the other members granted him the liberty to oversee the California recordings. Mark found that concentrating on vocals, keyboards, and arranging was more than enough responsibility. Perhaps the surprise of the resulting Out Through the In Door album was Vinny's guitar work. He had finally become himself with his style, and played some of his best guitar ever on the album. Then there was Carmine's excellent drum solo on "Moby Dick,"a tribute to his old drummer rival John Bonham.

By the fall, the record was mixed, mastered, and delivered to Escapi per the terms of their contract, whereupon the band was to receive the balance of its advance. Several weeks had passed and no money came. Tom and Carmine made calls and sent e-mails to Europe but all they got were evasions and excuses, hearing that "funds were being transferred from one company to another and the balance would be forthcoming shortly." Weeks turned into months, and as Mark soon learned, lies turned into bigger lies until they were notified that Escapi had gone belly up. There was no more money. Here was Vanilla Fudge with an excellent finished product and no one to market or distribute it. At that point, Mark didn't know whether to laugh, cry, or shake his head: How much bad luck can one band have over the course of all those years?

Efforts to sell the masters and perhaps get another label to take the project failed repeatedly, but they had the album, *Out Through The In Door* to sell over the internet. This was, they were learning, the major means of non-"star" bands selling their product. Even without major marketing, though, the album got some critical acclaim and the general comments were that the vocals and the playing were impressive.

Without a major label, and without the Fudge around him, Mark, then back in Florida, at the suggestion of Joe Lopez, entertained notions of again creating his own band. Lopez knew a trio of players and said they were great, a local band called Tripod that was popular on the South Florida scene. On bass was Steve Argy, who had played with the Big Man, Clarence Clemons in "Temple Of Soul." Jimmy Fiano was the guitarist. He had done gigs with Bad Company, and Jimmy Jack Tamburo played drums. Argy came over to Mark's condo and brought along his bass with a small amp per Mark's request. Mark wanted to play and, in essence, check out his chops. Argy was a natural, and he praised the other guys for their playing and vocal prowess and eventually everyone came over. Mark was impressed, thinking, "What a pleasant surprise! Three really nice guys that sang harmonies, perhaps every bit as well as the Fudge but with a slightly different texture." Mark set up a rehearsal at Other World and was hoping for a good sounding band. After two or three rounds of "Take Me For A Little While" and "You Keep Me Hangin' On," they already sounded strong. Fiano was a killer guitarist, obviously influenced by several of the greats. Mark found him to be a terrific lead player with powerful rhythms. Jimmy Jack had a good feel with excellent grooves, who held back at first until Mark asked him to solo. Then he exploded. He also had a voice similar to Mark's— in part because he listened to the Fudge a lot over the years. Jimmy Jack surprised Mark, knowing Fudge facts that even Mark had forgotten.

The group laid down some tracks with Wasilewski at the console, mainly so that Mark could get a good demo that he could send around to agents to try and get bookings. He could have gotten local gigs, but they didn't pay enough. Instead, he tried to get "The Mark Stein Band" (as he called it) booked as an opening act for one of the majors in the classic rock market hoping to break in on a good level again.

In the meantime, Vinny Martell called about this man he knew who was organizing what was to be the inaugural ceremony of the Long Island Music Hall of Fame. It would induct Vanilla Fudge along with a host of stars and artists from over the decades. Like so many other events that supposedly "were happening," this one struck Mark as another fly-by-night operation. Even Vitorino didn't think it would happen. But Vinny kept saying it was real, and that it would be a great event. Richard Hommideau, one of the organizers, contacted Mark and informed him that not only would the Long Island Music Hall of Fame induct Vanilla Fudge, but that it was to be a gala night. Billy Joel would attend, said Hommideau, along with so many celebrities, such as Joan Jett, Little Anthony & The Imperials, Dee Snyder and Twisted Sister, Gary "US" Bonds, the Stray Cats, the Harry Chapin family, and others. Television bandleader Paul Shaffer would be one of the presenters. Even Perry Como was to be honored. The list went on and on! Vitorino wasn't convinced. "I'll eat my hat if Billy Joel or even half of these artists show up at this thing," he announced. By then, Patty had found that, in fact, the event was genuine: she spoke to Joel's head of PR who she'd known over the years and indeed he was attending. Carmine wanted to be involved but Tim didn't want to make the flight from Los Angeles, even though all expenses were being picked up by the organizers along with hotels and limos. Felix Cavaliere of the Rascals was also going to be one of the speakers so Mark called him to say hello, and asked if he'd be into inducting the Fudge. "How appropriate would that be?" Mark asked. Felix agreed. Mark suddenly got a call from the New York Times with a request for an interview. Things were really heating up!

The event was to take place at the Patchogue Theatre for the Performing Arts on the evening of October 15, 2006. Patty and Mark flew in the night before and met with Vinny and Peg at the hotel after they drove in from south Jersey. The next day, while Mark hung out at the lobby, a white stretch limo pulled up in front of the hotel. A woman got out, Mark asked who was in the limo, and she replied "Shadow Morton." "Wow," Mark said, "It must be nice to travel in style like that!" "Yes, it is!" she answered sarcastically. Mark introduced himself and with a laugh she responded, "Oh my God! I'll tell George you're here." "No don't," Mark said. I'll go back in the lobby...don't say I'm here, I

236

want to surprise him when he comes in." Mark sat in the lobby for a while and after he saw Morton check in, Shadow came over and shouted, "who is that guy?" Morton was being inducted into the Hall of Fame as well. Then out of the elevator came Leslie Gold, "the Radio Chick." Carmine and Leslie were going together for several years now. She gave Mark a hug as he introduced her to Shadow Morton. She said that Carmine was in the gym on the treadmill, so Shadow and Mark went down the hall and through the glass they saw him. They burst into the room and Mark screamed "Dude! Look who I found!" They all exchanged greetings and spoke about the Out Through The In Door/Zeppelin tribute project they did. Shadow listened to the album on a portable CD player through earphones and was impressed.

Night came and the limo was waiting in front of the hotel to take Mark and the band to the theater. As he approached the venue, to his amazement, the streets were lined with people and screaming fans held back behind barricades. Mark, Vinny, and Carmine got out of the limo with their ladies by their sides and walked onto a red carpet leading into the theater while light bulbs flashed and reporters from everywhere stuck microphones into their faces and asked questions about the event. It had all the trappings of a Hollywood Premiere, and it was entirely unexpected. Patty said to Mark, "There's Billy Joel! Go over to him and say hi!" Mark walked over while Joel was being interviewed and extended his hand. "Hi Billy," he said. "I'm Mark Stein from Vanilla Fudge!" Joel barked back with a menacing look, "I know who you are!" Then, he abruptly added, "Are we going to jam tonight?" and the mood lightened. "That would be great," Mark replied and agreed to meet later in the evening.

Outside the theater in the back lot was a huge circus tent that housed a beautiful catering service with great food and an open bar. Mark topped off a few vodka tonics and spotted Joan Jett. He ran up to her like a crazed fan and introduced himself, telling her how much he appreciated her music. She returned the compliment, noting she was a Fudge fan herself. Dee Snyder and the guys from Twisted Sister, were also on the scene. Snyder remarked that it was about time the Fudge got some recognition. Mark also met Gary US Bonds, who he did a jingle with in the early 1980s when Bonds had his career revived by the Bruce Springsteen-produced album. Bonds's single from the early 1960s, "A Quarter to Three," remains one of Mark's favorite rock & roll records.

Leslie West also was there and performed Mountain's hit "Mississippi Queen "with his trio, Richie Scarlett on bass and Corky Laing on drums (Felix Pappalardi having died many years earlier, killed by his wife).[2] They were smokin'. This had turned into a great night.

Mark met with Felix Cavaliere backstage and they talked about how he'd introduce the Fudge and give them the award that accompanied their induction, which was a huge treble clef mounted on a beautiful base with Vanilla Fudge engraved on it. So Mark drank a little more and became more uninhibited, he listened to the speeches from the inductees and realized he'd better start putting together some things to say when the time came which was probably within the next hour and a half.

It all came to Mark when it was Vanilla Fudge's time. From the side of the stage as Felix said a few words about their history, a projection of one of their live concerts was up on the screen and he called the Fudge up. Mark accepted the award then gave Felix a hug with Vinny and Carmine right behind. They stood at the podium in front of a packed house of cheers and well wishes. Briefly Mark thanked Felix and acknowledged his influence on himself and the Fudge along with the Vagrants and all the bands that shared what was once called "The Long Island sound." Of course he thanked Patty for putting up with him through the long, arduous task of being behind and supporting a rock musician. Vinny spoke next and thanked a list of people a mile long while Carmine nudged Mark hoping he wasn't going to drag it out too long. But it was his night too and Mark always thought it was cool, Vinny thanking the veterans and all the armed forces that were engaged somewhere on their behalf. Carmine was short and sweet. Peter Criss from Kiss gave him a hug as they walked off and they all went back to the bar before they were to hold press conference with the media. Mark recalled "It was great hangin' with Little Anthony and Johnny Maestro as well….I mean these guys had a lot of early influence on me too."

The following day, Mark picked up a copy of the Sunday *New York Times* and there was a half page layout on the event containing his interview and a picture of himself along with Billy Joel, Joan Jett, Dee Snyder, Gary US Bonds and the late Harry Chapin. Excited, he showed it to Patty just as the phone rang and it was Mark's sister, Sharon calling to see how everything went. "It was an awesome night and pick up a copy of the Sunday Times, there's a great article in it!" Mark shouted.

Vinny and Peg drove the Steins back to Jersey where they were all walking on air for a few days. Mark had a conference call with Tim and Carmine; the crux of it was to try to set up dates to promote the *Out Through The In Door* CD, maybe get a buzz going but there was minimal income involved. It didn't make sense to Mark at this stage of the game. Tim was angry with him and took off while Vitorino and Carmine were trying to persuade Mark. All the time Mark was screaming at Vitorino to get the band on the David Letterman show. Paul Shaffer was just at the music awards and he was a Fudge fan and at the moment, Vanilla Fudge was hot in the New York area. Mark practically begged him to try—that kind of exposure would have been priceless and certainly would quickly lead to bookings, but Vitorino didn't agree. Mark was livid!

While all this was going on, Vinny's friend and agent Pat Horgan, who booked his solo band contacted Mark with an offer for the Fudge to go on the PBS "The 60s My Generation" series. This was a TV show that reached millions of viewers. He emailed Tom about it, but Vitorino responded with hostility and demanded Pat to cease and desist from contacting his artists. Vitorino argued that he was working on a possible special with the Doors and the Fudge for that very same station, but with so many unfulfilled promises of late from him, Mark wanted to take advantage of this opportunity. On and on they went and with the failure of cooler heads prevailing the two hung up on each other.

Horgan called Mark the next day and said "Listen.the producer of the PBS show said if Stein wants to do the show with Vinny, it would be fine with him since he's the lead singer. So Mark, sick of all this turmoil with rest of the band, agreed. Calling Steve Argy and Jimmy Jack, Mark asked them to join himself and Vinny on the PBS special. Of course they were excited to do it, and Vinny, after a little reassuring, accepted them as the band's new rhythm section. He never heard them play but he took Mark's word for it. Mark and Vinny met at Irving Plaza Club in downtown New York where the Shadows Of Knight were playing, and Vinny related the fact that Steve Van Zandt would be there along with Pat Horgan, the agent who got them the PBS show. Mark's brother-in-law, Bob Patterson drove with him into the city and upon arrival, Mark saw Little Steven talking to Vinny. He snuck up behind them and gave 'em both a big hello. "Don't worry about Argy or Jimmy Jack," Mark said to Vinny. "The instant we start to play, you'll feel like you're in the Fudge, and they got the harmony parts down as well!"

As the night went on, the Shadows asked the duo to jam, so they jumped on stage and rocked with them on the tune that almost every rock band learns as one of its first songs, the three-chord "Gloria": GLORIA . . .G-L-O-R-I--A- GLORRRIA! Van Zandt gave Mark a hug and said, "Man, you haven't lost a thing." Mark asked him to come to the Patchogue Theater on Long Island the following week where Vanilla Fudge was doing a show—the same place where the Music Hall Of Fame ceremony was being held. Van Zandt said he couldn't make it, and was Mark relieved that he didn't. Carmine and Tim weren't too happy about Mark and Vinny doing the upcoming TV show without them and they held nothing back in their resentment to them on stage that night. Mark recalled the nightmare: "Nobody looked at anybody. It felt just like the pre-breakup shows from early 1970. The vibe was horrible; it was every man for himself, they even had separate dressing rooms and after the gig took off without so much as a goodbye."

On Wednesday, November 8, 2006, Argy, Jimmy Jack, and Mark boarded a US Air jet in Fort Lauderdale to fly to Pittsburgh. There a limo drove them to the Mountaineer Resort Casino in West Virginia, where the PBS show was being taped. After a pleasant drive along the Ohio River, they arrived about an hour later, finding that Vinny and Peg were already there. Vinny was anxious to meet with the new band and to go over the vocals to "You Keep Me Hangin' On." He found himself instantly at ease after a few bars, with the harmonies sounding terrific. Rehearsal would begin at 9:30 a.m. the next day.

Everyone arrived at the arena, just across from the hotel around 9:00 AM and were quickly escorted to the dressing rooms where they were fed breakfast doughnuts and strong coffee. When they hit the stage, all the gear was in place and in minutes the camera and sound crew were in action like a well oiled machine. The sound balance on stage came together with just a few tweaks here and there. They ran through their classic hit for the first time as a band as Iron Butterfly and Rick Derringer looked on, seated in front awaiting their turn for sound check. Vinny winked at Mark with relief, pleased that Argy and Jimmy Jack proved to be the musicians that Mark had promised. From the sound check, they marched to the production office to sign all the union paperwork, releases, and other documents, then headed back to the dressing room for more coffee. Derringer appeared in the dressing room, saying, "Mark, if you closed your eyes, you'd think it was the original Fudge playing." For Mark, that was music to his ears and a great validation. A '60s group with a single megahit, "We Five," were rehearsing "When I Woke Up This Morning!...You Were On My Mind....You Were On My Mi-ii-ind." Female crooner Jackie De Shannon was also on the bill, with her hit, "What the World Needs Now, Is Love....Sweet Love," (featured prominently in the Elliot Gould/Dyan Cannon/Natalie Wood movie, "Bob and Carol and Ted and Alice."

Elsewhere, Mark saw a different configuration of his old idols, "The New Rascals" without Felix Cavaliere was on the show with Gene Cornish and Dino Danelli. Shaking hands with Gene, Mark heard typical band stories: Dino was arguing with the show's producers over the fact that they wanted them to play a certain sequence of their hits and he wasn't happy about it. It was rumored that if Vinny and Mark were going to close the show, the New Rascals were not too pleased about it. Dino Danelli purportedly threatened to not to go on at all if his demands were not met. Word spread like wildfire while Derringer approached Mark and quietly said, "With a shot like this for them to be on national TV, they

240

are acting like total idiots! Chances like this don't come around too often." (Mark could have silently agreed, given his long history with the Fudge's prima donna antics.) At any rate, the New Rascals worked it out, but the bad vibes they caused didn't enhance their image. In the middle of the mayhem, Mark introduced Jimmy Jack to Dino, and although the exchange was awkward, Danelli knew that the Rascals were one of the Fudge's early influences, and acknowledged Mark with a smile.

Strangely, with all the rockers present, Mark was most anxious to get re-acquainted with Marilyn McCoo and Billy Davis. Recalling the times when the Fifth Dimension was hot in the late 60s, and the occasions when Vanilla Fudge shared the stage with them, Mark spotted the pair in the dressing room and said hello. After a few photos, Mark told Marilyn that he had a picture of them all backstage in 1967 at a show in Seattle. After all those years, they were exactly the way Mark remembered them.

Vanilla Fudge's performance went well as they performed the seven minute version of "You Keep Me Hangin' On." The audience, all baby boomers, loved it and Mark and his band got on great with the production staff and all the artists. Later, Mark headed backstage on his way to watch Marilyn McCoo and Billy Davis perform with the house band. Before he could get to stage right, they began singing "Up Up and Away"....my beautiful, my beautiful balloon." McCoo's voice soared with every note Suddenly, Mark felt frozen in time, just standing there, alone, envisioning for a brief moment how it was so long ago. A wave of melancholy swept over him, realizing how practically a lifetime had flown by!

Some fourteen months passed before the special was aired. Then, overnight, it was on nationally, sometimes twice a day on heavy rotation. The first time Mark saw it he was happy with the editing and surprised when Michelle Phillips made the introduction: "And here is Mark Stein from Vanilla Fudge with his rendition of You Keep Me Hangin' On." He had guilt pangs that Phillips did not mention Vinny, and knew it would rightly bother him, as it would Mark if the shoe was on the other foot. But the camera was on him often, and his guitar sounded real good—indeed, the band as a whole came off great. Mark received numerous emails commenting on how good the "original band" looked and sounded, which made him laugh, seeing as though Vanilla Fudge was only half original. Some noticed, though, that "Carmine" wasn't shown enough. Yet even Carmine called Patty and said "Who is that bass player ...he looks and plays like a younger Tim!" Naturally, he didn't comment on Jimmy Jack. And shortly after, in the spring of 2007, the original Fudge got together again to play a few scattered gigs in the North East while the PBS show was airing. Mark anticipated problems psychologically among them, but Tim and Carmine had accepted matters, and had in fact heard from fans how great the Fudge were and seemed rejuvenated.

That July, Mark was in the gym swimming laps in the pool when he ran into a man named Adam Shuman, who was running a club in downtown Ft. Lauderdale called "Automatic Slims." He related that his father was a classic rock fan and he knew Vanilla Fudge. Mark told him about his solo band, and Shuman invited him to the club and offered to give Mark a shot at playing "The Revolution," a popular venue close to his place. He also mentioned that Deep Purple was at the Pompano Beach Amphitheater the upcoming weekend. When Mark related the history of the Fudge and Deep Purple, Shuman suggested he try to attend the show. That night, the two met at "Slim's," which was packed wall to wall with girls scarcely a day over twenty one. Some smiled at Mark like he was a father figure looking for a burst of youthful energy. Adam brought over a vodka tonic and introduced Mark to his disc jockey who blasted the club with dance tracks. Mark had brought a demo of his band and the DJ played the track "Back in My Arms Again," the classic Supremes hit. But this was, naturally, a rocked out version. The DJ pumped up the bottom end, and Mark swelled with pride, seeing the younger generation rockin' and dancin' to his music! It was 1968 all over again. Adam took Mark upstairs to the office where they spoke about Deep Purple. Although Jon Lord wasn't touring with the band, Mark asked Shuman to email Ian Paice to see if he'd get them backstage passes. Paice overnight got their names on the list.

When they arrived at the concert, the passes indeed awaited them at will call, and Shuman used his charm and connections to wheedle dressing room passes. Paice and Mark exchanged hugs, and the Deep Purple drummer introduced him to Don Airey, the great rock keyboardist who had now been touring with them. He was excited to meet Mark and the feeling was reciprocal. Bruce Payne, who had managed Purple well since the beginning, said "Stein, you look great! Would you like to come up and play with us? Come Up And Play 'Smoke on the Water.'" (This was, of course, the best-known Deep Purple song and a guitar lick that had so permeated the culture it became the basis for numerous commercials and comedy skits). To Mark, it was "beyond cool." Airey said it was in the key of "G," and although Mark never played it before (not being a guitarist, for whom the lick was mandatory training), he learned it on the fly. Then, the two Ians, Paice and (singer) Gillan, along with bassist Roger Glover started reminiscing about how they listened to Vanilla Fudge while sailing up and down the Thames River in England in the late '60s. Guitarist Steve Morse burst into the room, exclaiming, " Hey Mark, I hear you're gonna jam with us. Great!" The night got better and better as Mark saw Edgar Winter backstage (recalling that he had once embarrassed himself mistaking Edgar for his brother Johnny). Winter was the opening act. All the while Mark rehearsed "Smoke On The Water" in his head but he couldn't hear the chords to the chorus. He went searching for a keyboard somewhere to have a private moment to figure them out—to no avail. Time grew short and at the last minute Mark ran up to Steve Morse's young son, a budding guitarist who was also going to play onstage with his father, and screamed "Help me out. What are the chords to the chorus?" The boy shouted back, like a pro, "C to A flat!"

Gillan then announced to the audience that a surprise guest was about to join them and Payne told Mark to hit the stage. There he stood behind Don Airey's monster Hammond C3 rig that had two killer high-powered Leslies. He growled on it with a few windups to test it as Don stood to his right about to play supporting keys on a synthesizer. For Mark, it was classic rock heaven. The band tore through the tune flawlessly. Morse's guitar sound was huge as was the sound and power of the whole band. But on one of his windups, Mark ripped a callous on his left hand and some blood spewed over the keys. Later, he heard a comment that some of Purple's members said to "let Stein's blood dry on the Hammond—he'll be there forever ." Backstage after the show, Mark was introduced to Nicko McBrain, Iron Maiden's drummer. McBrain told Mark, in an odd statement, "when you see Carmine, tell him I hope there's no bad feelings."

Bruce Payne asked Mark, "What's Going On With Vanilla Fudge ?" Mark told him they still did shows from time to time. Payne replied, "If you can get the original group together, I'd like you to open for us next month at Radio City Music hall in New York." Mark could hardly believe it—yet another chance. Payne added, "I think the time is right for Vanilla Fudge to tour again. I'm going to check things out."

During the course of the evening, Mark also ran into Jeff Miller who at the time was a booking agent working with Steve Peck one of the executives at Fantasma, a top Agency located in South Florida. Payne told Mark when he received approval from the other Fudge members to put the Radio City gig together with them, everything would all fall into place. Mark called Carmine first thing when he got up the next day and shocked his former drummer. Then, he related the news to Tim and Vinny, and once he had approval from everyone, he let Miller know it was a "go." A few days later, Bruce Payne informed Mark everything was moving forward and that Deep Purple was happy that they were

243

doing the show together.

The concert was set for August 7, and the band rehearsed at Randy Pratt's house in Manhasset, Long Island two days before. Carmine had set it up and also hired a small crew. The basement was set up beautifully with a good PA, a Hammond, drums, amps, and everything a band could want. When Mark arrived, he walked into the kitchen and ran into Tim, who was a bit spaced from being up half the night .Then Carmine and Vinny walked in. "Here we are again," Mark thought, "with yet another shot at the brass ring." We all knew it and rehearsals went well—very well. On the afternoon of the show, Bob Patterson, Mark's brother-in-law, drove him into Manhattan along with Ryan, his nephew and young friend who, as a classic rock fan, was excited. When they got to the city, the ticker tape on the Radio City Hall marquee   kept flashing   DEEP PURPLE   AND THE ORIGINAL VANILLA FUDGE .TONIGHT! Patty had helped arrange this greeting with one of the heads of promotion at Madison Square Garden Productions. She also coordinated some of the load in and sound check times not only for the Fudge, but, as fate would have it, for Purple as well. Whenever confusion raised its ugly head and crew and band members start freaking out, Patty always has a way of getting things organized. She was leading this charge from back in Florida; she had to stay there because Dorie, their daughter-in-law was about to give birth to Mark's new granddaughter.

The sound check was 3 o'clock p.m. As they approached the venue, fans with a slew of albums to sign reached out to Mark with pens in hands. "That always felt good," he noted. As they found when they went to the dressing room, a huge log was given to Mark to sign. He learned this was an honor—it was signed by many artists from all walks of the entertainment business, from Frank Sinatra to Tony Bennett and just about half the rock stars in the universe .The Deep Purple crew were great as they got permission from Roger Glover to set his bass rig back so there would be room for a riser for Mark's keyboards.

It was now time for the sound check. Things were running a bit late and union rules said the band had about twenty minutes, which under normal circumstances would have been fine. But what's ever normal with this quartet? The drums started to sound fine in the monitors. Mark liked heavy kick and lots of snare, and the soundmen got the Hammond sounding good as well, along with Mark's Korg X -50 synthesizer that he used for orchestra sounds and cosmic effects. Vinny had his guitar sounding great, whereupon Tim suddenly said that there was something wrong with his bass rig. He said he couldn't hear any bass and then begins what was to be one of the most intense moments the band ever experienced! Screaming at the top of his lungs, he started demanding a different bass rig. He insisted that he could not hear his bass and cursed the crew and anyone that came near him. "What a fucking nightmare! It was The Taj Mahal all over again times a hundred," Mark thought. He was the only one that couldn't hear his bass, because everyone else heard it just fine. Mark was mortified as Tim carried on like a lunatic, grabbing Carmine—who seemed to have some sway over him, and pleaded with him to try and stop his madness. They were running out of time. Privately Mark fumed. "I couldn't believe he was pulling this shit in front of the whole Radio City entourage. Mark vowed to himself, "NEVER AGAIN." Suddenly, the monitor technician ran Tim's bass through the huge side fills, and that made him happy. Only by then, they only had five minutes to get the vocal mix. They ran through "People Get Ready "and the blend came quickly. What a scene. Mark was certain they'd never make it. He approached the monitor technician stage left and apologized for Tim's behavior. "Don't worry," he replied. "I've seen worse." Later, backstage a beautiful buffet was shared by everyone as the moment faded. But Mark was really upset with Tim when one of their crew guys George Fedden asked Tim to talk to Mark and cool out. They shook hands as he came over with a plate of food, apologizing for what had occurred. Mark said, "Look, let's get focused now on the show; that's what really matters. This could lead to a lot more for us," but deep down, he feared the damage might have already been done. I mean, the Purple people, the entire production crew, everyone witnessed Tim's meltdown.

"Good Evening and Welcome to the Most Famous Music Hall on the Planet," Mark screamed over the mike to a packed house after Leslie Gold, the Radio Chick introduced the Fudge. They played with confidence and great energy that night while the Purple members watched from both sides of the stage. During Carmine's drum solo on "Shotgun," Mark jumped off his riser and grabbed a towel and chugged down a bottle of water .This break in the action was always a welcome relief for him to catch his breath and rest for a few minutes. Walking over to Steve Morse, he said "What a great band! You guys have amazing energy" while Bruce Payne added "The audience really likes you, Mark. You've got a hell of a voice!" Just then, it was time for Mark to jump back on stage to finish the show. The Fudge played Led Zeppelin's "Dazed and Confused," which segued into Mark's keyboard solo, then into "Season Of The Witch,"one of the more intriguing and dynamic parts of the performance where Vinny sang his ass off. The show, of course, closed with "You Keep Me Hangin' On," where the band got the crowd to sing the chorus with them, and sing it and sing it they did while the house lights went up and all was standing at the finale. "WE DONE GOOD," Mark silently admitted.

After the show Mark met with his sister, Sharon along with cousins, nieces and yes, nephews who were waiting to say hello. He was pleased they all came out to support him and the band and it had to be an exciting night . . . for everyone.

Then, Mark heard the monster Hammond sound of Don Airey playing low-end fourths that came up from the belly of the theater. Quickly, he told his family that he had to watch the show. Deep Purple rocked like Deep Purple does. They had multitudes of fans worldwide, and they've never let a fan go home unhappy, certainly not on that night.

And so it was. The big night was over. Would it help to get Vanilla Fudge back on the touring map? Perhaps secure a spot, like so many classic bands had, for regular appearances in Las Vegas? Would the Purple gang invite them to open for them on future shows? Would the fact that they rocked the house, created a buzz, and had so many people talking about them all over New York City generate a resurgeance?

Upon his arrival back home in Florida, Mark was greeted by Dorie and Rich and his new-born granddaughter, Melody Stein who came into this world on August 9, 2007. Patty came walking out of the kitchen, a bit emotional. It was good to be back home—but it was good to be back on stage, in the limelight, as well. But as the days turned into weeks, no offers came . Mark made calls to all the agents he could muster and except for a few scattered appearances, Vanilla Fudge was out of work…..again…..again…..and so it was.

POSTSCRIPT

When author Larry Schweikart contacted Mark in 2008 after seeing his e-mail on the rescue dogs website, they talked about Patty's wish to see Mark get down his stories in a biography. After a few visits, and some heavy outlining by Mark, they began writing this book. Meanwhile, Larry had other, political history writing projects, one of which came out in 2010 called *Seven Events that Made America America*. That book had already been under contract for a year, and had a chapter called "A Steel Guitar Rocks the Iron Curtain," about rock music's influence and part in bringing down the Berlin Wall. Director Marc Leif and Larry had gotten together through a mutual friend, director Charles Carner, who had directed an award-winning television show, "Who Killed Atlanta's Children?" in the 1990s. Marc Leif and Larry saw a documentary film in the rock chapter, perhaps with other chapters made into documentaries later. Larry formed "Rockin' the Wall, LLC," a motion picture company to make the movie and began soliciting investors (something he knew almost nothing about) while Marc engaged in pre-production of the film.

They intended to interview three sets of people to tell the story: government officials and historians, who could offer general perspective; people from behind the Iron Curtain who lived under communism, whom they called "witnesses"; and most of all, rock and rollers who had played in Europe during the Cold War, on either side of the Iron Curtain. Mark and Vinny not only were natural interview subjects because the Fudge played in Europe, but Mark's contacts for the book now blossomed into other interview subjects for the film, including Robby Krieger, Rudy Sarzo, Jimmy Haslip, David Paich of Toto, and others. Filming began in the spring of 2010, and the camera crew arrived in Fort. Lauderdale to film Mark and his band record and perform four songs that "Rockin' the Wall" contracted with them for the movie: Mark's originals "We Are Survivors," "Break It Down," and covers of the classics, "Ball of Confusion" (by the Temptations) and "People Got to Be Free" by the Rascals. Initially, Felix Cavaliere had agreed to fly down and do the session as well, but as the time approached, the deal never materialized, so Mark sang the classic song himself.

Employing his familiar mates, Jimmy Jack, Steve Argy, and guitarist Jimi Fiano, Mark's band pounded out the four songs in what seemed record time, all of them with the energy and power reminiscent of both the Fudge and Mark's "Boomerang" band. They were prominently featured in ads and promotion for the film, which as of this writing was just being marketed to buyers in America and Europe.

About the Authors

Mark Stein, lead vocalist and keyboardist of the classic rock band, Vanilla Fudge, has spent most of his life in the world of rock music. During the musical and cultural renaissance of the 1960's , Vanilla Fudge set the stage for many great artists of that era , from Led Zeppelin, Deep Purple, Alice Cooper, Three Dog Night, Janis Joplin and beyond. At present, he still brings his dynamic approach to rock entertaining thousands around the world. He lives in Fort Lauderdale, Florida.

Larry Schweikart, professor of history at the University of Dayton, is a former rock drummer who opened for Steppenwolf, the James Gang, and other noted rock acts. He is the co-author (with Michael Allen) of the New York Times #1 bestselling book, *A Patriot's History of the United States* and has authored numerous other bestselling books, including *Seven Events that Made America America*, He produces documentary films, including "Rockin' the Wall," the story of rock music's part in bringing down the Iron Curtain, and "Other Walls 2 Fall," about music's part in penetrating and transforming radical Islam. He lives in Centerville, OH.

Acknowledgments

We would also like to thank Brian Bennett, who oversaw the formatting of this book, and Adam Schweikart, who conducted research for some of the chapters. We would also like to thank Patty Stein for organizing the interviews and photos for this book. And, thank you to Jack Langer for believing in our vision for this book. And a special thanks to Ned Levine for all his support and creativity.

R I P... Mike Kovins, Vince Wasilewski, Tony "Red" Ruffino, Ronnie James Dio, Bruce Gary, and Clarence Clemons

Chapter One Notes

1. Charles R. Cross, *Room Full of Mirrors: A Biography of Jimi Hendrix* (New York: Hyperion, 2005).

2. Mike Evans, *Rock 'n' Roll's Strangest Moments: Extraordinary Tales From Over 50 Years of Rock Music History* (London: Robson Books, 2006), 116.

3. Robert Christgau, "Anatomy of a Love Festival," *Esquire*, January 1968, and reprinted in his *Any Old Way You Choose It: Rock and Other Pop Music, 1967-1973* (Baltimore: Penguin, 1973).

4. David Suisman, *Selling Sounds: The Commercial Revolution in American Music* (Cambridge, MA: Harvard, 2009).

5. Ibid., 19-20.

6. Robert S. Lynd and Helen Merrell Lynd, *Middletown: A Study in Modern American Culture* (New York: Harcourt Brace, 1929).

7. Ray Manzarek, *Light My Fire: My Life With the Doors* (New York: Berkeley Boulevard, 1999), 24.

8. Keith Emerson, *Pictures of An Exhibitionist* (London: John Blake, 2004), 27.

9. Manzarek, *Light My Fire*, 28-9.

10. Interview with Billy Joel, February 24, 2010.

11. Ibid.

12. Interview with Phil Chen, June 17, 2010.

13. Elijah Wald, *How the Beatles Destroyed Rock and Roll* (New York: Oxford, 2009), 206.

14. Wald, *How the Beatles Destroyed Rock and Roll*, 193.

15. David P. Szatmary, *Rockin' in Time: A Social History of Rock-and-Roll*, 6th ed. (Upper Saddle River, NJ: Pearson, 2007), 85.

16. Interviews with Mark Stein, February 26-7, and various dates, 2009.

17. Brian Wilson with Todd Gold, *Wouldn't It Be Nice: My Own Story* (New York: HarperCollins, 1991), passim.

18. Interview with Alice Cooper, July 29, 1009.

19. Peter Ames Carlin, *Catch a Wave: The Rise, Fall, & Redemption of the Beach Boys' Brian Wilson'* (New York: Rodale Books, 2006).

20. Ibid., 91.

21. "Parents, Don't Worry—This Music Will Never Last," *San Diego Union Tribune*, July 25, 2004.

22. Glenn C. Altschuler, *All Shook Up: How Rock 'N' Roll Changed America* (Oxford: Oxford U. Press, 2003), 175.

23. Richard Starkey (Ringo Starr), "It Don't Come Easy," Apple Records, 1971. (Ironically, Brian Wilson would perform with Starr on his 1992 album, "Time Takes Time."

24. Forrest White, *Fender: The Inside Story* (San Francisco: Backbeat Books, 1994).

25. Jonathan Gould, *Can't Buy Me Love: The Beatles, Britain, and America* (New York: Harmony Books, 2007), 61.

26. Interview with Felix Cavaliere, March 10, 2009.

27. Interview with Billy Joel, February 24, 2010.

28. For example, author's interview with Mark Stein, keyboardist with Vanilla Fudge, February 26, 2009. Stein was widely regarded as one of the best Hammond organ players in the country. But the same could be seen with guitarist Jimi Hendrix, who learned to play as a backup guitarist in a half-dozen bands.

29. Interviews with Ian Paice, June 16, 2010, and Liberty DeVitto, June 17, 2010.

30. Interview with Liberty DeVitto, June 17, 2010.

31. Interview with Ian Paice, June 16, 2010.

32. Larry Schweikart, *The Entrepreneurial Adventure: A History of Business in the United States* (Ft. Worth, TX: Harcourt, 2000), 397.

34. Szatmary, *Rockin' in Time*, 140.

35. Altschuler, *All Shook Up* (Oxford: Oxford U. Press, 2003), 178.

36. Interview with Tony Bongiovi, March 25, 2010.

37. Gould, *Can't Buy Me Love*, 147.

38. Altschuler, *All Shook Up*, 183.

39. Aerosmith with Stephen Davis, *Walk This Way: The Autobiography of Aerosmith* (New York: Itbooks, 1997), 95.

40. Aerosmith, *Walk This Way*, 95.

41. Rudy Sarzo, *Off the Rails: Aboard the Crazy Train in the Blizzard of Oz* (San Francisco: TooSmartPublishing, 2008), 80.

42. Interview with Dave Mason, April 14, 2009.

43. Interview with Pete Rivera, July 22, 2009.

44. Interview with Vince Martell, April 21, 2009.

45. Interview with Jerry Corbetta, July 19, 2009.

46. Barry Miles, *Zappa: A Biography* (New York: Grove Press, 2004), 150-1, 222.. This was a continuation of the legendary tour where during a Mothers concert in Monteux, Switzerland, a fire broke out and burned down the casino. Deep Purple, who had been in the audience and were booked to record an album in the casino ballroom, scampered back to their hotel and watched the flames from their rooms, where Roger Glover jotted down the words to their biggest hit ever, "Smoke On the Water."

47. Interview with Robby Krieger, July 1, 2009.

48. Interview with Chuck Negron, September 17, 2009.

49. Interview with David Paich, June 25, 2009.

50. Eric Clapton, *Clapton: The Autobiography* (New York: Broadway Books, 2007), 42.

51. Wald, *How the Beatles Destroyed Rock 'n' Roll*, 13.

52. Ibid., 13.

53. Ibid., 2.

54. Fred Kaplan, "Teen Spirit," *Slate*, February 6, 2004.

55. E-mail with Mark Stein, April 21, 2009.

56. E-mail with Felix Cavaliere, April 7, 2009.

57. Manzarek, *Light My Fire*, 94-5.

58. Gould, *Can't Buy Me Love*, 221. The influence of the Beatles on American the American music scene was, in an understatement, massive. West Coast rockers such as Doors keyboardist Ray Manzarek and east coast "white soul" singer/keyboardist Mark Stein of Vanilla Fudge identified the Beatles as one of the most important influences in their music (interviews with Mark Stein, various dates, 2008-9). Dave Mason, of Traffic, observed "they were raw, brand new, everyone copied them" (interview, April 14, 2009). The impact was not universal: Doors guitarist Robby Krieger cited more edgier British bands, such as the Rolling Stones and Animals, as his primary influence; and David Paich of Toto leaned toward American jazz and blues artists (interview with Robby Krieger, July 1, 2009; interview with David Paich, June 25, 2009).

59. Fred Goodman, *The Mansion on a Hill: Dylan, Young, Geffen, Springsteen, and the Head-on Collision of Rock and Commerce* (New York: Times Books, 1997), 27.

Chapter Two Notes

1. James Miller, *Flowers in the Dustbin: The Rise of Rock and Roll, 1947 1977* (New York: Simon & Schuster, 1999), 57-61; Carlo Wolff, *Cleveland Rock and Roll Memories* (Cleveland, OH: Gray & Company, Publishers, 2006); John A. Jackson, *Big Beat Heat: Alan Freed and the Early Years of Rock & Roll* (Indianapolils, IN: Schirmer Books, 1991); Wes Smith, *The Pied Pipers of Rock 'N' Roll: Radio Deejays of the 50s and 60s* (Athens, GA: Longstreet Press, 1989).

2. Glenn C. Altschuler, *All Shook Up: How Rock 'N' Roll Changed America* (Oxford: Oxford UniversityPress, 2003), 21.

3. Ibid., 148-9.

4. Ibid., 151.
5. James F. Dunnigan and Albert A. Nofi, *Dirty Little Secrets of World War II* (New York: Quill/William Morrow, 1994), 26.

6. Larry Schweikart and Lynne Pierson Doti, *American Entrepreneur: The Fascinating Stories of the People Who Defined Business in the United States* (New York: Amacom, 2010), 335-42. Auto historian John Heitmann, in conversations with the author, has speculated that the push-button car radio, with its pre-set station tuning, was connected to the timing of traffic lights. See his book *The Automobile in American Life* (New York: Macfarland, 2009).

7. Mick Brown, *Tearing Down the Wall of Sound: the Rise and Fall of Phil Spector* (New York: Vintage, 2008), 41.

8. Altschuler, *All Shook Up*, 126.

9. Ibid., 176.

10. Elijah Wald, *How the Beatles Destroyed Rock 'n' Roll: An Alternative History of American Popular Music* (New York: Oxford, 2009), 158.

11. Altschuler, *All Shook Up*, 82.

12. Ibid.

13. David Crosby, *Since Then: How I Survived Everything and Lived to Tell About It* (New York: Putnam's, 2006), 166.

14. Interview with Jerry Corbetta, July 19, 2009.

15. Scott later changed his name to Neil Bogart and headed Casablanca Records during its heyday, in the process discovering Donna Summer and launching the career of the queen of disco. He also saw the potential of an obscure band and odd-looking band named Kiss.

16. Keith Emerson, *Pictures of an Exhibitionist* (London: John Blake, 2004), 35.

17. Ibid., 35.

18. Ray Manzarek, *Light My Fire: My Life With the Doors* (New York: Berkley Press, 1997), 163.

19. Ibid.

20. Michael Beschloss, *The Crisis Years: Kennedy and Khrushchev, 1960-1963* (New York: Edward Burlingame Books, 1991); Sheldon M. Stern, *The Week the World Stood Still: Inside the Secret Cuban Missile Crisis* (Stanford, CA: Stanford University Pres, 2005).

21. Ray Manzarek, "The Doors: Myth and Reality," on-line interview, n.d.; Interview with Vince Martell, April 21, 2009.

22. Manzarek, "The Doors: Myth and Reality" and *Light My Fire*, 158; interview with Robby Krieger, July 1, 2009.

23. Larry Schweikart and Michael Allen, *A Patriot's History of the United States from Columbus's Great Discovery to the War on Terror* (New York: Sentinel, 2006), 676-79, 680-95. For some of the myths of Vietnam, see Larry Schweikart, *America's Victories: Why the U.S. Wins Wars and Will Win the War on Terror* (New York: Sentinel, 2006), passim.

24. Kenneth J. Bindas and Craig Houston, "'Takin' Care of Business': Rock Music, the Vietnam War, and the Myth of the 1960's," *The Historian*, 52, November 1989, 1-23.

25. Interview with Robby Krieger, July 1, 2009.

26. "Jimi's Private Parts," http://www.thesmokinggun.com/archive/0803051jimi1.html; Charles Cross, Room Full of Mirrors (New York: Hyperion, 2005) claims Hendrix faked being a homosexual to get a discharge, but Hendrix told reporters he was discharged because he broke his ankle. In all likelihood, it was a combination of Hendrix's attitude and injury that led to his discharge.

27. Charles R. Cross, *Room Full of Mirrors: A Biography of Jimi Hendrix* (New York: Hyperion, 2005), 66.

28. Steven Roby, *Black Gold* (North Hollywood, CA: Billboard Books, 2002), 15.

29. Cross, *Room Full of Mirrors*, 248.

30. Ibid.

31. Peter Doggett, *There's a Riot Going On: Revolutionaries, Rock Stars, and the Rise and Fall of the '60s* (New York: Canongate, 2007), 26.

32. Ibid.

33. Ibid., 79.

34. "Beatles Song 'Inspiration' Dies," BBC News, September 28, 2009, http://news.bbc.co.uk/2/hi/uk_news/england/8278785.stm

35. Doggett, *There's a Riot Going On*, 87.

36. Jeff Tamarkin, *Got a Revolution! The Turbulent Flight of Jefferson Airplane* (New York: Atria Books, 2003), 114.

37. Doggett, *There's a Riot Going On*, 88.

38. Fred Goodman, *The Mansion on a Hill: Dylan, Young, Geffen, Springsteen, and the Head-on Collision of Rock and Commerce* (New York: Times Books, 1997), x.

39. BBC's Chris Welch interview with Mark Stein, November 2006, transcript in Mark Stein's possession.
40. Interview with Liberty DeVitto, June 17, 2010.

41. Richard Williams, *Phil Spector: Out of His Head* (Auckland, NZ: Abacus, 2003), ch. 5, passim.

42. Interview with George "Shadow" Morton, September 20, 2009. Morton was sure the band was still playing traditional cover songs, but Mark was certain by then Vanilla Fudge had begun doing its first album "show."

43. Interview with Liberty DeVitto, June 17, 2010.

44. Stephen Davis, *Hammer of the Gods: The Led Zeppelin Saga* (New York: Harper Entertainment, 2008), 62.

45. Wald, How the Beatles Destroyed Rock and Roll, 197.

46. Ibid.

47. Bill Graham and Robert Greenfield, *Bill Graham Presents: My Life Inside Rock and Out* (Cambridge, MA: Da Capo Press, 2004), 159.

48. Ibid., 254.

49. Ibid.

50. Ibid., 257.

51. Ibid., 181.

52. Ibid., 172.

53. Marc Shapiro, *Carlos Santana: Back on Top* (New York: St. Martin's, 2000), 25. Shapiro claimed Santana "blew the Atlantic audition on purpose" because the group

wanted to sign with Columbia (26).

54. Goodman, *Mansion on a Hill*, 268.

55. Tamarkin, *Got a Revolution!*, passim.

56. Dave Marsh, *Before I Get Old: The Story of the Who* (New York: St. Martin's, 1983), 260.

57. Ibid., 456.

58. Graham and Greenfield, *Bill Graham Presents*, 172.

59. Interview with Peter Lewis, http://www.sundazed.com/scene/exclusives/peter_lewis 3.html.

60. Interview with Peter Lewis, http://www.terrascope.co.uk/MyBackPages/Peter_Lewis.pdf.
61. Holly George-Warren and Patricia Romanowski, eds., *The Rolling Stone Encyclopedia of Rock and Roll* (New York: Fireside/Rolling Stone Press, 2001), 913-4; "Sonny Bono," http://en.wikipedia.org/wiki/Sonny_Bono. Rev. 2/13/2011

Chapter Three Notes
1. Eric Clapton, *Clapton: The Autobiography* (New York: Broadway Books, 2007), 90.

2. Dave Thompson, *Smoke on the Water: The Deep Purple Story* (Toronto: ECW Press, 2004), 33.

3. Ibid., 47.

4. Interview with Ian Paice, June 16, 2010.

5. Aerosmith with Stephen Davis, *Walk This Way: The Autobiography of Aerosmith* (New York: Itbooks, 1999), 143.

6. Ibid., 150.

7. Michael David Harris, *Always on Sunday: Ed Sullivan, an Inside View* (New York: Signet, 1968), 153.

8. Jake Austen, *TV a-go-go: Rock on TV from American Bandstand to American Idol* (Chicago: Chicago Review Press, 2005), 16.

9. Joel Selvin, *For the Record: Sly and the Family Stone: An Oral History* (New York: Quill, 1998), xi.

10. Marc Shapiro, *Carlos Santana: Back on Top* (New York: St. Martin's, 2000), 86.

11. Ibid., 87.

12. Ibid., 90-1.

13. Ibid., 100.

14. David Szatmary, *Rockin' in Time: A Social History of Rock-and-Roll*, 6th ed. (Upper Saddle River, NJ: 2007), 154.

15. Ibid.

16. Ibid.

17. Bill Graham and Robert Greenfield, *Bill Graham Presents: My Life Inside Rock and Out* (Cambridge, MA: Da Capo Pres, 2004), 243.

18. Ibid., 244.

19. Ibid., 244.

20. Clapton, *Clapton: The Autobiography*, 134.

21. Stephen Davis, *Hammer of the Gods: The Led Zeppelin Saga* (New York: Harper Entertainment, 2008), 303-4.

22. Ray Manzarek, *Light My Fire: My Life with the Doors* (New York: Berkeley Boulevard Books, 1998), 292.

23. Clapton, *Clapton: The Autobiography*, 157.

24. Ibid., 156-7; 176.

25. Dave Marsh, *Before I Get Old: The Story of the Who* (New York: St. Martin's, 1983), 396.

26. Ibid., 396-7.

27. Ibid., 397.

28. Rick Wakeman with Martin Roach, *Grumpy Old Rock Star* (London: Preface, 2008), 174.

29. Ibid., 175.

30. Interview with Richard Supa, May 6, 2010.

31. Shapiro, *Carlos Santana*, 99.

32. Rudy Sarzo, *Off the Rails: Aboard the Crazy Train in the Blizzard of Oz* (San Francisco: TooSmartPublishing, 2008), 222.

33. Don Felder with Wendy Holden, *Heaven and Hell: My Life in the Eagles (1974-2001)* (New York: John Wiley, 2008), 166.

34. Ibid., 167.

35. Gary Herman, *Rock 'N' Roll Babylon* (Norfolk: Fakenham Press, 1982), 44; Bill Wyman, *Rolling With the Stones* (New York: DK Publishing, 2002), 326.

36. Marsh, *Before I Get Old*, 397.

37. See Gavin Edwards, *'Scuse Me While I Kiss This Guy and Other Misleading Lyrics* (New York: Fireside, 1995).

38. Interview with Tony Ruffino, May 5, 2009.

39. Ibid.

40. Ibid.

41. Interviews with Mark Stein, various dates, 2008-09.
42. Interview with George "Shadow" Morton, September 20, 2009.

43. Ibid.

44. Clapton, *Clapton: The Autobiography*, 98.

45. Chris Welch, "Vanilla Fudge, 'Out Through the In Door,'" 2006.

46. Ibid.

47. Davis, *Hammer of the Gods*, 77.

Chapter Four Notes

1. This claim is made by Dave White in his "About.com" writeup of Cream, http://classicrock.about.com/od/bandsandartists/p/Cream.htm.

2. David Dalton, "Finally, the Shocking Truth About Woodstock Can be Told, or Kill It Before It Clones Itself," the *Gadfly*, August 1999, http://gadfly.org/1999-08/toc.asp, and conversations with David Dalton and cited in Larry Schweikart and Michael Allen, *A Patriot's History of the United States from Columbus's Great Discovery to the War on Terror* (New York: Sentinel, 2006), 703-4.

3. Jonathan Gould, *Can't Buy Me Love: The Beatles, Britain, and America* (New York: Harmony Books, 2007), 566.

4. David Dalton, "Finally, the Shocking Truth About Woodstock Can be Told."

5. Bill Graham and Robert Greenfield, *Bill Graham Presents: My Life Inside Rock and Out* (Cambridge, MA: Da Capo Pres, 2004), 288.

6. Ibid.

7. Ellen Sander, "It's the Sound," *L.A. Free Press*, September 5, 1969.

8. Abbie Hoffman, *Woodstock Nation* (New York: Vintage, 1969), 91; Peter Doggett, *There's a Riot Going On: Revolutionaries, Rock Stars, and the Rise and Fall of the '60s* (New York: Canongate, 2007), 275.

9. Hoffman, *Woodstock* Nation, 4-5; Doggett, *There's a Riot Going* On, 270.

10. Doggett, *There's a Riot Going* On, 516.

11. Ibid., 512.

12. Ibid., 513.

13. Jeff Tamarkin, *Got a Revolution! The Turbulent Flight of Jefferson Airplane* (New York: Atria Books, 2003), 73.

14. Ibid., 73.

15. Ibid., 75.

16. David P. Szatmary, *Rockin' in Time: A Social History of Rock-and-Roll*, 6th ed. (Upper Saddle River, NJ: 2007), 229.

17. Ibid.

18. Ibid.

19. Artemy Troitsky, "Rock in the USSR: The True Story of Rock in Russia," http://www.planetaquarium.com/eng/pub/doc_at1.html

20. Timothy W. Ryback, *Rock Around the Bloc: A History of Rock Music in Eastern Europe and the Soviet Union* (New York: Oxford, 1990), 26.

21. Ibid., 42.

22. Ibid., 58.

23. All this material is from Ryback, *Rock Around the Bloc*, 50-58 and passim. See also Tony Mitchell, "Mixing Pop and Politics: Rock Music in Czechoslovakia before and after the Velvet Revolution," *Popular Music*, 11, 187-203.

24. Ryback, *Rock Around the Bloc*, 63-4.

25. Doggett, *There's a Riot Going* On, 95.

26. Ibid.

27. Keith Emerson, *Pictures of an Exhibitionist* (London: John Black, 2004), 122.

28. Interview with Chuck Negron, September 17, 2009; e-mail from Chuck Negron, October 6, 2009.

29. Interview with Billy Joel, February 24, 2010.

30. Interviews with Leslie Mandoki, various dates, January 2010, as seen in "Rockin' the Wall," Larry Schweikart and Marc Leif, producers.

31. Tamarkin, *Got a Revolution!* 143.

32. Fred Goodman, *The Mansion on the Hill: Dylan, Young, Geffen, Springsteen, and the Head-on Collision of Rock and Commerce* (New York: Random House, 1997), 237.

33. Tamarkin, *Got a Revolution!* 143.

34. Don Felder with Wendy Holden, *Heaven and Hell: My Life in the Eagles (1974-2001)* (New York: John Wiley, 2008), 166.

35. Ibid., 167.

36. Mary Cross, *Madonna: A Biography* (Westport, CT: Greenwood Press, 2007), 60.

37. Ginger Baker and Ginette Baker, *Ginger Baker, Hellraiser: The Autobiography of the World's Greatest Drummer* (London: John Blake, 2009), 232.

38. Tamarkin, *Got a Revolution!* 58-9.

39. Ibid.

40. Ibid., 60.

41. Ibid., 60-1.

42. Goodman, *The Mansion on the Hill*, 310.

43. Ibid.

44. Stephen Davis, *Hammer of the Gods: The Led Zeppelin Saga* (New York: Harper Entertainment, 2008), 164-5.

45. Ibid.

46. Ibid.

47. Gould, *Can't Buy Me Love*, 436.

Chapter Five Notes

1. Dave Marsh, *Before I Get Old: The Story of the Who* (New York: St. Martin's Press, 1983), 456.

2. Ibid.

3. Interviews and e-mails with Rudy Sarzo, various dates, 2009-1010. See also Rudy

Sarzo, *Off the Rails: Aboard Crazy Train in the Blizzard of Oz* (San Francisco: TooSmartPublishing, 2008).

4. Marc Shapiro, *Carlos Santana: Back on Top* (New York: St. Martin's, 2000), 175.

5. Tom McGrath, *MTV: The Making of a Revolution* (Philadelphia: Running Press, 1996).

6. Ibid., 39.

7. Ibid., 96.

8. Ibid.

9. "Ann Wilson of Heart Undergoes Weight Loss Surgery," http://www.youtube.com/watch?v=18G8fqZgYMc

10. "Ozzy Bites Head Off Bat!" http://www.rollingstone.com/Mythozzy

11. McGrath, *MTV*, 118.

12. Ibid., 134.

13. Ibid., 144.

14. Interview with Tony Bongiovi, March 25, 2010.

15. Mick Brown, *Tearing Down the Wall of Sound* (New York: Vintage, 2007), 3.

16. Ibid., 81.

17. Greg Milner, *Perfecting Sound Forever: An Aural History of Recorded Music* (New York: Faber and Faber, 2009), 152-3.

18. Ibid., 153.

19. Ibid.

20. Ibid.

21. Brown, *Tearing Down the Wall of Sound*, 110.

22. Ibid., 6.

23. Ibid., 51.

24. Ibid., 61.

25. Ibid., 6.

26. Ibid., 75-6.

27. Ibid., 179.

28. Peter Ames Carlin, *Catch a Wave: The Rise, Fall & Redemption of the Beach Boys' Brian Wilson* (New York: Rodale, 2006), 44.

29. Ibid., 45.

30. Ibid., 140.

31. Ibid., 45.

32. Ibid., 46. Interestingly, though, neither the names "Beach Boys" or "Brian Wilson" appear in Dave Zimmer's 40th anniversary edition of CSN's biography, *Crosby, Stills & Nash* (Philadelphia: Da Capo Press, 2008).

33. Joe Stuessy and Scott Lipscomb, *Rock and Roll: It's History and Stylistic Development*, 6th edition (Upper Saddle River, NJ: Pearson, 2009).

34. Brown, *Tearing Down the Wall of Sound*, 179.

35. Ibid.

36. "Johnny Ramone Stays Tough: Ramones Guitarist Reflects on Dee Dee's Death and the Difficult Eighties," *Rolling Stone*, June 24, 2002; "Phil Spector, the Ramones, and a Gun," http://new.music.yahoo.com/blogs/stopthepresses/22948/phil-spector-the-ramones-and-a-gun/

37. *New York Post*, April 13, 2009.

38. Aerosmith with Stephen Davis, *Walk This Way: The Autobiography of Aerosmith* (New York: Itbooks, 1997), 2-3.

39. Ibid., 2-3.

40. Ibid., 252-3.

41. Ibid., 260, 291.

Chapter Six Notes

1. Elijah Wald, *How the Beatles Destroyed Rock 'n' Roll* (New York: Oxford, 2009), 2.

2. Jonathan Gould, *Can't Buy Me Love: The Beatles, Britain and America* (London: Piatkus, 2008), 560.

3. Interview with Andy Johns, June 15, 2010.

4. Ibid.

5. Ibid.

6. Interview with George "Shadow" Morton, September 20, 2009.

7. Gould, *Can't Buy Me Love*, 600-1.

8. Wald, *How the Beatles Destroyed Rock 'n' Roll*, 4.

9. Jeff Tamarkin, *Got a Revolution: The Turbulent Flight of Jefferson Airplane* (New York: Atria Books, 2003), 221-222.

10. Dave Marsh, *Before I Get Old: The Story of the Who* (New York: St. Martin's Press, 1983), 349.

11. Ibid.

12. Ibid., 354.

13. Ibid., 350.
14. Stephen Davis, *Hammer of the Gods: The Led Zeppelin Saga* (New York: Harper, 2008), 277.

15. Legs McNeil and Gillian McCain, *Please Kill Me: The Uncensored Oral History of Punk* (New York: Grove Press, 1996), passim.

16. Ibid., 225.

17. "Biography Channel: The Sex Pistols," December 5, 2009. The official web site says "He fatally overdosed . . . most likely by accident. . . ." http://www.sexpistolsofficial.com/index.php?module=biography&biography_item_id=29

18. McNeil and McCain, *Please Kill* Me, passim.

19. Ibid., 228.

20. Ibid.

21. Ibid.

22. Ibid., 245.

23. Ibid.

24. Marsh, *Before I Get Old*, 230-1.

25. Piero Scaruffi, *A History of Rock and Dance Music: From the Guitar to the Laptop From Chicago to Shanghai*, 2 vols. (Milan, Italy: Omniware Publishing, 20009), quoted at http://www.scaruffi.com/history/cpt34.html.

26. Larry Harris with Curt Gooch and Jeff Suhs, *And Party Every Day: The Inside Story of Casablanca Records* (New York: Backbeat Books, 2009).

27. David, *Hammer of the Gods*, 322-3.

28. McNeil and McCain, *Please Kill* Me, 334.

29. Ibid., 299.

30. John Robb, *Punk Rock: An Oral History* (London: Ebury Press, 2006), 97; Jon Savage, *Anarchy, Sex Pistols, Punk Rock and Beyond* (New York: St. Martin's Press, 1992), 108-112.

31. McNeil and McCain, *Please Kill* Me, 125.

32. Interview with Alice Cooper, March 17, 2009.

33. Ibid.

34. Ibid.

35. George Kimball *Rolling Stone*, August 19, 1971.

36. "Con Air," 1997, http://www.imdb.com/title/tt0118880/quotes

37. Interviews with Mark Stein, various dates, 2008-2009.

38. Author Larry Schweikart's bands often alternated nights at the Aquarius Club in Phoenix, Arizona, with Tommy Bolin's "Energy" in the early 1970s.

39. Greg Prato, *Touched by Magic: The Tommy Bolin Story* (New York: Greg Prato, 2008), 134.

40. Interview with Jimmy Haslip, June 18, 2009.

41. Prato, *Touched by Magic*, 155.

42. Ibid.

43. Interview with Glenn Hughes, November 16, 2009.

44. Ibid.

45. Prato, *Touched by Magic*, 155.

46. "Song Review," Stewart Mason, http://allmusic.com/cg/amg.dll?p=amg&sql=33:3vfixvq5ld0e.

47. David P. Szatmary, *Rockin' in Time: A Social History of Rock-and-Roll*, 6th ed. (Upper Saddle River, NJ: 2007), 233.

48. Jack Banks, *Monopoly Television: MTV's Quest to Control the Music* (Boulder, CO: Westview Press, 1996); R. Serge Denisoff, *Inside MTV* (New Brunswick, NJ: Transaction, 1991); Ann Kaplan, *Rocking Around the Clock: Music Television, Postmodernism, and Consumer Culture* (London: Routledge, 1987); and Andrew Goodwin, *Dancing in the Distraction Factory: Music Television and Popular Culture*

265

(Minneapolis: University of Minnesota Press, 1992).

49. Marsh, *Before I Get Old*, 230.

50. Interview with Alice Cooper, March 17, 2009.

51. Interviews with Mark Stein, various dates, 2009-2009.

52. Marsh, *Before I Get Old*, 261.

53. Tamarkin, *Got a Revolution!* 313.

54. Marsh, *Before I Get Old*, 298.

55. Tamarkin, *Got a Revolution!* 295.

56. Marsh, *Before I Get Old*, 367.

57. Ibid., 299.

Chapter Seven Notes

1. Interviews with Mark Stein, various dates, 2010.

2. Larry Schweikart and Lynne Pierson Doti, *American Entrepreneur* (New York: Amacom Press, 2009), 410.

3. Ibid., 398.

4. Joel Kotkin and Russ C. DeVol, "Knowledge-Value Cities in the Digital Age," *Milken Institute Study*, February 13, 2001, in authors' possession.

5. David Szatmary, *Rockin' in Time: A Social History of Rock-and-Roll* (Upper Saddle River, NJ: Pearson, 2007), 287.

6. Ibid.

7. Greg Kot, *Ripped: How the Wired Generation Revolutionized Music* (New York: Scribner, 2009), 45.

8. David Suisman, *Selling Sounds: The Commercial Revolution in American Music* (Cambridge, MA: Harvard, 2009).

9. Muzak Company History, http://www.fundinguniverse.com/company histories/MuzakCompanyHistory.html.

10. "The Soundtrack of Your Life: Muzak in the Realm of Retail Theatre," *The New Yorker*, April 10, 2006.

11. Suisman, *Selling Sounds*, 14.

12. Kot, *Ripped*, 194.

13. Interview with Denny Somach, August 4, 2009.

14. Kot, *Ripped*, 7.

15. Suisman, *Selling Sounds*, 204.

16. Kot, *Ripped*, 18-19.

17. Ibid., 22.

18. Ibid., 16.

19. Ibid., 23.

20. Ibid., 10.

21. Aerosmith with Stephen Davis, *Walk This Way: The Autobiography of Aerosmith* (New York: Itbooks, 1999), 434.

22. Kot, *Ripped*, 150.

23. Ibid., 155.

24. Ibid., 25.

25. Ibid.

26. Ibid., 36.

27. Ibid., 202.

28. Ibid., 203.

29. *MGM Studios, Inc. V. Grokster, Ltd.*, 545 U.S. 913 (2005).

30. http://www.grokster.com/

31. Kot, *Ripped*, 53.

32. Ibid., 153-4.

33. Ibid., 209.

34. Ibid., 210.

35. Ibid.

36. Interview with Tony Bongiovi, March 25, 2010.

37. Szatmary, *Rockin' in Time*, 365.

38. Ibid.

39. Ibid.

40. Kot, *Ripped*, 16.

Chapter Eight Notes

1. Chris Welch, "In Through The Out Door."

2. In 20011, Leslie West had a leg amputated due to a long battle with diabetes. "Mountain's Leslie West Loses Leg to Diabetes," http://new.music.yahoo.com/blogs/amplifier/89341/mountains-leslie-west-loses-leg-to-diabetes/

D

E

S

Stevie Winwood, 41, 67
Stevie Wonder, 7, 188
Stuart Sutcliffe, 24
Sylvester Stallone, 143

T

Tawny Kitaen, 162
Ted Mack, 12
Ted Nugent, 159, 162
Terry Meeuwsen, 14
Terry Melcher, 38
The Monkees, 5, 38, 193
Tim Bogert, 6, 7, 8, 21, 30, 31, 40, 49,
  50, 51, 53, 56, 57, 59, 60, 73, 88,
  89, 90, 91, 94, 95, 96, 106, 138,
  142, 145, 146, 147, 148, 158, 160,
  162, 163, 184, 185, 186, 189, 213,
  220, 221, 222, 223, 224, 225, 229,
  230, 231, 232, 234, 236, 238, 239,
  241, 243, 244
Tina Turner, 42, 97
Toly Anderson, 101
Tom Cruise, 139
Tom Scott, 198
Tom Vitorino, 228, 229, 231
Tom Wolfe, 153
Tommy Aldridge, 161
Tommy Bolin, 69, 188, 190, 191, 198
Tommy Boyce, 38
Tommy Dorsey, 9
Tony "Red" Ruffino, 82
Tony Asher, 19
Tony Bongiovi, 26
Tony Bennett, 208, 244

U

Uncle Willie, 10

V

Van Dyke Parks, 19

Van McCoy, 176
Vince Furnier, 182
Vince Waslewski, 229, 234
Vince Martell ("Vinny", born Vincent
  Martemucci), 6, 27, 31, 40, 44, 46,
  48, 49, 50, 51, 52, 53, 59, 60, 71,
  75, 86, 88, 90, 91, 94, 95, 98, 106,
  138, 142, 143, 144, 145, 148, 159,
  162, 163, 173, 186, 197, 220, 221,
  222, 225, 228, 229, 231, 232, 233,
  234, 236, 237, 238, 239, 240, 241,
  243, 244, 245, 248, 253, 255

W

Wayne Fontana, 37
Wayne Newton, 14, 101
Whitey Ford, 226
Whitey Glan, 194
Whitney Houston, 221
William Benton, 209
William Shatner, 73
Willie Dixon, 184
Wilson Pickett, 4, 50
Wolf Biermann, 103
Wolfman Jack, 36, 211
Wolodia Grajonca, 57
Woody Guthrie, 13, 47

Y

Yoko Ono, 168

Z

Z Z Top, 4
Zakk Wylde, 9
Zsa Zsa Gabor, 28

YOU KEEP ME HANGIN' ON

CPSIA information can be obtained at www.ICGtesting.com
Printed in the USA
BVOW08s0526170716

455836BV00001B/2/P